Oedipus in the Trobriands

OTHER BOOKS BY MELFORD E. SPIRO

An Atoll Culture
(coauthored with E. G. Burrows)

Context and Meaning in Cultural Anthropology
(editor)

Kibbutz: Venture in Utopia

Children of the Kibbutz
(with the assistance of Audrey G. Spiro)

Gender and Culture: Kibbutz Women Revisited

Burmese Supernaturalism

Buddhism and Society

Kinship and Marriage in Burma

Melford E. Spiro

Oedipus
in the
Trobriands

The University of Chicago Press

Chicago and London

The University of Chicago Press, Chicago 60637
The University of Chicago Press, Ltd., London

Library of Congress Cataloging in Publication Data

Spiro, Melford E.
  Oedipus in the Trobriands.

  Bibliography: p.
  Includes index.
  1. Ethnology—Papua New Guinea—Trobriand Islands.
2. Oedipus complex. 3. Ethnopsychology. 4. Malinowski,
Bronislaw, 1884–1942. Sex and repression in savage
society. 5. Family—Papua New Guinea—Trobriand Islands.
I. Title.
GN671.N5S64   306.8′74   82–7032
ISBN 0–226–76988–7 (cloth)   AACR2
ISBN 0–226–76989–5 (paper)

MELFORD E. SPIRO, professor of anthropology at the
University of California, San Diego, and a member
of the National Academy of Science, is the author of
numerous works including *Kibbutz: Venture in Utopia;
Children of the Kibbutz; Gender and Culture: Kibbutz
Women Revisited; Burmese Supernaturalism; Buddhism
and Society;* and *Kinship and Marriage in Burma.*

To the memory of A. Irving Hallowell

Contents

Preface

This book is about the Oedipus complex. That yet another book should be added to the vast literature on this topic[1] testifies to its persistent claim on the interest of those who are concerned with understanding the human condition. I do not use that overworked expression lightly, for, as the controversies over the Oedipus complex indicate, what is at issue is the existence not merely of some passing episode in the psychological development of the child, but rather—if its proponents are correct—of a pivotal event in the human career which has far-reaching consequences for our understanding of society, culture, and human nature. Although the towering figure of Sigmund Freud initiated these controversies, the less prominent figure of the anthropologist Bronislaw Malinowski has stood behind many of them ever since the publication of his work on the Trobriand Islands more than fifty years ago. Because of the influence of these two men, it is perhaps understandable that psychoanalysis and anthropology have been among the more active participants in these controversies over the last five decades.

For psychoanalysis the Oedipus complex is a cornerstone of its theory of personality formation, as well as the lens through which it observes many of the psychological dimensions of society, culture, and human nature. For anthropology, the discipline that has been singularly attentive to the cross-cultural diversity in human affairs, the Oedipus complex has been an example, par excellence, of the cultural relativity of human na-

---

1. A recent bibliography of the Oedipus legend, characterized by its compilers as "only a beginning," runs to ten pages (Edmunds and Ingber 1977).

ture (as well as the ethnocentric bias of Freudian theory), at least since the publication of Malinowski's classic *Sex and Repression in Savage Society*. The evidence of that book, which argues that the Oedipus complex is absent in the Trobriand archipelago, is the cornerstone for the thesis propounded by relativists of all persuasions —anthropological and nonanthropological, Freudian as well as anti-Freudian—that the existence of the Oedipus complex (assuming that it might exist somewhere) is a product uniquely of Western institutions and, more particularly, of the Western "patriarchal" family structure.

This book challenges that thesis. On the basis of a reanalysis of Malinowski's data, it argues that if the existence of the Oedipus complex is culturally variable, the Trobriands, at least, do not constitute evidence for such a thesis. The argument comprises two parts. The first (and shorter) part—chapters 1 and 2—argues that there are no convincing grounds for Malinowski's contention that, in the Trobriands, the nuclear complex (as he calls it) consists of a psychological constellation in which the boy, unlike the case in the Oedipus complex, loves his sister and hates his mother's brother. Indeed, if the grounds that Malinowski had offered for the existence of the Trobriand *Kula*, for example, or for matriliny, had been of the same order as that which he advanced for the existence of the matrilineal complex (the term by which he refers to the psychological constellation comprising the Trobriand nuclear complex), it would have been rejected out of hand by all competent scholars.

The second (and larger) part of the argument (chapters 3–5) contends, pace Malinowski, that there are strong grounds for believing that the Oedipus complex comprises the nuclear complex in the Trobriands and that, moreover, both of its dimensions (love for the mother and hatred of the father) are if anything even stronger in the Trobriands than they are in the West. In pursuing this argument, I present the theoretical and empirical grounds for the development of this hypothesis and then test the hypothesis using two sets of predictions, one related to the determinants of the Oedipus complex, the other to its psychological concomitants. The final chapter discusses some wider implications of the Trobriand findings, particularly regarding the long controversy concerning the universality of the Oedipus complex.

Although this book is about the Oedipus complex, it is also an exemplification of one mode of symbolic interpretation. Now "symbol," "symbolic meaning," "symbolic interpretation," and the like are enormously ambiguous expressions, conveying a wide range of meanings concerning which there is little consensus. As I shall employ the term, a symbol, like other signs, is an object or event which stands for or represents something else. Hence, not only is it the case that by cultural designation certain objects and events—the flag, for example, or the Lord's Supper—are stipulated to be symbols whose meanings are similarly stipulated, but also it is the case that objects or events that are not designated as symbols can also evoke symbolic meanings, both shared and idiosyncratic, in social actors. A president, for example, by psychological processes akin to the construction of metaphors, may be perceived as a father figure; hence, he may arouse feelings and reactions appropiate to a father.

Symbols, whether culturally designated or associatively constructed, may have unconscious as well as conscious meanings. Thus, the Madonna might unconsciously represent one's mother, just as a teacher might unconsciously represent one's father. Such unconscious symbolic representations are usually formed when beliefs and motives are too painful to remain in consciousness and, having been repressed, are then represented and gratified, respectively, by means of unconscious symbol formations.

Since an adult (unlike a child) Oedipus complex is, by definition, an unconscious psychological constellation, its existence can only be discovered insofar as it is represented in such unconscious symbolic formations. Hence, much of the evidence that is presented in support of the Trobriand Oedipal hypothesis consists of a wide range of cultural beliefs and social forms together with their putative unconscious symbolic meanings. These meanings, however, are derived neither from a symbolic code book nor yet again from any assumptions about the existence of universal unconscious symbols. Rather, they are derived initially from structural analyses of the cultural beliefs or from theoretically deduced predictions from the social forms, and they are accepted only after they are tested by empirical procedures which are explained in a later chapter.

Though a solitary enterprise, scholarship is yet a cooperative one. In an important sense, the author of a book, one of this type at least, is merely the conduit for the channeling of many influences, both conscious and unconscious. To acknowledge by name all those whose influence is represented in this book—teachers and students, colleagues and informants, parents and children—would be a conceit, but to fail to mention some because one cannot possibly mention all would be equally egregious. In my case the most important single influence is that of A. Irving Hallowell, to whose memory this book is dedicated. It was his example that led to my interest in the interface between anthropology and psychoanalysis, and it was his guidance that directed my attention to both Malinowski and Freud.

More immediately, I am grateful to Edwin Hutchins, Benjamin Kilborne, Donald Kripke, Michael Meeker, Marc Swartz, and Donald Tuzin, whose criticisms of an earlier draft of this book provided the required incentive to improve its deficiencies. I am also indebted to Janet Loomis, Kae Knight, David Marlowe, Barbara Boyer, and Marian Payne who patiently typed and retyped the many drafts of a manuscript which eventually became this book. In addition I wish to acknowledge the National Institute of Mental Health for its support of a comparative study of culturally constituted defense mechanisms, which (by a long and twisting intellectual route) led to the writing of this book.

1

The Problem Posed

Introduction

That the male Oedipus complex, even granting that it might exist somewhere, is a phenomenon restricted to Western-type societies is one of the most widely accepted generalizations in anthropology. Its wide acceptance is the singular achievement of Bronislaw Malinowski, who, as every (anthropological) schoolboy knows, demonstrated that the male Oedipus complex is not found in the Trobriands and, by extrapolation, in other societies whose family structures do not conform to that of the Western type.

With some few exceptions (Barnouw 1973: chapter 5; Fortes 1977; Gough 1953; Jones 1925; McDougall 1975; Róheim 1950) Malinowski's argument for existence of an alternative "nuclear complex" (as he calls it) in the Trobriands has convinced anthropologists and psychoanalysts alike. Thus, the Trobriand case is offered as disproof of the universality of the Oedipus complex not only in anthropology textbooks (Beals 1979:345; Ember and Ember 1973:322–23; Hoebel 1972:43; Honigmann 1967:273–74; Kottak 1978:19; Richards 1972:228), but also in the work of psychological (Campbell and Naroll 1972:437–41; Rohner 1977:6–7) and psychoanalytic (Parsons 1969:1–14) anthropologists, as well as of classical (Fenichel 1945:97) and neo-Freudian (Kardiner 1939:chapter 3; Fromm 1949) psychoanalysts. This is all the more surprising since, in 1957, H. A. Powell, the first anthropologist to study the Trobriands following Malinowski's classic study, wrote a doctoral dissertation on Trobriand kinship in which *en*

1

passant he takes issue with Malinowski's thesis concerning the Oedipus complex. "The facts of the pattern of upbringing in the Trobriands," he observes in one passage, "are, so far as the development of the Oedipus complex is concerned, at least, no different from those of upbringing in any elementary family, whether under a patrilineal or a matrilineal kinship system" (Powell 1957:137). Again, in a later passage, he writes: "The Oedipus or any other type of complex is as likely to occur, and have the same basic form, in Trobrianders as in any other people" (Powell 1957:143).

That Powell's comments have been ignored by the scientific community in the quarter-century since he wrote his thesis may be attributed perhaps to two factors. In the first place his dissertation (to which I had access only after completing this manuscript) has not been widely available. But this cannot be a sufficient explanation for overlooking Powell's work, for his dissertation has long been known and referred to by Melanesian and kinship specialists, and for those who might not have been aware of its existence, he reiterated the same view in an article published some few years prior to the publication of the anthropology textbooks referred to above (Powell 1969, especially pp. 184–85). It can only be assumed, therefore, that a second reason for ignoring Powell's comments is the difficulty of rejecting a scientific tradition, especially if it is initiated (as this one was) by a highly influential scientific figure.

Like most other anthropologists trained in the post-Malinowski era, I too had accepted the Trobriand case as established truth until a few years ago when, for a seminar on the incest taboo, I assigned *Sex and Repression in Savage Society* (Malinowski [1927] 1955) as one of the readings. Although I had read Malinowski's ethnographic monographs while a graduate student, I had not studied this work, the *locus classicus* of received anthropological opinion concerning the Oedipus complex, with special care. In studying this book for the seminar, however, it became increasingly apparent to me that its argument was seriously flawed and its data frustratingly thin. When a rereading of the relevant sections of *The Sexual Life of Savages* (Malinowski 1929) underscored these impressions, I was finally led to conclude that although the Oedipus complex may not be universal, the Trobriand case is a slim reed on which to base this judgment.

Malinowski was an outstanding anthropologist because he usually recognized an important problem, and having recognized it, he almost always formulated the relevant research question. The present case is no exception. Thus, in *Sex and Repression in Savage Society* (hereafter referred to as *SR*) he put the problem which concerns us here squarely: "Do the conflicts, passions and attachments within the family vary with its constitution, or do they remain the same throughout humanity?" (*SR*:19). Having stated the problem, he proceeded to formulate the research question which (rare for his day) he put in the form of a testable hypothesis: "If they vary, as in fact they do, then the nuclear complex of the family cannot remain constant in all human races and people; it must vary with the constitution of the family." This being so, the Oedipus complex (so he argued) is only one type of nuclear complex, viz., that type which "corresponds essentially to [our] patrilineal Aryan family with the developed *patria potestas*, buttressed by Roman law and Christian morals, and accentuated by the modern economic conditions of the well-to-do bourgeoisie" (*SR*:20). In the Trobriands, on the other hand, in which descent is matrilineal, jural authority is vested in the mother's brother, the father (who is not even taken as genitor) is kindly and nurturant, and children are allowed free expression of their sexual impulses, another type of nuclear complex is found. Although the boys' motives in both complexes are the same, their targets, to quote Malinowski's famous formulation, are different: "In the Oedipus complex there is the repressed desire to kill the father and marry the mother, while in the matrilineal society of the Trobriands the wish is to marry the sister and to kill the maternal uncle (*SR*:76).

Before proceeding to a detailed examination of Malinowski's thesis, it is perhaps desirable to briefly summarize the contours of the Oedipus complex. This summary will address not only those dimensions that were addressed by Malinowski, but some others as well that Malinowski did not address and whose neglect perhaps led him to ignore certain manifestations of the Trobriand Oedipus complex which he might otherwise have perceived. At the same time, however, it will deal primarily with Freud's description of this psychological constellation since it is Freud's paradigm with which Malinowski is concerned. Moreover, the summary will be confined to the boy's Oedipus complex because, inasmuch as the nuclear complex of the Trobriand girl, so Malinowski contends, is "very similar" to that of the girl in Western society (*SR*:69), this book will deal with the male Oedipus complex exclusively. To be sure, despite Malinowski's contention, it would be important and desirable to include the female Oedipus complex as well, but unfortunately the data on Trobriand girls are too scanty to permit an adequate analysis.

The Freudian Oedipus Complex

The male Oedipus complex, according to Freud, basing his description on clinical evidence, is a *triangular* constellation involving a boy, his father, and his mother, in which the boy's *sexual desire* for the mother, whose love he wishes to monopolize, *leads* to hostility toward his father (and his siblings), whom he views as a rival for the mother's love. As a result of his wish to possess the exclusive love of the mother, the boy moreover develops the wish to kill the father and to replace him in his relationship with the mother. (In the mind of a little boy, of course, "to kill" means to eliminate, to banish, to be rid of.)

Love and hatred for his mother and father, respectively, are not the only feelings that the boy has for them. On the contrary, his feelings are highly ambivalent. Since typically the mother spurns the boy's erotic advances, her seeming preference for his rival, the husband-father, also evokes the boy's hostility toward her. Similarly, although the boy hates his father because he perceives him to be a rival for the love of the mother, he also loves and admires him for his protection and nurturance.

The boy's ambivalence aside, it is important at the outset to emphasize the two characteristics of Freud's formulation of the Oedipus complex which are italicized above. In the first place, unlike Malinowski and others who view the male Oedipus complex as consisting of two separate diadic constellations, one comprising the boy and his mother (whom he loves), the other comprising the boy and his father (whom he hates), Freud formulates the Oedipus complex as one triangular constellation in which, loving his mother, the boy hates his father, whom he views as his rival. In short, it is not that the boy hates his father *and* loves his mother, but rather that he hates his father *because* he loves his mother. This is not to say that there are no other sources of filial hostility to the father related specifically to their diadic relationship. On the contrary, the boy may develop hostile feelings toward him for any number of reasons related to their diadic relationship—his authority, his power, his punitive socialization, etc.—but his specifically *Oedipal* hostility toward the father has its source in his rivalry with him for the love of the wife-mother. According to Oedipal theory, therefore, so long as his father is simultaneously his mother's lover, the boy will develop Oedipal hostility toward him even if other sources of hostility are absent from their diadic relationship.

Given this basis for the boy's Oedipal hostility, there is a second characteristic of Freud's formulation of the Oedipus complex which must be appreciated. The Oedipus complex is brought into being not by the boy's hatred of the father, but by his love—and specifically his sexual love—for the mother, his "first love-object." To be sure, the mother initially becomes his love-object not because of his sexual desire for her, but "as a result of her feeding him and looking after him" (Freud [1931] 1968:228). At this early ("oral") stage of psychosexual development, however, the boy's love for the mother is "pre-Oedipal;" his *Oedipal* love for her is associated with a later ("phallic") stage of psychosexual development, the stage at which—toward the end of the third year of life—the genitals achieve libidinal primacy. It is at this time that the boy's hostility to the father, whom he now perceives as his rival for the love of the mother, comes into being. Seeing that the Oedipus complex is initiated by the boy's sexual love for the mother, both of its dimensions—the sexual and the hostile—may be exacerbated by his witnessing of parental intercourse ("the primal scene"). This experience "simultaneously creates a high degree of sexual excitement" and "the impression that sex is dangerous" (Fenichel 1945:92).

Although Freud views the Oedipus complex as a triangular constellation, he typically stresses the role of the boy as its initiator. In focusing on the son, he often neglects the complementary role of the parents in initiating this constellation, despite the fact that the Greek myth from which he borrowed his term for this constellation begins with the father, Laius, ordering the death of his infant son, Oedipus[1]—although neither he nor other classical psychoanalytic theorists (Fenichel 1945:91–97) dispute their role. In order to redress the imbalance in Freud's treatment, it is important to emphasize here that the role of the parents is often central in initiating the Oedipus complex.[2] Thus, the mother is often "seductive" toward the child, thereby arousing his sexual feelings toward her, which may lead him to fantasies of actual seduction. Similarly, the father often views the son as a rival for the love of the wife-mother, and in expressing his hostility toward him arouses the latter's fear and enmity. Indeed, the "complementary Oedipus complex" of the parents, as Devereux terms it, is sufficiently present for him to have concluded that "the Oedipus complex appears to be a consequence of the child's sensitiveness to the parents' sexual and aggressive impulses" (Devereux 1953:139).

It may be suggested, then, that the lack of resolution of the Oedipus complex in the parents greatly exacerbates the Oedipus complex in the son. For if a girl remains frustrated in her incestuous desires for her father, she may, as a mother, put her son in his place and act all the more "seductively" toward him, as is often the case in Bengali mothers (Roy 1975). Similarly, if a boy remains frustrated in his wish to monopolize his mother, he may, as a husband, put his wife in her place and act all the more aggressively toward his son whom he views as his rival, as seems to be the case in Dahomey (Herskovits and Herskovits 1958).

The Oedipus complex not only begins in childhood, but typically is also resolved in childhood, usually by the beginning of the sixth year, when, because of the fear of castration, "the child's ego turns away from the Oedipus complex" (Freud [1924] 1968:176). The fear of castration may result from actual castration threats (as the threatened punishment for masturbation, for ex-

1. Interestingly enough, the Indian (Ramanujan 1972), as well as many Oceanic (Lessa 1956) and Dahomeyan (Herskovits and Herskovits 1958) "Oedipus" myths, among others, also emphasize the role of the father as initiating the subsequent events.

2. Within a span of a single decade—in one of those convergences that frequently marks the history of science—four different scholars from separate disciplines, each working independently of the other, published papers on the need to redress this imbalance in Freud's treatment of the Oedipus complex (Devereux 1953; Lessa 1956; Herskovits and Herskovits, 1958; Mandler, 1963).

ample), from the working of the talion principle (the penis, as the offending organ, being the fantasied object of punishment), or from the perception of female genitalia (which the boy may interpret as the consequence of castration). In any event, motivated by castration anxiety (the fear that he might be castrated), the boy gives up his wish to kill his father and, instead, identifies with him. In the process of identifying with the father, the boy also "introjects" his authority, thereby forming the nucleus of his superego "which takes over the severity of the father and perpetuates his prohibition against incest . . . [His] incestuous wishes are in part desexualized and sublimated . . . and in part inhibited in their aim and changed into impulses of affection" (ibid.:177). Having given up his mother as a sexual object, the boy later replaces her with someone who either "resembles her or is derived from her" (Freud [1931] 1968:228).

It is the formation of the superego, then, that "secures the ego from the return of the libidinal object-cathexis" (Freud [1924] 1968:177), i.e., a resumption of his sexual love for the mother. Ideally, this is achieved by the "destruction and abolition" (ibid.) of the boy's sexual desire for her, but often it is achieved by the repression of this desire, in which case it persists unconsciously, though with diminished intensity (Fenichel 1945:108). Despite the resolution of the Oedipus complex in childhood, however, unconscious Oedipal conflicts are usually revived during puberty (ibid.:110–13), following which (in the normal case) they are again, and finally, resolved. If, however, the Oedipus complex is not resolved in childhood, it is during puberty that its "pathogenic effect" (Freud [1924] 1968:177) will become evident. An unresolved Oedipus complex (including persistent, but unconscious, incestuous longings for the mother) is at the core of almost every adult neurosis. Even in the latter case, however, it is not the mother of his adult years who is the unconscious object of his sexual desires; rather, it is his mental representation of the young mother of his childhood upon which he remains (unconsciously) fixated.

The Trobriand Matrilineal Complex

The first difference between the Oedipus complex and the matrilineal complex of the Trobriands, as the latter is described by

Malinowski, is that the former comes to an end before the latter even begins. Although in the latter society, too, the young child develop "very definite sentiments" toward his mother and father, nevertheless "nothing suppressed, nothing negative, no frustrated desire forms a part of them" (*SR*:72). It is not until puberty, "in fact almost exclusively then, that . . . the child [is] submitted to the system of repressions and taboos which begin to mould his nature" (*SR*:74). Hence, in the Trobriands it is not until puberty that "any complex is formed," and—to come to the second difference between the Oedipus and the matrilineal complex—its actors consist of the teenage boy, his mother's brother, and his sister. Malinowski supports this contention by the following argument.

The father plays no role in the formation of the matrilineal complex because in matrilineal systems—at least in that of the Trobriands—he is uniformly loving and kind. He protects and plays with the children, and he helps and nurtures them, but he does not punish or exercise authority over them. This being so, the hostility dimension of the matrilineal complex is not found in the father-son relationship. Rather, it is found in the relationship between the boy and his mother's brother, for it is the latter who is the locus of jural authority, and it is he who inculcates duty and imposes constraints. Nevertheless, since his authority is principally exercised when the boy attains puberty, it is not until then that he becomes an important object—indeed, *the* object—of the boy's hostility. To be sure, the boy's attitude toward his maternal uncle is not unambivalent. On the one hand, "the efforts which [the uncle] demands and the rivalry between successor and succeeded introduce the negative elements of jealousy and resentment," which, however, are manifested only "indirectly" and in a "repressed hatred" (*SR*:75). On the other hand, it is the maternal uncle who also introduces the boy to social ambition, traditional glory, and promises of wealth and prestige, all of which "make life bigger, more interesting, and of greater appeal" (*SR*:50).

The mother, no less than the father, is excluded from the matrilineal complex, despite the fact that the early relationship between mother and child in the Trobriands is the same as in the West. In infancy, the "biological adjustment of instinct" and the "social forces of custom, morals, and manners" serve to "bind" mother and infant to each other, "giving them full scope for the passionate intimacy of motherhood" (SR:32). Weaning initiates the first important difference between Western and Trobriand society, for, unlike the former, weaning takes place in the latter at a relatively late age—between the age of two and three—after the child has already become relatively independent. Nevertheless, the mother continues to relate to the child "quite as lovingly" as during the preweaning stage, the infant continuing to cling to the mother "with undiminished passionate desire for her presence, for the touch of her body and the tender clasp of her arms" (SR:34).

The age between four and six years marks the second, and crucial, developmental difference between the Trobriands and the West. (This is the age, it will be remembered, which marks the peak of the Oedipus complex and its subsequent resolution.) Since, as a result of their "close bodily contact," the young boy "reacts sexually" to the mother (SR:42), there must be some way of handling his sexual impulses;[3] and whereas in the West as a result of paternal pressures, the boy's erotic feelings for the mother (and everyone else) undergo repression, in the Trobriands this does not occur (SR:43). Rather, children of this age are permitted complete sexual freedom. They not only play at being "husband and wife," but such play freely includes sexual activity. (For the extent of these activities, see Malinowski's *Sexual Life of Savages* [hereafter referred to as *SLS*], pp. 51–59.) That the boy does not take his mother as a sexual object, despite his complete sexual freedom and the lack of repression of his erstwhile "passionate" feelings for her, is not the result of his fear of the father (castration anxiety), but of the "mother's withdrawing completely but gradually from the boy's passionate feelings" (SR:67). Put differently, "all of the infantile craving of the child for its mother is allowed gradually to spend itself in a natural, spontaneous manner" (SR:75).

That the mother is not a libidinal object for the boy does not mean, however, that a libidinal dimension is absent from the matrilineal complex. Rather, in this nuclear complex the sister replaces the mother as the principal object of the boy's erotic

3. The first section of *Sex and Repression*, from which this summary is taken, was originally published as an article in *Psyche* (4 [1923]:98–128). In a footnote, which Malinowski added to the article as republished in *SR*, he disavows this statement, characterizing it as "absurd" (p. 241).

desires. Thus, in a formulation impressive for its structural elegance, Malinowski contends that whereas the sexual feeling of the boy for his mother is repressed in the West but spontaneously disappears in the Trobriands, the reverse occurs in the brother-sister relationship: in the West the early "intimacy [between a boy and his sister] gradually cools off and changes into a somewhat restrained relation," while in the Trobriands it is "systematically repressed from the outset" (*SR*:68).

That the sexual feeling of the boy for his sister requires repression (while that for the mother disappears gradually and spontaneously) is not explained by matriliny, as such, nor can it be attributed to the punitive intervention either of the father or of the mother's brother. Rather, so Malinowski claims, it results from the special strength of the brother-sister incest taboo. The prohibition of brother-sister incest is the "supreme taboo" (*SLS*:519), the one that is applied not only "most stringently" (*SR*:75), but even "with great brutality" (*SR*: 101). In short, "the loudness and stringency of the [mother-son] taboo is by no means so great as in the brother-sister incest" (*SR*:94–95).

It is the special severity of the brother-sister taboo which causes the boy's erotic desire for the sister to be singularly intense, and its intensity requires that it be repressed. This is so for two somewhat different reasons. First, the severity of this taboo "causes the thought of the sister to be always present as well as consistently repressed" (*SR*:75). Second, since "the taboo against the sister is imposed with great brutality and kept up with rigid strength, the real inclination to break the strong taboo is much more actual" than in the case of the mother (*SR*:101).

It will be noticed, then, that in addition to the difference between the Oedipus and the matrilineal complex in their cast of characters, there is an important difference in the relationships among them. In the Oedipus complex, the boy sustains a triangular relationship with the other two actors in that his hostility to the father is motivated by his rivalry with him for the love of the wife-mother. In the matrilineal complex, the boy sustains a diadic and separate relationship with each of the other actors, his love for the sister having no bearing on his hostility to the mother's brother.

Compelling though it seems to be, Malinowski's case for a distinctively matrilineal complex, as an alternative to the "patrilineal'' Oedipal complex, in the Trobriands is seriously flawed on three accounts. First, most of the data offered in refutation of a Trobriand Oedipus complex are not evidential because, based on a misunderstanding of the latter complex, they are not germaine to the issue. Second, the structural characteristics of the Trobriand family are insufficiently different in their essential dimensions from those of the Western type to sustain the argument that, in principle, each should produce a different kind of nuclear complex. Third, and most important, the data presented as evidence for the existence of a matrilineal complex are not only meager in the extreme, but just as easily susceptible of a contrary interpretation. Each of these arguments will be examined in detail in the next chapter.[4]

4. Although Malinowski argues that the absence of neurosis in the Trobriands constitutes yet another reason for believing that the Oedipus complex is absent in matrilineal societies (*SR*:83–87), I shall not discuss this argument for two reasons. First, Malinowski erroneously assumes that, according to Freud, an Oedipus complex is a sufficient condition for the development of a neurosis. Freud, however, claimed that it is necessary but not sufficient. Second, since Malinowski himself agreed that he was not competent to make valid diagnostic judgments (Ibid.:84), his claims concerning the absence of neurosis in the Trobriands are hardly reliable. I heartily agree, however, with his methodological suggestion that systematic studies of mental illness in "matrilineal and patriarchal communities of the same level of culture" (*SR*:86) would be illuminating.

2

The Trobriand Matrilineal Complex:
A Critique

Mother-Son Relationship

The Boy and His Mother

Despite the fact that Malinowski shows that in the Trobriands (as elsewhere) the mother is the boy's first love-object, he nevertheless argues that the Oedipus complex does not exist in the Trobriands. His argument rests on two grounds, one having to do with the relationship between the boy and his mother, the other with that between the man and his mother. We shall examine each of these grounds in turn.

So far as the boy is concerned, Malinowski claims that at the very age—between three and six—when the Western boy is struggling with his incestuous desire for the mother, the Trobriand boy's "passionate feeling" for her has already been extinguished. Its extinction, Malinowski further claims, is not a result of pressure from, or fear of rivalry with, the father, for in the Trobriands there is "no repression, no censure, no reprobation of infantile sexuality of the genital type" (*SR*:43). Rather, the boy's "infantile craving" for the mother spends itself in a "natural" and "spontaneous" manner. This being the case, in his relationship with the mother (as well as the father) there is "nothing suppressed, nothing negative, no frustrated desire" (*SR*:72).

In view of Malinowski's rather strong claims concerning the boy's maternal relationship—nothing is suppressed, nothing is negative, there are no frustrated desires—it is more than a little disappointing that he offers *no* evidence in their support. Thus, following his description of the relationship between infant and mother, Malinowski proceeds to a description of adolescence, thereby bypassing the very developmental age which, alone, is germaine for the assessment of these claims. For this age there is no description of any kind regarding the boy's actions, feelings, or fantasies regarding the mother. In the absence of such data, some degree of skepticism concerning Malinowski's claims is perhaps not entirely unwarranted. For given the young boy's erstwhile "passionate feelings" for her, is it implausible to assume that his "infantile sexuality of the genital type" might at least sometimes take the mother as its object? And if it does not, then seeing that his "infantile craving" for her allegedly comes to an end at the very age at which he commences his otherwise uninhibited sexual activities, is it implausible to assume that repression, censure, reprobation, and the like may not be entirely absent from the boy's relationship with his parents?

Since, however, there are no data concerning the boy's relationship with his mother at this age, there is little point in continuing with these questions. Let us, instead, turn to the adolescent, for here Malinowski reports two observations in support of his contention that the infantile craving of the boy for his mother is already dissipated in early childhood. The first observation is that "the personal friendship, the mutual confidences and intimacy which is so characteristic of the mother-to-son relationship in our society" is not found in the Trobriands (*SR*:66).[1] The second observation is that, unlike the West, where the boy's emerging sexuality at puberty "estranges him from his progenitors, embarrasses their relations and creates deep complications" (*SR*:67), these characteristics are not found in the Trobriands.

Now even granting the dubious assumption that each of these observations, taken individually, constitutes evidence for the claim that the young boy's sexual feeling for the mother spends itself naturally and spontaneously, taken jointly they cancel themselves out because they are clearly contradictory. The sec-

1. Although there is no basis to doubt Malinowski's characterization of the Trobriand situation, I suspect that many Westerners—adolescents and former adolescents alike—would be rather startled by his characterization of the situation in the West.

ond observation, moreover, is contradicted yet again by Malinowski's comment, in a later theoretical discussion, that the
"bashfulness and awkward attitude of children to their parents
in matters of sex" seems to be a transcultural phenomenon inasmuch as it is found "even among the essentially 'unrepressed'
Trobrianders [among whom] the parent is never the confidant
in matters of sex" (*SR*:241). This contradiction aside, a clinical
perspective would suggest that a child's discomfort concerning
sexual matters in the presence of parents is symptomatic of his
sexual feelings (conscious or unconscious) for them.

Whatever we make of these observations, however, none of
them casts any light on the status of the boy's "passionate feelings" for the mother during the period which is crucial for the
argument, the period of the onset of "infantile sexuality of the
genital type." And since, so Malinowski claims, the disappearance of these early feelings is not only "spontaneous," but "gradual," this would seem to imply that they are present at least at
the beginning of this period—the Oedipal period, according to
Freudian theory.

Since, then, the *evidence* offered in support of the claim that
the boy's sexual feeling for the mother disappears prior to the
conventional Oedipal period is scanty, contradictory, and irrelevant, let us turn instead to Malinowski's *arguments* for why its
disappearance is theoretically expectable. His first argument is
that since Trobriand weaning is relatively late—occurring between the ages of two and three—it takes place "when the child
neither wants nor needs the mother's breasts anymore." Hence,
the "first wrench" experienced by the Western child when separated from the mother—the wrench of abrupt independence—
"is eliminated" in the case of the Trobriand child (*SR*:35).[2] This
argument, however, hardly addresses the issue at hand. Since
genitality and dependency are separate variables, it is hard to
understand how the ease of the boy's "detachment" from his
dependency on the mother might affect the detachment of his
libidinal desire for her. Indeed, in the Trobriand situation, even
the dependency argument is weak. During the two or more
years in which the child is nursed, he and the mother sleep

2. According to Edwin Hutchins (personal communication), however, Trobriand mothers talk of the anger of the child at being denied the breast.

together, both being separated from the father. When the process of weaning begins, however, the infant is separated from the mother, and sleeps with the father or grandmother (*SLS*:235), which means that though he may not experience the wrench of abrupt weaning, he experiences the wrench of abrupt separation at the very time that weaning also occurs.

But wrench or no wrench, dependency, as I have said, is not the relevant issue so far as the Oedipal question is concerned. According to the Freudian paradigm with which Malinowski is taking issue, the Oedipus complex does not come into being until the "phallic" stage of psychosexual development—the stage at which the penis supersedes the oral cavity as the primary organ of libidinal pleasure. If, then, the boy is weaned at the lower end of the age range mentioned by Malinowski—about two years—it should have little effect on the boy's genital desire for the mother, which, *ex hypothesi*, has not yet achieved libidinal primacy. If it does have an effect, Malinowski offers no data which indicates that this might be so. If, on the other hand, the boy is weaned at the upper range of the weaning period—about three years—then he may enter the phallic stage while still being nursed. If so, then whatever the effect gradual weaning might have on the boy's dependency needs, Oedipal theory would predict that such prolonged nursing would, if anything, intensify the boy's libidinal desire for the mother. And not only Oedipal theory. For if, according to Malinowski, the infant "reacts sexually" to his "close bodily contact" with the mother (*SR*:42), the prolongation of such bodily contact occasioned by protracted nursing should lead to the persistence, if not exacerbation, of his sexual reactions. In short, if late weaning is a relevant variable, Malinowski's argument can be turned on its head, which is all the more reason to regret the absence of any data for this period of Trobriand child development by which these competing claims might be evaluated.

Malinowski's second argument for the theoretical expectation that in the Trobriands the boy's sexual feeling for the mother disappears at the very age at which he enters the period of genital sexuality was offered six years after the first. Since, so he argued, the boy is given complete sexual freedom, his "relation to the mother and the sexual relation are kept distinct and allowed to run side by side. The ideas and feeling centering around sex on the one hand, and maternal tenderness on the other, are differentiated naturally and easily, without being separated by a rigid taboo. [Hence] since normal erotic impulses find an easy outlet, tenderness towards the mother and bodily attachment to her are naturally drained of their stronger sensuous elements" (*SLS*:523).

This argument is no more cogent than the first. That as a consequence of an "easy outlet" for his erotic impulses the boy's tender and sexual feelings for the mother are differentiated "naturally," or that his attachment to her is "naturally" drained of its sensuous elements—these are neither self-evident propositions, nor are they empirically supported. Kibbutz children of the same age, for example, who are to a large degree separated from their parents, who never experience the intense physical and emotional relationship to the mother that is found in the Trobriands, and who, like Trobriand children, enjoy a sexually permissive regime, nevertheless (according to Nagler) take the mother as the main object of their sexual impulses (Neubauer 1965:260). Indeed, it is precisely *because* of the free expression of their sexual impulses that (according to Lewin) the sexual attachment to the mother, as measured by the late resolution of the Oedipus complex, is so strong in the kibbutz (ibid.:85). The kibbutz evidence, however, is not the only empirical grounds for rejecting Malinowski's argument. In a detailed study of sexual latency in the United States Sarnoff (1976) shows, inter alia, that the absence or relative absence of latency does not mean that either the sexual or the aggressive dimension of the Oedipus complex is absent in the child.

But there is no need to turn to other cultures to show that Malinowski's argument is not self-evident, for it is refuted by his own data. Thus, if it is the case that the boy's sexual attraction to the mother is dissipated by his sexual freedom, we would expect that his attraction to his sister and that the attraction of the daughter to the father would be similarly dissipated. Yet in these relationships, so Malinowski reports, the sexual attraction persists throughout childhood and into adulthood when it is then repressed. If there is a satisfactory explanation for this apparent anomaly, Malinowski, as we shall see, does not offer one. I shall confine my remarks to what he tells us about the father-daughter relationship, not only because that between brother and sister is examined in detail in a later section, but because the former relationship, involving as it does a parent-child tie, is more instructive for assessing Malinowski's argument concerning the mother-son relationship.

Despite the alleged early dissipation of the boy's sexual attachment to the mother, the girl's sexual attachment to the father, "although not quite identical" with that found in the Oedipus complex of the Western girl, is yet, so Malinowski reports, "very similar" to it (*SR*:69). More than that, this attachment persists into puberty, at which time the "intimacy" between them "is fraught with some temptation" (ibid.). That this is so, Malinowski argues, may be inferred from the strong taboo on father-daughter incest. But this argument, surely, should also be applicable to the mother-son relationship, as well. Why may it not be inferred from the taboo on mother-son incest that the boy's sexual attraction to the mother also persists into puberty, rather than being dissipated in early childhood? Malinowski's response to this challenge is that in a matrilineal system the sexual prohibition between mother and son is but a special case of the general rule of clan exogamy, while that between father and daughter exists despite the fact that it does not violate the exogamic rule (*SR*:69–70). Hence, whereas the father-daughter taboo is a measure of their incestuous desires, that between mother and son is not.

Now without entering a long-standing anthropological controversy I would merely observe that Malinowski's response rests on sheer dogma. For whatever the causes or functions of the parent-child incest taboo, there is no evidence whatsoever to support the contention that, in a matrilineal society, the taboo on father-daughter incest prohibits the expression of their libidinal desires, while that on mother-son incest is merely a logical entailment of a general exogamic rule. The detailed evidence presented by Gough (1953:section 5) for strong incestuous desires for the mother in the matrilineal Nayar is sufficient to confound such a contention. The Nayar aside, however, even if we were to accept this dogma as fact, it still leaves the question with which we began unanswered: since boys and girls alike achieve an "easy outlet" for their respective libidinal feelings for their parents, why are the boy's feelings for his mother drained of their "stronger sensuous elements," while those of the girl for her father persist with undiminished strength? Malinowski's answer to this question is even less satisfactory. The prohibition on father-daughter incest, he argues, not only is a measure of, but actually increases, their libidinal bond (*SR*:69). Dubious as this answer might be, if it holds for the father-daughter prohibition, we should expect it to apply with equal force to the mother-son prohibition. On this point, however, Malinowski is silent.

In sum, since the evidence he offers in support of his claims is not germaine to the issue, and since his theoretical arguments raise more problems than they resolve, Malinowski's contention that the Trobriand boy's infantile craving for his mother is given up gradually, spontaneously, and naturally even prior to the age at which the Western boy enters the Oedipus complex rests on a flimsy empirical and theoretical foundation. To what extent the boy's libidinal tie to the mother might rather be given up (whether through extinction or repression) because of his relationship with his father (as Oedipal theory would expect) will be addressed in a later chapter.

The Man and His Mother

Malinowski's case for the early dissipation of the Trobriand boy's libidinal tie to his mother is not confined to his remarks about childhood. His case is finally proved, so he contends, by the total absence of conscious incestuous desires for the mother on the part of adults. Neither in dream nor in deed is incest found between a mother and her adult son. So far as the former is concerned, not only do adult males not only report no dreams of mother incest, but all queries concerning the existence of such dreams evoke "a calm and unshocked negation" (*SR*:91). Similarly, not only are there no known cases of actual mother-son incest, but the latter is regarded as "almost impossible" (*SLS*:524).

To clinch his argument, Malinowski quotes his informants as saying that since the mother is an "old woman," only an "imbecile" would desire to have sexual relations with her (*SR*:91). This argument—the centerpiece of Malinowski's thesis that the male Oedipus complex is absent in the Trobriands—is entirely misplaced. If, for any society, the existence of the Oedipus complex is evidenced by the conscious sexual desire of adult sons for their mother, it would follow that it is absent in normal males not only in the Trobriands, but in the West (in which, according to Malinowski, the Oedipus complex is present) as well. But normal adult males in the West, no less than in the Trobriands, regard mother-son incest as "almost impossible," and they too, moral qualms aside, find their mother no more desirable sexually than any other elderly woman. That Malinowski should have thought otherwise—that he should have thought, that is, that psychologically healthy adults in the West have a conscious incestuous desire for their mothers, or (on the improbable assumption they did) that they consciously attempt to gratify this desire either in dream or in deed, or that Oedipal theory would expect either of these conditions to obtain—reflects a degree of misunderstanding concerning Western males and of naiveté concerning the Oedipus complex that is difficult to credit.

Oedipal theory, it will be recalled, does not claim that (normal) adult males have a conscious sexual desire for their mothers. It claims, rather, that this desire is confined to early childhood, beginning around the age of three and ending (either by its extinction or repression) around the age of six (as a result of castration anxiety). Hence, the persistence of the son's conscious incestuous desire for the mother beyond early childhood, or its eruption into consciousness in adulthood following its repression in later childhood, is expected only in cases of psychopathology. Assuming, moreover, that this desire is repressed rather than extinguished in childhood, it is not the mother of his adult years, but the mental representation of the mother of his childhood who, as we have seen, is normally the object of the son's unconscious incestuous desire. This being the case, any conscious sexual desire on the part of an adult for his contemporary mother, including actual attempts to act upon such a desire, is expected only in severe psychosis. In short, Malinowski's finding concerning the absence of conscious incestuous desires for the mother in Trobriand adult sons not only is consistent with Oedipal theory, but—contrary to his assumption—is required by it.

Not only does Oedipal theory require it, but Western findings concerning mother-son incest duplicate these Trobriand findings. Thus, on the basis of all available data concerning Western incest, Lindzey (1967:1056) concluded that mother-son incest, though not totally absent, is extremely rare. The latter finding, moreover, has been reported in every study, both of normal and clinical populations, which I have been able to examine. Thus, for example, in what is still the most extensive study of incest in a nonclinical population—a study of 203 incest offenders brought to the attention of the authorities in the state of Illinois—Weinberg (1955:74) discovered only 2 cases of mother-son incest. Again, in more recent large-scale studies of incest reported by Frances and Frances (1976), only 3 cases of mother-son incest were discovered in Northern Ireland, three in Japan, and one in Czechoslovakia. The findings for clinical subjects are no different. Thus, in a recent study of a clinical population, Meiselman (1978:74) found only 2 cases of mother-son incest in a sample of 50 cases of incest. Moreover, Western findings concerning mother-son incest conform to the expectations of Oedipal theory not only in regard to its incidence, but also in regard to the pathology of the incestuous son. Thus, in a review of all available studies of mother-son incest, Meiselman (1978:299–300) reports that the sons exhibit severe psychopathology, typically schizophrenia and other forms of psychosis.

We may conclude, then, that the evidence on adults adduced by Malinowski for the absence of an Oedipus complex in the Trobriands, at least so far as its libidinal dimension is concerned, is (if anything) even less convincing than the childhood evidence. Since mother-son incest is not expected by Oedipal theory, and since (consistent with the theory) its absence in the Trobriands is duplicated in normal populations in the West, the Trobriand finding can hardly be attributed to the matrilineal "constitution" of the Trobriand family, nor can it be taken as evidence for the absence of an Oedipus complex. Indeed, on the basis of the clear relationship that has been established in the West between mother-son incest and severe psychopathology, the only firm inference to be drawn from the absence of mother-son incest in the Trobriands is that severe pathology of this type is not found in Trobriand males.

Lest I be misunderstood, I wish to emphasize that I am not proposing the absurd thesis that the absence of mother-son incest is evidence for the presence of an Oedipus complex in the Trobriands. Rather, I am arguing, pace Malinowski, that it does not constitute evidence for its absence. It may well be, therefore, that despite Malinowski's invalid argument for the absence of a male Oedipus complex in the Trobriands, he is nevertheless correct in claiming that the primary object of the male's libidinal desire is the sister rather than the mother. Hence, we may now examine his argument on behalf of that thesis.

Brother-Sister Relationship

That the brother-sister relationship, like that between parent and child, includes a libidinal dimension is a proposition that all incest theorists, from Tylor to Lévi-Strauss, insist upon. What is at issue, therefore, in the case of the Trobriands is not whether the sister is an incestuous object for her brother—that is something they would all expect—but whether she is his primary incestuous object, so that (as Malinowski contends) the sister takes the place of the mother in the Trobriand nuclear complex. That this is indeed the case is proved, Malinowski argues, by a variety of data: the severity of the brother-sister incest taboo, dreams and deeds of brother-sister incest, an obscenity pattern, and a myth of brother-sister incest. Let us examine each in turn.

Malinowski holds, it will be recalled, that the brother-sister incest taboo is the most stringent of all the incest taboos, and that its stringency is the *cause* of the brother's singularly strong sexual feelings for his sister. For him to then argue, however, that the stringency of this taboo is a *measure* of the strength of these feelings is, of course, invalid—it begs the very question to be answered. Rather than lingering, however, over this petitio principii, let us instead examine the grounds for Malinowski's claim for the special stringency of this taboo, for if this claim is not justified, the taboo can be adduced neither as a cause nor as a measure of the boy's greater sexual feeling for his sister than his mother.

Unfortunately, Malinowski's argument for the special stringency of the brother-sister taboo is perhaps the most frustratingly inconsistent and contradictory of all his arguments. Whereas in one passage (*SR*:74) he tells us that the boy "is submitted" to this taboo only at puberty, on the very next page (*SR*:75) he writes that "it enters the boy's life in infancy." Although the first statement supports Malinowski's crucial thesis that in the Trobriands (unlike the West) the nuclear complex does not come into being until puberty, and the second supports his claim for the stringency of this taboo, taken together they are clearly contradictory. Since, however, he later escalates his stringency thesis by claiming that the sister taboo is "imposed with great brutality" (*SR*:101), and since his ethnographic descriptions indicate that the latter taboo is inculcated at an early age, it is probably safe to accept the earlier age (which, however, contradicts his thesis that the nuclear complex does not begin until puberty).

In support of the special stringency of the sister taboo (and the brutality of its imposition) Malinowski offers the following evidence. From an "early age" not only are the boy's advances toward his sister "reprimanded and punished," but the adults react to such advances with "horror and anguish" (*SLS*:520). Moreover, brother and sister are forbidden to be present at the same time in any form of play, let alone in children's sexual games (ibid.). In addition, to assure their continuous sexual avoidance, brother and sister are required to live apart from each other beginning with the onset of puberty (*SR*:58; *SLS*:519). Here again, however, we are confronted with another contradiction, for in another context we are told that it is the boys, "especially," who must leave home, and the reason is not to assure sexual avoidance of the sister, but "so as not to hamper by their [the boys'] embarrassing presence the sexual life of their parents" (*SLS*:62).

It should be added, however, that even if we accept the first reason for the extrusion of the boy from the home, this would not support the hypothesis that the brother-sister incest taboo is more stringent than the son-mother taboo, nor that this is evidence for a matrilineal complex. In village Burma, for example, where the mother-son taboo is more stringent than the brother-sister (and the father-daughter more stringent than either), brother-sister (but not son-mother) avoidance is practiced, although descent is bilateral and the father's authority is "patriarchal" (Spiro 1977: chapter 5). Nor is Burma exceptional in this regard, for as Murdock (1949:277) reports in his cross-cultural study of avoidance taboos, institutionalized brother-sister avoidance is second only to that between a man and his mother-in-law as the most frequent type of kin avoidance, a finding which holds regardless of descent system. Moreover, mother-son avoidance is absent in all the societies in his sample.

This is another example of Malinowski's attributing to matriliny a structural characteristic which is widespread in human societies in general.

Malinowski's previously cited argument for the special stringency of the brother-sister taboo fares no better. Although the boy is not permitted to be present when his sister is engaged in sexual games, he must also be absent, as has been noted, from the "sexual games" of his parents. And although his advances toward his sister are reprimanded and punished, it is probably safe to assume—though Malinowski is silent on this question—that his advances toward his mother are hardly encouraged. Thus, considering that the early feeling of the boy for the mother (but not for the sister) is characterized by Malinowski as "passionate," and considering that nevertheless any type of sexual relationship between them is prohibited, the mother taboo can hardly be a trivial one. Indeed, in one of his more startling contradictions Malinowski admits as much when he writes that among adults, "the idea of mother incest is as repugnant to the native as sister incest, *probably even more*" (*SR*: 100–101, italics mine). To be sure, in another passage, written six years later, he writes that although "incestuous inclinations toward the mother are regarded as highly reprehensible, as unnatural and immoral, there is not the same feeling of horror and fear as toward brother-and-sister incest" (*SLS*:523–24), but again, no evidence is offered in support of either statement. Since by this time, however, the contradictions are so numerous and confusing, perhaps the best thing to do is to proceed to Malinowski's other arguments for his claim that the libidinal dimension of the Trobriand nuclear complex inheres in the brother-sister, rather than the mother-son, relationship.

Malinowski's next two arguments concern the relative incidence of mother-son and brother-sister incest, both in dream and in deed. Although, as we have already seen, Trobriand males never report dreams of mother incest, they do report dreams of sister incest, which, moreover, "haunt and disturb" them (*SR*:91). In addition, whereas queries concerning mother incest dreams arouse no affect, those regarding dreams of sister incest produce a "strong affective reaction . . . of indignation and anger" (ibid.). Similarly, in contrast to the absence of reported cases of mother-son incest, there are known cases of brother-sister (*SR*:91–95; *SLS*:528–29), and even a few of father-daughter, incest (*SR*:70, 95).

We have already observed that mother-son incest neither is expected by Oedipal theory nor occurs any more frequently in the West (in normal populations) than in the Trobriands. We may now observe that just as the absence of mother-son incest does not constitute evidence for the absence of an Oedipus complex in the Trobriands, so too the existence of some few cases of brother-sister incest does not support the conclusion that the boy's "repressed attitude of incestuous temptations can be formed only toward his sister" (*SR*:76), because the same relative incidence of mother and sister incest is also found in the West, where, according to Malinowski, the mother is the primary incestuous object. Indeed, the relative incidence of all three forms of reported or known nuclear family incest exhibits precisely the same pattern in the West that Malinowski reported for the Trobriands: brother-sister incest is much more frequent than that between father and daughter, while mother-son incest is all but nonexistent. Thus, in his survey of the Western evidence alluded to above, Lindzey (1967:1056) estimated that brother-sister incest is five times more common than father-daughter incest, which, in turn, is much more frequent than that between mother and son.

It should be added that in the West, at least, the relative incidence of incest within the nuclear family is correlated with the relative intensity of the psychopathology of the male actors. Thus, in a review of all available studies of brother-sister incest, Meiselman (1978:293) concluded that an incestuous brother—it is the brother who almost invariably initiates the incest—"has no outstanding neurotic or psychotic symptoms and is not alcoholic or mentally defective." In contrast to incestuous brothers, however, incestuous sons and fathers—again, it is they who, overwhelmingly, initiate mother-son and father-daughter incest, respectively—show many forms of social and psychological pathology, those of the fathers being less severe than the sons'. Unlike the psychotic tendencies which, as was noted in the last section, characterize incestuous sons, the tendencies incestuous fathers are more likely to exhibit are psychopathic behavior (Meiselman 1978:95), pathological obsession with sex (ibid.), and paranoia (ibid.:103), as well as dull normal or below normal intelligence (ibid.:88–90).[3]

Since, then, the relative incidence of incest with mother and sister is no different for the Trobriands than for the West (in which, Malinowski concedes, the mother is the male's primary incestuous object), neither can the Trobriand finding be offered in support of the thesis that the sister (rather than the mother) is the boy's primary incestuous object, nor can it be attributed to the matrilineal "constitution" of the Trobriand family. Indeed, the only society not only in which brother-sister incest was widely practiced, but in which its institutionalization in marriage is reported to have been common—Roman Egypt—is one in which the family "constitution" was not matrilineal, but patriarchal (Hopkins 1980). We shall return to this example in the final chapter. Similarly, marriage between brothers and sisters of the same father but different mothers occurred in both medieval Japan (Sofue 1981:2) and ancient Israel (Bakan 1979:68–69), both of which were "patriarchal."

That the relative incidence of sister-brother and mother-son incest (and marriage) is the same in societies as different and as remote (in time and space) as the Trobriands, Roman Egypt, and the modern West may perhaps, then, reflect a general characteristic of the human personality, which (as a result of certain invariant dimensions of family experience) views mother-son incest as more frightening, either morally or in its punitive consequences, than brother-sister (or father-daughter) incest.

It need only be further remarked here that the differential emotional reaction of the Trobrianders to queries concerning dreams of mother and sister incest which Malinowski adduces as evidence for the greater strength of the incestuous attachment to the sister is more simply explained by the fact that overt dreams of sister incest occur in the Trobriands while those of

3. In some special cases, however, incestuous fathers exhibit little psychopathology. Thus, in a review of 1,025 cases of father-daughter incest, Bagley (1969) discovered that in some of them incest was associated not so much with psychopathology as with two conditions of *social* pathology. In one condition, the family was isolated, and in lieu of a sexual partner, the father turned to his daughter, who, in effect, became his wife. Such cases are also reported for nineteenth-century rural Sweden and Utah, as well as for rural Japan today. The second condition consisted of overcrowding and social disorganization, Chicago and immediate postwar Germany being the most important examples.

mother incest do not. Why this should be so is addressed in the following chapter, in which sister incest dreams will be reexamined from a different perspective. But whatever its explanation, before leaving this subject it should be observed here that Malinowski's findings regarding incest constitute another refutation of his claim concerning the special stringency of the brother-sister incest taboo. For if this taboo is all that stringent, why is it violated not infrequently, both in dreams and in deeds, while the taboo on incest with the mother is never violated in either?

Malinowski's next argument for his claim that the sister rather than the mother is the primary incestuous object in the Trobriands can be dealt with briefly. There is, he tells us, a gradient of abusive obscenity in the Trobriands, according to which the expletives "cohabit with thy mother," "cohabit with thy sister," and "cohabit with thy wife" constitute, respectively, a "mild term," "a most serious offense," and the "worst" (*SR*:99–100). This gradient—so Malinowski argues—reflects the greater strength of the incestuous desire for the sister compared to the mother, for since the most insulting of these sexual imputations (the one concerning husband and wife) is the one in which the sexual relationship is legal, the insult gradient reflects the relative "likelihood of reality corresponding to the imputation." In short, it indicates that the desire for the sister is the strongest of the man's sexual desires. It is not clear to me, however, what such sparse data indicate. Nevertheless, even agreeing that Malinowski's interpretation is correct, this gradient is not a function, uniquely, of "mother-right," nor does it constitute evidence for the absence of an Oedipus complex. The Bedouin of the Sinai, for example, a patrilineal group, and one of the most "patriarchal" in the world, have an insult gradient of precisely the same type as the Trobriands'.

This brings us to the last, and, according to Malinowski, "the most telling evidence" for his thesis that in the Trobriand nuclear complex the libidinal desire of the boy is directed primarily to the sister rather than the mother. Since he twice claims that this evidence—a myth in which the origin of love magic is allegedly attributed to brother-sister incest—is the "most telling" (*SR*:112, 114), it merits special scrutiny. According to the relevant aspects of this myth, a boy prepared a concoction of love magic in his hut. Later, his sister entered the hut and accidentally brushed against the vessel containing the concoction, causing some of it to fall on her. As a result she was consumed with lust for her brother and, despite his repeated attempts to elude her, she relentlessly pursued him until, finally, he capitulated to her desires, and they committed incest. (See *SR*:114–16 for a précis of the myth, and *SLS*:541–45 and 551–65 for the full text.)

It is difficult to understand the grounds for Malinowski's claim that this myth attributes the origin of love magic to brother-sister incest since, according to the text, the brother already knew of and prepared love magic prior to the incestuous act with his sister. Indeed, in *SLS* (p. 545) Malinowski no longer claims that the myth accounts for the origin of love magic; he (properly) claims, instead, that it accounts for its transfer from one island (Kiatava) to another (Iwa). It would appear, then, that the "most telling evidence" for the influence of the matrilineal complex is not telling at all. Indeed, rather than reflecting the special power of the libidinal attraction of the boy for his sister, the myth shows the special power of this type of love magic to overcome inhibitions arising even from the incest taboo.

Although in *SLS* (p. 546), Malinowski, too, interprets the myth as demonstrating the power of love magic, he nevertheless continues to claim that it is evidence for the special power of the boy's sexual desire for his sister, for—so he argues—it proves that the magic is so powerful that it "can even break down the *terrible barriers* which separate brother and sister and persuade them to commit incest" (ibid.:italics mine).[4] Seeing, however, that the myth neither states nor implies that the barrier to incest between brother and sister is more "terrible" than that between mother and son—nor do any of the native glosses on the text indicate that this might be so—there is no evidence for this claim. Rather, Malinowski deduces it from his argument for the special stringency of the brother-sister taboo, which, as we have already

---

4. Actually, this symmetrical formulation does violence to the asymmetry of the text, according to which it is the girl who lusts after the brother, the latter only submitting to her importunities after much struggle. His resistance, of course, is only natural since it was she, not he, who brushed against the magical potion.

seen, is rather weak.[5] In short, a *speculation* concerning one cultural domain is used as *evidence* to support an interpretation concerning a finding from another domain.

Whether or not this myth proves the special power of love magic or its origin in brother-sister incest, Malinowski contends that it shows that brother-sister incest is the prototypical incest myth in matrilineal societies, replacing the mother-son (Oedipal) myth of "patriarchal" societies. This demonstrates, he argues, that in matriliny the libidinal dimension of the nuclear complex is found in the brother-sister, rather than the mother-son, relationship. Unfortunately, a comparative study of myth does not support Malinowski's contention. In his survey of Oedipal myths in Micronesia, Indonesia, and Melanesia, Lessa (1961:chapter 18) discovered that myths of mother-son incest are found in both matrilineal and patrilineal societies. Indeed, in the matrilineal society studied by Lessa himself—the Micronesian atoll of Ulithi—in which brother-sister avoidance is, if anything, even more stringent than in the Trobriands (ibid.:53), not only is there a myth of brother-sister incest, but also there is a classical Oedipal myth of mother-son incest in which, moreover, mother and son live together in a permanent incestuous relationship following the latter's murder of his father (ibid.:49–51).[6] This myth, as we shall see below, is reminiscent of a Trobriand myth of the same type.

To conclude this section, I would say that, on the evidence presented by Malinowski, the claim that the sister, rather than the mother, is the principal object of the boy's libidinal desires

5. Playing the devil's advocate, one might make the opposite claim. Since it is the girl, rather than the mother, who by brushing against the magical potion violates the incest taboo, this might suggest that though the potion is sufficiently powerful to overcome the prohibition on brother-sister incest, it is not powerful enough to overcome that on mother-son incest.

6. As another typical illustration of the anthropological misunderstanding of psychoanalysis, Lessa argues that this Ulithi Oedipus myth refutes the psychoanalytic theory of the Oedipus complex because Ulithi is matrilineal, while psychoanalytic theory claims that Oedipus myths are confined to "patriarchal" societies! This claim, of course, is Malinowski's, not Freud's. The latter would claim, on the contrary, that such myths should be found in both types of society inasmuch as (for him) the Oedipus complex is universal. In short, far from refuting the psychoanalytic claim, the Ulithi myth supports it.

in the Trobriands must be received with more than a little skepticism.

Relationship of the Son to His Mother's Brother

While conceding that the mother is the primary sexual object for the boy in the West, Malinowski nevertheless contends that the hostility dimension in the Oedipus complex is to be explained not by the boy's rivalry with the father for the love of the wife-mother, but by the father's authority, which (as we shall see below) is viewed by Malinowski as brutal and sadistic. Since, then, unlike the "patriarchal" societies of the West, it is the mother's brother who is the locus of authority in matrilineal societies, the boy's hostility in the Trobriands, Malinowski contends, is directed not to the father, but to the mother's brother.

Despite the almost universal acceptance of this contention, it is nevertheless difficult to evaluate because nowhere does Malinowski offer any direct evidence for the boy's hostility to the uncle, and his inferential evidence is as amenable to the sexual rivalry as to the jural authority hypothesis.

The inferential evidence consists of two ethnographic observations. First, in "prophetic dreams of death" (the frequency of occurrence of which we are not told) it is "usually the sister's son who will foredream his uncle's death" (*SR*:95). Second, the first victim of disease-causing sorcerers must fall in the category of "near maternal relatives" (*SR*:95). The latter argument is rather disingenuous (if not misleading) because the uncle is never singled out as one of the "near maternal relatives." Thus, in the passage just quoted Malinowski writes that the "near maternal relative" is "very often" the mother, and in an earlier, nonpolemical book, he explicitly gives primacy to the mother and sister (without even mentioning the mother's brother). Sorcery, he writes, "must first be practiced on his [the sorcerer's] mother or sister, or any of his maternal kindred" (Malinowski [1922] 1961:74). In effect, then, we are left with a single ethnographic observation—prophetic dreams of death—in support of the thesis that the uncle, rather than the father, is the principal object of the boy's hostility.

Even, however, if both observations were to be accepted, they would hardly constitute formidable evidence for the thesis of widespread hostility to the maternal uncle; at most the generalization would apply to a few dreamers and even fewer sorcerers. But even if it were conceded that hostility to the maternal uncle is widespread, on what basis can it be inferred that this hostility is grounded in the latter's jural authority? In principal, at least, it could just as plausibly be grounded in sexual rivalry. For if it is true, as Malinowski claims, that the incestuous desires of brother and sister persist (albeit in a repressed state) in adulthood, and that the boy is aware of his mother's repressed feelings for her brother, his hostility toward his mother's brother could just as well be attributed to sexual rivalry with him as to his jural authority. (On this point, see also Parsons 1969:12–14.) Whether the one or the other, since Malinowski provides no direct evidence for his claim that the maternal uncle is the principal object of the boy's hostility, and since the indirect evidence is not excessively strong, it would be better to leave this discussion of the boy's feelings for his uncle and turn instead to their social relationship. For it is on the basis of one dimension of their relationship—the uncle's jural authority—that Malinowski *postulates* the boy's hostility to him.

Although there is no doubt that in matrilineal systems in general, and in the Trobriands in particular, the mother's brother is the locus of jural authority, the degree to which this structural fact engenders hostility in his sister's son depends in large measure on the manner in which the uncle's authority is manifested in their relationship . It is rather exasperating, therefore, that on this critical point we encounter yet another lacuna in the ethnography. Nowhere in any of his writings does Malinowski provide an on-the-ground description of the relationship between the boy and his uncle. Instead, he states jural norms and formulates abstract generalizations. The following examples are typical, though not exhaustive. A woman's brother is "the head of her family . . . and as such exercises great influence, especially over the boys" (*SLS*:521). What this "influence" might be, or how it is exercised, Malinowski does not tell us. Again, "the authority over the children is vested in the mother's brother" (*SR*:23); it is he who "wields over them the direct potestas" (*SR*:24). Here, too, there is no further elaboration. Similarly, although we are told that the mother's brother "represents the principle of discipline, authority, and executive power within the family" (*SR*:24), no description of his behavior is offered. Even when his actual behavior is alluded to—thus, the mother's brother not only "wields the potestas," but "makes ample use of it" (*SR*:48)—no examples are presented.

In the absence, then, of any description of the manner in which the mother's brother expresses his potestas, let us take yet another tack. If the uncle's jural authority accounts for his becoming the principal target of the boy's hostility, there must presumably be sufficient opportunity for him to express this authority in some kind of ongoing interaction with him. From Malinowski's description, however, their interaction would appear to be infrequent at best. Until he moves at puberty to the bachelors' house, the boy lives with his natal family (*SLS*:61; *SR*:66), which means (since residence is virilocal) that during his childhood he and his uncle live not only in separate households, but in different villages (*SR*:24, 48). This indicates, as Malinowski admits, that the uncle's authority must be "exercised from a distance" (*SR*: 48).

To be sure, beginning at the age of six the boy is required to help his uncle in the gardens, which is a source of "constraint" for him (*SR*:49). Moreover, since every adult male periodically visits the home of his sister, this presumably offers yet another occasion for his exercise of "constraint." Unfortunately, we are not told how frequently either occurs, nor what the nature of the "constraint" might be, but from the little information Malinowski does provide, it seems safe to infer that it is slight.

In the first place, because the uncle's authority is exercised "from a distance," it cannot—as Malinowski admits in a highly revealing throwaway line—"become oppressive in those small matters which are *most* irksome" (*SR*:49, italics mine). Since, moreover, we are elsewhere told that it is the father with whom the boy interacts "in daily execution of nine-tenths of all the pursuits and interests of life" (Malinowski 1926:109), would it be unreasonable to infer that it is the father, rather than the uncle, whose authority has that consequence? In the second place, in claiming that the matrilineal complex does not commence until puberty, Malinowski stresses that "*only* at this period is the child submitted to the system of repression and taboos" (in this case, "the submission to matriarchal tribal law") which is "brought about by the influence of the mother's brother" (*SR*:74–75, italics mine). This being the case it seems safe to infer that the "constraints" imposed by him prior to puberty are not very severe.

Again, since even prior to puberty many of these repressions and taboos "have already been inculcated into the boy by the parents" (*SR*:49), it would seem that they, rather than the uncle, impose those "constraints" on the child. To be sure, Malinowski hastens to add that it is the uncle who is "always held up as the real authority behind the rules" (*SR*:49), but this claim too is contradicted by yet another claim. For if it is a "regular institution" (Malinowski 1926:109) for adolescent boys to remain in their natal village (rather than moving to their uncle's), and if this serves to "*prolong* paternal authority" (ibid.:108, my italics), this can only mean that it is the father's, not the uncle's, authority that is present all along.

If, then, the "constraints" imposed by the mother's brother before puberty do not appear to be very severe, how severe are those imposed by him during or after puberty? Apparently not very. For although in one passage Malinowski (*SR*:75) reports that puberty is the period when the boy first develops "repressed antagonisms" toward his uncle—and this despite the fact that it is a "regular institution" for boys to remain in their natal village even after puberty—in another passage he writes that puberty is the period in which, because the uncle instructs him in tribal lore, the boy's "interest in his mother's brothers . . . is greatest and their relations are at their best" (*SR*:67). Hence, it is not at puberty after all, but somewhat "later on," that "friction with the maternal uncle makes its appearance" (*SR*:67). Malinowski does not tell us how much "later on," but by this time the account is so confusing that I am not sure it would make much difference.[7]

In sum, I would submit that despite the fact that, jurally, the mother's brother has authority over the boy, the extent to which his authority is exercised, the age at which it is operative, the degree to which it is frustrating, and the intensity of the hostility which it consequently arouses in the boy—all of these questions

7. Malinowski seems to have been aware of the confusions in his account because in a footnote appended at this very juncture in his argument he writes that the relationship between a young man, his father, and his maternal uncle

remain maximally problematic. This being so, we seem to be confronted with the following alternatives. On the one hand we can grant that jural authority is the basis for the arousal of the hostility dimension of the nuclear complex, and since the mother's brother is the locus of jural authority, it is he who is the principal target of the boy's hostility in the Trobriands. Since, however, on the basis of Malinowski's description it can safely be claimed that there is nothing in the behavior of the mother's brother that even approximates the brutality and sheer sadism of the Western father as Malinowski describes him (see below), it would be quixotic to believe that the mother's brother is to the matrilineal complex what the father is to the Western Oedipus complex. That is, if it is the authority of the mother's brother that arouses the hostility of the Trobriand boy, the hostility found in the Trobriand nuclear complex is a pale imitation of that found in the nuclear complex in the West (as Malinowski portrays it).

If we were to grant, on the other hand, that the Trobriand boy does indeed harbor powerful feelings of hostility to the mother's brother (but that Malinowski simply failed to provide the evidence to support this contention), then, from the mild "constraints" that he suffers at the latter's hands, it can hardly be possible for those feelings to be aroused by the mother's brother himself. It would be more reasonable to assume that they are aroused elsewhere, and that the mother's brother is merely the object for their displacement. In Jones's (1924) analysis, these feelings are aroused by the father. Which of these alternatives is the more probable cannot be decided until the boy's relationship with the father is examined more closely.

Father-Son Relationship

In evaluating Malinowski's treatment of the father-son relationship in the Trobriands, it may be well to begin by recalling that, as Freud describes it, the boy's Oedipal relationship with his

---

"are in reality somewhat more complicated than I have been able to present here" (*SR*:242), and he promises to discuss it once again in his "forthcoming" book on kinship (which, however, was never published). It might be added that much of the confusion in Malinowski's account may be a result of the fact that his generalizations concerning the Trobriands are based on observations directed mostly at the lineages of chiefs, which, on some important dimensions, differ from those of commoners.

father is a *triangular* one in which, taking the mother as his primary love-object, the boy hates his father because he views him as a rival for her love. For Malinowski, however, the boy's Oedipal relationship with his father is a *diadic* relationship only. That is, while agreeing that the mother is the boy's primary love-object in the West, Malinowski contends that he hates his father not because the latter is his rival for the love of the wife-mother, but because he is an oppressive authority figure.

Now Freud, it will be recalled, also assigns an important Oedipal role to the father's authority, but for him it is important as an explanation not for the origin, but for the resolution of their Oedipal relationship. That is, motivated by fear of the father's authority, the ultimate expression of which is castration, the boy gives up his Oedipal hatred of the father—as well as his Oedipal love for the mother—by introjecting the father's authority and establishing a superego. Since for Malinowski, however, the father's authority is the origin of the son's Oedipal hostility, and since in the Trobriands, so he believed, it is the mother's brother who is the primary authority figure, the father, Malinowski contends, cannot possibly be the target of the boy's hatred in the Trobriands.

In sum, having rejected the notion that the Western boy might be hostile to the father because the latter is his rival for the love of the wife-mother, Malinowski does not allow for the possibility that although the Trobriand father may not be an authority figure, the son might still hate him as a rival for his love of the wife-mother. Nor, for the same reason, does he allow for the possibility that the apparent absence of an incestuous desire for the mother in the Trobriands might be explained not by the lack of such a desire, but by its repression attendant upon the fear of a powerful rival (whether that rival be father or mother's brother). That he would not entertain these notions even as possibilities may perhaps be explained by his starkly contrasting perceptions of Western and Trobriand fathers.

Although the Trobriand father, as we saw in the previous section, exercises much more authority over the son than Malinowski allowed—indeed by our interpretation of the available evidence he seems to be the primary authority figure—he is nevertheless a very benevolent father indeed. Thus, he is variously characterized by Malinowski: he is a "beloved, benevolent friend" (*SR*:23); he is "only loving . . . and tender" (*SR*:24); he is "a hard working and conscientious nurse . . . always interested in the children, sometimes passionately so [who] performs all his duties eagerly and fondly" (*SR*:33); with the infant, he is "tender and loving," and with the child, he plays, "carries it, and teaches it such amusing sports and occupations as takes its fancy . . . with a strong affection" (*SR*:38); as they grow older, he "continues to befriend the children, to help them, to teach them what they like and as much as they like" (*SR*:48).

Such a near-idyllic portrait, of course, cannot help but arouse at least a modicum of skepticism in the reader. Can we fully credit the reliability of extravagant generalizations—the father is "only" loving, "always" tender, and the like—which on their face have the ring of hyperbole? If, however, we understand that the book from which these passages are quoted was explicitly written as a polemic, the hyperbole then makes sense as an attempt by Malinowski to reinforce his polemical aim of proving that the hostility of the Western son is to be explained, pace Freud, by the father's oppressive authority. Whatever his aim, however, and even after discounting for the hyperbole, the Trobriand father still emerges from Malinowski's portrait as a warm and kindly person. Hence, having rejected the Oedipal hypothesis that the son might hate even this type of father because of his perception of him as a rival for the mother's love, it is understandable that Malinowski should have concluded that hostility is absent from the Trobriand son's relationship with his father.

At the same time, given his perception of the Western father it is also understandable that Malinowski should have rejected the Oedipal explanation for the son's hatred of the father in the West. As Malinowski sees him, the Western father, "irrespective of nationality and social class," is an "absolute ruler" who is "liable to become a tyrant." He is the "origin of punishment" and therefore "becomes a bogey." He is the "perfect being for whose benefit everything has to be done," and the " 'ogre' whom the child has to fear." If he is "loving," he will assume the "former role of a demi-god," and if he is "pompous," he will "earn the suspicion and even hatred of the nursery." If, moreover, he is a worker or a peasant, the "friction" is "much more acute and chronic." Often drunk, he "vents his ill-temper on the family, and bullies mother and children." In more extreme, but nevertheless "numerous," cases he will, when drunk, "beat the children for sheer pleasure, or drag them out of bed and send them into the cold night" (*SR*:36–37).

That some fathers of this type might be found in the West (though perhaps not uniquely in the West) can hardly be denied, and that by their brutality and sadism they would arouse their sons' hatred is understandable enough. Given, then, his view that fathers of this type represent the *typical* Western father, it is also understandable that Malinowski should have believed that the boy's wish to monopolize the love of his mother, even if true, is irrelevant as an explanation for the hostility dimension of the Oedipus complex. That, however, Malinowski could have held the extraordinary view that such relentlessly brutal fathers represent (or even represented in Malinowski's time) the typical Western father suggests once again that he may have been motivated, perhaps unconsciously, by the polemical aim of proving that very belief. For if hatred toward the father is present only when (like this putative Western father) he is brutal, and absent when (like the Trobriand father) he is benign, could it then be doubted that rivalry for the mother plays no role in the boy's Oedipal hostility in the West or, more generally, that it is the person who serves as the authority figure for the boy who becomes the hated figure in the nuclear complex?

Although the logic of this argument is unassailable, it is factually vulnerable to serious criticism in regard to the West and the Trobriands alike.

To begin with the West, even granting that the father is as brutal as Malinowski makes him out to be, this argument does not address the question of whether, in addition to the fear and hatred that is aroused in the boy by his father's oppressive authority, he might not also hate him because he perceives him as a rival for the love of the wife-mother. And by failing to address that question, the argument also fails to address the prior question of whether the father's putatively harsh treatment of the son might not be motivated, at least in part, by his own rivalry with him for the love of the wife-mother, so that the boy's fear and hatred of him might therefore be "Oedipal" in that it is a response to the father's "complementary" Oedipus complex. Finally, this argument neglects to address the question of whether Western sons whose fathers do not conform to the putatively typical Western father—surely there must be some atypical Western fathers—might not nevertheless be hostile to them.

That Malinowski failed to address these questions can probably be explained by the assumption that in his view all three, but most especially the third, are counterintuitive and therefore not worth addressing. And yet until they are addressed, the grounds for filial hostility in the West, I would submit, remain problematic. Or at least they would have remained problematic had Malinowski been our only source of data concerning the father-son relationship in the West, which, fortunately, is not the case. Although the available data make it difficult (though not impossible) to address the first two questions, it is much less difficult to address the third. In fact, we know of at least a few Western fathers—even from the era in which Malinowski was writing—who approximate Malinowski's description of Trobriand fathers: fathers who are friends of their children, who play with them, who perform their duties fondly, who show them strong affection, and so on. And yet such fathers, according to clinical evidence, also arouse a hostility in their sons whose motivation, moreover, is typically Oedipal. (The latter finding is hardly surprising given the fact that these fathers are benign, and that their sons' hostility could have hardly been motivated by their "authority.") Indeed, the first psychoanalytic account of the Oedipus complex, the case of "Little Hans," is an account of a five-year-old boy whose father was a perfect exemplar of fathers of this type. It might be noted that this case (Freud [1909] 1968) was published almost twenty years before Malinowski published his own views on the Oedipus complex.

Malinowski's argument concerning the grounds for filial hostility is vulnerable to criticism not only in regard to the Western, but to the Trobriand nuclear complex as well. Although Malinowski contends that the boy's feelings for the father are uniformly warm and loving in the Trobriands, and that he harbors no hostility toward him, he presents no evidence, direct or indirect, in its support. Rather, it is a conclusion deduced from his observations concerning the father's treatment of the boy. For Malinowski it is all but self-evident that the warm and loving Trobriand father, at least as he portrays him, could not possibly arouse any hatred in his son. This conclusion, however, is contradicted not only by the Western evidence adduced above; more importantly, it is contradicted by the Trobriand evidence itself.

In the first place, it is contradicted by evidence presented by Powell, who, on the basis of observations of father-child relations in the Trobriands, reports that "the *psychological* relation between father and child is essentially the same under the Trobriand matrilineal as under a patrilineal system of kinship" (Powell 1957:142, italics mine), which presumably means that, among other things, the boy's hostility to the father in the Trobriands is little different from what it is in the West. A more troublesome contradiction, since it is based on Malinowski's own data, is Malinowski's report that Trobrianders regard the "bonds of fatherhood [and marriage] . . . as artificial and untrustworthy under any strain" (*SLS*:161). That the untrustworthy quality of their bond might indicate some hostility in the father-son relationship is strongly supported by yet another of Malinowski's findings, and the most important contradiction of all. According to Trobriand belief, Malinowski (ibid.) reports, every death— except for one caused by suicide or a visible accident—is caused by sorcery, and in the case of a male's death "the principal suspicion of sorcery attaches always to the wife and children" (*SLS*:161). Contrary, then, to Malinowski's view, the Trobrianders themselves believe that the boy does harbor hostility to the father, that it persists into adulthood, and that it is sufficiently strong to lead to (magical) patricide.[8]

Such limited contradictory findings, I hasten to add, do not in themselves permit us to conclude that the Trobriand son harbors hostile feelings for his father or, if he does, that they have their source in the son's Oedipal rivalry with him. Both contentions require much more evidence in order to be accepted. At the very least, however, these findings are sufficient to cast serious doubt on Malinowski's contrary contention that there is no hostility to the father in the Trobriands.

8. Malinowski is more than a little perplexed by this belief, not, however, because it contradicts his view that the son harbors no hostile feelings to the father—he does not comment upon this contradiction—but because he cannot understand why the Trobriand son would want to kill his father, despite the fact that his death causes him to suffer economic loss (*SLS*:161)!

Summary and Conclusions

Since the evidence adduced on its behalf is slim, confusing, and contradictory, I argued in the foregoing assessment that the Trobriand matrilineal complex is essentially unsupported. In short, on the basis of that evidence I concluded that it is highly unlikely that the early libidinal feelings of the son for the mother disappear gradually and spontaneously, that the sister is the primary object of his libidinal desires, that the mother's brother is the primary target of his hostility, and that he harbors no hostility toward his father.

To preclude any misunderstanding of this assessment, I wish, however, to explicitly disavow two inferences that might erroneously be drawn from it. Having rejected Malinowski's case for a Trobriand matrilineal complex, it cannot thereby be concluded that the Oedipus complex therefore exists in the Trobriands, let alone that the latter complex is produced by every conceivable type of family. Rather, from the foregoing assessment it can only be concluded that (1) if, as Malinowski claims, the Oedipus complex exists in Western actors, then on the basis of the data he presents concerning Trobriand actors it does not follow (as he argues) that this complex could not be present in the Trobriands; (2) if, as he further claims, the Oedipus complex is produced by a family structure of the Western type, then from his description of the Trobriand family it does not follow (as he argues) that this complex could not be produced by a family structure of the Trobriand type.

It must be stressed, however, that these limited conclusions are based on the data that Malinowski marshaled on behalf of the matrilineal complex. If, however, the data base is widened by drawing upon additional Trobriand materials which Malinowski ignored in arguing his case, I would then contend that these conclusions are too restricted in their claims, and that a stronger case can be made for the existence of an Oedipus complex in the Trobriands than I have thus far allowed. In the following two chapters I attempt to make that case.

3

The Trobriand Oedipus Complex:
A Hypothesis

Methods of Inquiry

If, following upon the suggestion made at the end of the last chapter, we wished to discover whether a male Oedipus complex existed in the Trobriands, what kinds of data would we look for? Inasmuch as this psychological constellation is formed in childhood, ideally we would look for evidence of its existence in the behavior and fantasies of boys roughly between three and six years of age. Since, however, Malinowski (like other anthropologists of his time) collected few data of that type, such a procedure is impossible to adopt. There is, however, another route that can be followed. Typically, according to Oedipal theory, the childhood Oedipus complex undergoes two fates: it is either extinguished in later childhood, or else it is repressed and persists, albeit as an unconscious constellation, into adulthood. The latter does not occur in the Trobriands, according to Malinowski, for since the Oedipus complex is not formed in childhood, adult thoughts and feelings regarding Trobriand parents contain "nothing repressed, nothing negative, no frustrated desire" (SR:72). This conclusion would not, of course, constitute evidence for the absence of a childhood Oedipus complex because the latter might, instead, be extinguished. Assuming for the moment, however, that contrary to Malinowski's assertion such a psychological constellation is formed in Trobriand childhood, and that rather than being extinguished it is repressed, what kinds of data would constitute evidence for the existence of an unconscious Oedipus complex in Trobriand adults?

Ideally, of course, such evidence would consist of the same kinds of data—unconscious fantasies, dreams and dream associations, and transference reactions—that are used by clinicians to discover such an unconscious psychological constellation in their subjects. Since, however, data of this kind—except for dreams, but without dream associations—are unavailable for the Trobriands (as well as for all other societies studied by the ethnographic method exclusively), the only data available to us are ethnographic. Our question then becomes, To what extent are data of the latter type evidential for establishing the existence of an unconscious Oedipus complex or any other unconscious psychological constellation?

The answer to the latter question is, I think, fairly obvious. Ethnographic data can provide only indirect evidence for the existence of such a psychological constellation, for inasmuch as the latter exists in the private and inner world of individual actors, its existence can only be inferred from the social and cultural "facts" which make up their public and external world. If, then, it were to be argued—as some social scientists do indeed argue—that there is no relationship (or, at best, an adventitious one) between the private psychological world of individual actors and their public sociocultural world, any attempt to infer the existence of any psychological constellation from ethnographic data would be impossible.

Malinowski, of course, did not subscribe to this view. Indeed, it is to his great credit—many, of course, would say that it is to his discredit—that Malinowski was one of the first anthropologists to recognize that social and cultural systems bear systematic relationships to, and therefore provide important evidence concerning, the minds of their bearers and transmitters. Indeed, except for dreams, his construction of the matrilineal complex was based almost exclusively on myths, customs, religious beliefs, folklore, cultural norms, and the like. Moreover, although he himself did not use the term, he may also have been the first anthropologist to view—and therefore to use—these cultural symbol systems as "projective systems."

Although (as is evident from my critique in the previous chapter) I have generally disagreed with Malinowski's psychological interpretations of the social and cultural data which he employed for his construction of the matrilineal complex, I entirely agree

with him that ethnographic data of this kind, even though indirect, constitute important and relevant evidence for the cognitive and motivational characteristics of social actors. I also
agree with him that since cultural symbol systems are, in large
part, projective systems, they are especially important in this
regard. Hence, in this and the following chapter I wish to reex-
amine the ethnographic—as well, of course, as the psychological—data which Malinowski published on the Trobriands for
the evidence they might provide for the existence of an Oedipus
complex. Although in this chapter we shall make as much use
of psychological data (dreams) as ethnographic, the data used
in the following chapter are exclusively ethnographic. Insofar,
then, as the ethnographic data in both chapters are important
for us because of their symbolic meanings, and insofar as these
meanings are interpreted projectively, before proceeding with
this reexamination, it is important to indicate what is meant
when we say that cultural symbol systems may be viewed as
"projective systems."

Although, as mentioned above, Malinowski used cultural
symbol systems as projective systems to support his case for a
Trobriand matrilineal complex, the term itself is Kardiner's, and
it was he who most systematically explicated the concept (Kardiner 1939, 1945). It was Kardiner's assumption that given common childhood experiences, the members of small, culturally
homogeneous societies develop common fears, wishes, and fantasies. It was his further assumption, following Freud's lead,
that fears, wishes, and fantasies that are threatening to the ego
are repressed, i.e., rendered unconscious. Although repressed
at the individual level, they are projected and represented in
disguised form, so Kardiner further proposed, in culturally constituted cognitive systems (such as religious and magical beliefs),
in culturally constituted fantasies (such as myths, legends, and
folktales), and in certain kinds of culturally patterned social behavior. This being so, in addition to their public and conscious
meanings, social and cultural systems have unconscious and
private symbolic meanings which, like dreams, reflect the unconscious motivational dispositions and mental representations
of the social actors. (For a more extended discussion of this
theme, see Spiro 1982.)

These, roughly, constituted the set of assumptions that were used implicitly by Malinowski for constructing a matrilineal complex from Trobriand social and cultural data, and they are the ones that I shall use explicitly for constructing a Trobriand Oedipus complex. Although using the same assumptions, Malinowski and I differ in our conclusions because my interpretations, unlike his, are based on psychodynamic formulations. If one is concerned with the putative unconscious meanings of cultural symbols—which is what it means to view these symbols projectively—it is necessary to understand unconscious processes in general, and in my view psychodynamic theory, especially its treatment of inner conflict and defense, is the one which can best help us to understand these processes.

Now the notion of projective systems is often suspect in more conventional anthropological analysis because it smacks of psychologizing. But all claims to the discovery of symbolic meanings in cultural beliefs—or, even, for that matter, in explicitly stipulated cultural symbols—involve psychologizing inasmuch as their meanings reside not in these beliefs and symbols themselves, but in the minds of social actors who attribute these meanings to them. In that general sense all symbolic meanings are "projective."

Technically, however, the notion of a projective system refers to the manner in which unconscious symbolic meanings are expressed, and it is in that more limited sense that it is being used here. If, so it is assumed, belief and wishes are threatening to the self—evoking a sense of shame or guilt or lowered self-esteem—they will be repressed. But since unconscious beliefs and wishes, no less than conscious ones, seek expression and gratification, respectively, they are then, according to projective theory, unconsciously projected and displaced in social and cultural systems, and are thereby expressed and gratified in symbolic disguise—unless of course they are symbolically represented in those individual symbol formations called neurotic symptoms. In short, to say that some cultural belief or social form serves as a projective system is merely to say that in addition to its conscious meanings (symbolic or otherwise) it also has unconscious symbolic meanings.

Having stated my assumptions, it is important, before proceeding to an examination of the data, to describe my methods of inquiry. A psychological construct such as the Oedipus—or the matrilineal—complex, whether it be sought in the minds of analysands or in its ethnographic expressions, is not found as a ready packaged constellation of psychological or sociocultural variables. Rather, the psychoanalyst and anthropologist, alike, find disparate "traces" (to use Malinowski's term) of it, which they must then piece together to construct the constellation. Hence, although already upon my first reading of the Trobriand data from which Malinowski constructed the matrilineal complex, I had caught glimpses and hints of Oedipal material, they made little impression on me until, toward the end of *Sex and Repression*, my attention was arrested by a passage in which Malinowski claimed that nowhere in the Trobriand data were there even any "traces" of the Oedipus complex. Here is the passage:

> If, as has been proved, there are no traces of [the Oedipus complex] either in Trobriand folklore or in dreams or visions, or in any other symptoms; if in all these manifestations we find instead the other complex—where is then the repressed Oedipus complex to be found? (*SR*:130).

This passage took me very much by surprise since, as I have said, I had indeed discerned "traces" of the Oedipus complex in some of those "manifestations," which, however, I had ignored. Stimulated now by Malinowski's sweeping claim, I decided to scrutinize these traces closely, and in doing so I discovered still others, both in the data that Malinowski had used and in many others that he had neglected. Although none of these traces in itself constitutes evidence for an Oedipus complex, when taken together they strongly suggested, so I concluded, that Malinowski's rhetorical question had a ready answer: it is in these very "manifestations" in which Malinowski had detected none of its traces that the repressed Trobriand Oedipus complex is to be found. In presenting those traces here, I shall proceed by recapitulating the steps by which I finally arrived at that conclusion.

These steps began, as is often the case in scientific inquiry, in a "context of discovery," and ended in a "context of validation." I first discerned "traces" of the Trobriand Oedipus complex in a set of cultural and psychological data which revealed a pattern I have come to call the "absent-father pattern." This pattern arrested my attention because it contains a paradox: why, given the warm father-child relationship in the Trobriands, is the father virtually absent from three universally important domains—myths, dreams, and reproduction beliefs? Exploring this pattern systematically, I concluded that it provides evidence for the existence of hostility to the father, that this hostility is Oedipal in its motivation, and that, moreover, its intensity is of more than ordinary strength. Oedipal hostility toward the father, of course, implies incestuous attraction to the mother, but however compelling an implication might be, without supporting evidence it does not in itself constitute a finding. I then recalled having discerned traces of such evidence in some Trobriand dreams which Malinowski had reported. When, upon reanalyzing these dreams, the traces of an incestuous attachment to the mother became much more evident, I concluded that there was now sufficient evidence to seriously entertain the hypothesis that an Oedipus complex exists in the Trobriands.

Since, if they are to be accepted, hypotheses must be confirmed, it was now necessary to shift from the "discovery" mode of inquiry to the "validation" mode, and I decided to test the Oedipal hypothesis in a rigorous manner, by using the hypothetico-deductive method. A set of predictions concerning the expected consequences of the Oedipus complex were deduced from Oedipal theory all of which, as it turned out, were supported by the Trobriand ethnographic data that were used to test them. It only remained to test the further hypothesis, suggested by the analysis of the absent-father pattern, that the Trobriand Oedipus complex was of more than ordinary intensity. According to Oedipal theory, such an outcome should be produced by a highly seductive mother, and this hypothesis too was tested by the hypothetico-deductive method. Specifically, a set of predictions concerning the expected antecedent and consequent conditions of a highly seductive mother were deduced from Oedipal theory and, as in the case of the first set, these predictions too were supported by the data. Both hypotheses, in short, were confirmed.

In this chapter, we shall examine those data in which traces of the Oedipus complex were initially discerned and whose analysis led to the hypothesis that such a constellation exists in the Trobriands. In the next chapter, we shall describe the predictions that were formulated to test this hypothesis, as well as the results of these tests. Let us begin, then, with the absent-father pattern.

The Absent-Father Pattern

Although Trobriand fathers may not be the paragons of fatherhood that Malinowski, writing in a polemical context, purports them to be, it is nevertheless a fair assumption that, stripped of his hyperbole, they occupy a position near the upper end of any cross-cultural scale of paternal nurturance and benevolence. It is all the more remarkable therefore—indeed, it would be remarkable even if this were not the case—that the Trobriand father is virtually *nonexistent* in three of the most important human domains: dreams, myths, and reproduction beliefs. Let us see.

Despite the fact that there exists in the Trobriands a rich corpus of myths, the father—so Malinowski informs us in one of his throwaway lines—"is *never* mentioned, and does not exist in *any* part of the mythological world" (*SR*:102, italics mine). Although, unlike the case of myths, Malinowski does not explicitly state that the father never appears in dreams, since he goes out of his way to describe the relative frequency of sister and mother dreams, it seems safe to infer from his silence that father dreams are virtually absent. That the father does not exist in Trobriand reproduction beliefs is, of course, one of the most widely known ethnographic facts concerning the primitive world. Rather than resulting from sexual intercourse, conception, so the Trobrianders believe, results from an ancestor entering the woman's womb in the form of a "spirit child" (Malinowski [1927] 1955:170–79).

Before examining each of these cases of the absent father in detail, I wish to underscore the importance, both substantively and methodologically, of their joint occurrence. There may be some few other societies in which the father is absent from the cast of actors involved in myths, dreams, and reproduction, taken separately. That in the Trobriands, however, he is absent from all three domains not only is a rare, if not a unique, phenomenon, but means that father-absence is a *cultural pattern*. As in the case, therefore, of the parts of any pattern, no explanation for the absence of the father in anyone of these domains can be accepted as valid unless it can simultaneously explain the more general pattern of father-absence of which it is a constituent part.

Taking this methodological premise as our point of departure, I would now argue that the absence of the father not only from one, but from three domains in which, in cross-cultural perspective, his presence is both expected and prominent cannot be explained by the theory of cultural relativism—each culture just happens to provide a unique perspective on the world—if indeed that fatuous theory could ever explain anything. Indeed, since, in the light of the cross-cultural evidence, this *pattern* suggests that the father is not simply "absent" from these domains, but that he has been eliminated from them, I would argue rather vigorously that such a pattern can only be explained as a response to some strong motivational determinant(s).

A possible clue to the identification of such a motive or motives is suggested by the fact that in all three domains present in this pattern—myths, dreams, and reproduction beliefs—strong and often conflicting emotions (love and hate, compassion and envy, sympathy and jealousy) are frequently aroused and expressed toward the same person, object, or event. This being so I would now suggest that the Trobriand pattern of father-absence is simultaneously motivated both by unconscious feelings of hostility toward the father and—since the Trobriand father is also an object of love and strong regard—by the wish to avoid the arousal and expression of these feelings. Although it might be difficult to credit the notion that the Trobrianders (or anyone else) might wish to eliminate the father from these three domains, let alone that such a wish might be motivated by contradictory feelings of love and hate, that is nevertheless the hypothesis that I now wish to explore in attempting to explain the pattern of the absent father in the Trobriands.

We shall begin our exploration with dreams, for which we have the least information, and whose explanation will therefore be the most speculative, and then proceed to myths and reproduction beliefs, for which the information is more abundant. Unlike the case of myths (in which our analysis will be guided by structural principle) and of reproductive beliefs (in which our analysis will be guided by symbolic meanings and expressive behavior) we have no corpus of Trobriand dreams—nor even one paradigmatic dream—by which we might be guided. In short, in this case we can chart our course only by the use of theoretical assumptions.

Let us begin with Malinowski's comment that "it is a remarkable and characteristic feature of [the Trobrianders], in which they seem to differ from other savages, that they apparently dream little," so that when they were asked to recount their dreams, "the answer was usually negative" (*SR*:889). Since we have learned only subsequent to Malinowski's death that REM sleep (the portion of total sleep during which dreaming normally takes place) occurs from four to six times a night, we can hardly fault him for not distinguishing between the frequency of dreaming, on the one hand, and the frequency with which dreams are recalled (let alone reported), on the other. Nevertheless, since (on the basis of this new knowledge) we now do know that it is not dreaming, but the recall of dreams, that is infrequent in the Trobriands, Malinowski's claim, that the paucity of Trobriand dreams indicates that the Trobrianders are a "non-repressed society," must be turned on its head. For if, as we now know, the Trobrianders dream as frequently as anyone else, then, by Malinowski's hypothesis they are at least as repressed as any other people.

In fact, however, the relationship between dreams and repression is not so simple as Malinowski suggested, for contrary to what he believed it is not the dream itself, but the disguise found in the dream that is instigated by repressed—and, therefore, forbidden—thoughts. Hence, it is not that the Trobrianders dream as much as anyone else that indicates that they are repressed, but rather that they only infrequently recall their dreams. For if a dream expresses forbidden, and therefore repressed, thoughts, the dream itself is repressed upon awakening only if, as sometimes happens, the manifest content of the dream does not sufficiently disguise those thoughts. In short, the persistent failure to recall dreams is a defense against some psychological threat—guilt, anxiety, fear, shame, and the like—attendant upon the repressed dream-thoughts entering consciousness. Although we can only speculate, of course, about the forbidden dream-thought(s) that account for the repression of dreams in the Trobriands, I would suggest that they are related in part to a double anomaly posed by the absence of the father in these dreams.

That fathers are absent from recalled dreams in the Trobriands, despite the fact that they are kindly and nurturant figures, poses the first anomaly. That in other societies, in which fathers are not that nurturant and kindly, they are nevertheless frequently represented in recalled dreams (cf. Hall and Nordby 1972:42) poses the second. Considering these anomalies, it is at least plausible to assume that the paucity of recalled dreams of any type in the Trobriands might be a function, in part, of a high incidence of father dreams that, being threatening, are repressed. Since, then, the Trobriand father is a kindly and nurturant figure, one for whom consciously the son has warm and loving feelings, it might be further suggested that father dreams are threatening because they express hostile wishes toward him which are insufficiently disguised, and since their recall would arouse strong guilt, they are repressed.

According to this explanation, then, the absence of father dreams in the Trobriands may be taken as one sign of repressed hostility toward the father. Although entirely speculative, this explanation has three merits: (*a*) it is consistent with the general theory of dreams; (*b*) it accounts, in part, for the curious paucity of recalled dreams in the Trobriands (later in this chapter we shall offer an additional explanation for this curious finding); (*c*) it resolves the double anomaly of father-absence in dreams. To be sure, this explanation does not account for the basis for the filial hostility that, putatively, is expressed in Trobriand dreams, but perhaps that might be discovered in the analysis of the other domains included in the absent-father pattern. Let us, then, turn to those other domains—myths and reproduction beliefs—beginning with myths.

Unlike dreams, we do have a small corpus of Trobriand myths, a fact which makes our analysis of father-absence in this domain much less speculative. For if, in any context whatsoever, there is a persistent pattern of the absence of a person (or object) whose presence is normally to be expected, and if, instead, some other person (or object) has taken his place, the clue to his absence is often provided by his replacement. Applying this structural principle to the absence of the father in myths, we may begin to get a handle on this curious phenomenon by discovering who takes his place in those particular myths in which, structurally, his presence would be expected. To illustrate this structuralist method, I shall first analyze one myth in detail, which can then be used as the paradigm for subsequent interpretations. The myth I have chosenfor analysis is paradigmatic for another reason: it is the one that Malinowski singled out as the paradigmatic family myth for a matrilineal society. Above all others, so he claims, this myth not only reflects "the pattern of the matrilineal family" (*SR*:103), but is one which "contains a typical matrilineal drama" (*SR*:105). Moreover, since it is part of a complex of myths—a mythic cycle—which recounts the career of a Trobriand culture hero, it is well known. In addition, the themes elucidated by the analysis of this myth are consistent, as we shall see below, with the themes of other types of oral narratives in which, unlike myths, the father is present.

This paradigmatic myth recounts the early life of the culture hero, Tudava by name, who was born of a virgin, and who grew up—as he was born—without a father. In this myth, the happy life enjoyed by the early residents of the Trobriand Archipelago is disrupted by the cannibalistic ogre Dokonikan, who has consumed the inhabitants of one village after another. As Dokonikan approaches the village of Laba'i, inhabited by Tudava, the latter's mother's brothers flee, leaving Tudava and his mother behind. His mother raises Tudava by herself, teaching him martial arts and magic. When he grows up, Tudava kills Dokonikan (with the aid of the magic his mother had taught him) and cuts off his head. Tudava disguises the head in a taro pudding, which he presents as a gift to one of his maternal uncles. Reacting with "horror and dismay," and "seized with fear and remorse" at having abandoned his sister and nephew, the uncle atones for his neglect by acceding to Tudava's request to take his daughter as his wife.

For Malinowski this myth reflects a crucial strain in the matrilineal family, namely, the strain induced in the adult male by the expectation that he serve as the protector, not of his wife and his own son, but of his sister and her son, despite the fact that it goes against his "natural tendency" (*SR*:104). Although this myth may reflect such a strain, by making this the focus of his analysis, Malinowski ignores not only the main plot of the myth and the focus of its dramatic action, but also its most important structural characteristic—the absence of a father from its dramatis personae. For if, as Malinowski claims, the myth reflects the "pattern of the matrilineal family," then, inasmuch as the father is one of its prominent members, as well as the most important male in the family household (the one who is purported never to shirk his responsibility to his children, but who cares for them eagerly and fondly), his absence from Tudava's family is all the more conspicuous. To be sure, Tudava was born of a virgin, but since in the Trobriands no children are believed to have genitors, there is no reason that he, like they, should not have had a pater. In short, since the matrilineal family comprises four important statuses—child, mother, mother's brother, and father—the absence of a representative of one of these statuses, that of father, must surely be accounted as the most conspicuous *structural* feature of the myth. That the status of father is replaced by that of cannibalistic ogre—in addition to mother, son, and mother's brother, Dokonikan is the only other character in the myth—must be accounted, therefore, as the most conspicuous *sociological* feature of the myth.

Although the absence of the father from the corpus of Trobriand myths was noted by Malinowski merely in passing, he himself was sufficiently perplexed by the absence of the father in the Tudava myth to have felt constrained to explain this structural anomaly. In fact, he offered not one, but two explanations. According to his first explanation the myth has one theme—the hostility of the brother to his sister and her son. This is demonstrated, so he argued, by the fact that when the uncle saw the head of Dokonikan in the taro pudding, he reacted with horror and dismay (rather than with joy), suggesting an "association or connivance" between the uncle and Dokonikan. "In reality," therefore, the myth contains "one villain and one conflict distributed over two stages and duplicated into two persons" (*SR*:105). That is, the cannibalistic ogre and the mother's brother are really one and the same person, and the latter's destructive wishes toward his sister and her son are disguised by being attributed to the former.

Malinowski, however, was not entirely satisfied with this interpretation of the identity of Dokonikan, and he immediately offered another, a "historical," interpretation.

But I wish to suggest that the figure of Dokonikan is not altogether explained by his association with the matriarch

[MoBr], that he may be a figure handed from a patriarchal culture into a matriarchal one, in which case *he might represent the father and husband* (*SR*:105, italics supplied).

But having gingerly approached a structural explanation by clothing it in historical garb, Malinowski beat a hasty retreat. Aware that this explanation contradicts his central thesis that in a matrilineal system there can be no hostility between father and son, he immediately denied that Dokonikan represents "the father and husband" in the contemporary Trobriand context. Instead, he argued, the persistence of the figure of Dokonikan in a matrilineal culture, in which (by a priori assumptions) he does not belong, demonstrates "how the prevalent cast of a culture moulds and transforms persons and situations to fit them into its own sociological context" (*SR*:105). In short, although Dokonikan may be a disguised representation of the father when the myth is embedded in a "patriarchal" culture, he can only represent the mother's brother when the myth is acquired by and becomes embedded in a "matriarchal" one.

If, how ever, we are not wedded to the a priori assumption that there can be no hostility between father and son in a matrilineal system, we are not constrained to follow Malinowski's tortuous explanation for the transformation of Dokonikan from father to mother's brother. The latter explanation not only is based on conjectural history, but does not attend to the structural anomaly of father-absence in this myth. Nor, it must be added, does it attend to the more general absence of the father from Trobriand myths, let alone to the Trobriand pattern of the absent father. If, then, we focus our attention on the structural features of the myth, its anomaly consists not in the fact that one of its characters, who might be a disguised representation of the husband-father, is a cannibalistic ogre, but rather in the fact that in a myth which, according to Malinowski, reflects the pattern of the Trobriand family, the husband-father is nowhere in evidence.

Whether it is then viewed in the context of a previous "patriarchal" culture, or in that of the contemporary "matriarchal" one, the interpretation of the figure of Dokonikan as constituting the disguised representation of the husband-father not only resolves this structural anomaly, but proceeds from the firm ground of the structural features of the myth rather than (like

Malinowski's interpretation) from the quicksand of the imputation of motives to its characters.[1] It might be added that, if
symbolic representation in myth is similar to that in dreams, this
structural interpretation of the identity of Dokonikan is supported by a symbolic one, for according to the findings of current
dream research, hostile animals and male strangers are often the
symbolic representations of the feared father (Hall and Nordby
1972:22). (An ogre, I assume—though Malinowski does not describe Dokonikan—is bestial in certain respects.)

If, then, this structural analysis of the identity of Dokonikan
is correct—the latter being a disguised representation of the
father—the Tudava myth would seem to indicate that the Trobriand father is unconsciously viewed as (among other things)
a dangerous and terrifying figure toward whom the son, in turn,
harbors murderous wishes. If so, this would indicate why the
father as such is absent from the myth, patricidal and filicidal
wishes being too threatening to acknowledge even when attributed to the characters in a myth.

To be sure, this structural interpretation of the identity of
Dokonikan entails the psychological conclusion that even in a
matrilineal society, the father (though benign and nurturant)
may be unconsciously perceived by the son as a hostile and
dangerous figure, toward whom he harbors intensely hostile—
even homicidal—repressed wishes.[2] Although rejected by Malinowski, this conclusion is consistent both with other Trobriand

1. In this regard, Malinowski's imputation is doubly hazardous. His claim that
the cannibalistic ogre is the disguised representation of the mother's brother is
based not only on the assumption that the latter alone can be hostile to the
sister's son, but also on his (the uncle's) "horror and dismay" upon seeing the
head of Dokonikan in his taro pudding. The uncle's reaction, Malinowski argues,
shows either that he and Dokonikan are one and the same person, or that they
were in collusion. Neither interpretation, however, is entailed by the text. On
the contrary, the uncle's "horror and dismay" are more simply explained as the
natural reaction of anyone confronted with a severed head in the food he is
about to eat.

2. It is not only in matrilineal societies that the unconscious hostile wishes of
the son toward the father are expressed in a disguised form in legends and
myths. Thus, in an ingenious analysis of some Sanskrit epics, combining great
textual learning, ethnographic knowledge, and theoretical acumen, Goldman
(1978) was able to show that the repressed Oedipal hostility of the son toward
the patriarchal Indian father is disguised in these epics in acts of aggression
directed toward gurus, sages, and elder brother, all of whom, he demonstrates,
are unconscious symbolic representations of the father.

myths which Malinowski overlooked in his account of the father-son relationship, as well as with those found in other matrilineal societies. Let us begin with the former.

In the class of myths to be examined here the father appears in an undisguised form. Perhaps this contradiction of Malinowski's claim that the father is absent from all Trobriand myths can be resolved by classifying such oral narratives as "legends," rather than "myths." Although Malinowski ignored these legends in his discussion of the absence of hostility in the father-son relationship in the Trobriands, we cannot ignore them in our present analysis. The most important narrative in this connection is the well-known Kula legend which recounts an undisguised (though unsuccessful) attempt to commit not only patricide, but filicide as well. The existence of a legend of this type is especially significant in the light of Stephens's statistical finding that overt father-son conflict is a "rare" theme in the folktales of "nearly all" societies, at least those making up his cross-cultural sample (Stephens 1962:159).

According to this legend (Malinowski [1922] 1961:322–25) a man, his son, and his grandson took part in a Kula expedition in the course of which the man obtained a prized necklace from his Kula partners, which he concealed from his son. Angered by his father's treachery, the son abandoned him on a sandbank and sailed for home without him. In revenge, the father then attempted to drown his son and the latter's companions by sinking their canoe, but he failed in his attempt. Later, with the assistance of various stellar bodies, the father returned to their village, and out of "bitterness" became an evil spirit.

Since, then, a legend of *undisguised* (though unsuccessful) patricide and filicide can exist in the Trobriands, it surely makes little sense for Malinowski to have rejected the notion that the Tudava myth, in accordance with his second interpretation, is an account of *disguised* patricide, in which Dokonikan represents the father. It makes even less sense, moreover, in the light of both the Trobrianders' attitude toward actual patricide and their practice of magical patricide. Although noting that there are no recorded cases of patricide in the Trobriands, such an event, Malinowski remarks, "would be no special tragedy, and would be merely a matter to be settled with the father's own clan" (*SR*:96). As for magical patricide it has already been mentioned that, according to Trobriand belief, almost all deaths are caused by sorcery and that in the case of a man it is his wife and children who are always the principal suspects. Neither of these ethnographic data—the cavalier attitude toward the actual murder of the father and the belief that a man's death might be caused by his son's sorcery—seems consistent with Malinowski's claim regarding the uniformly positive sentiments of the son toward the loving matrilineal father, nor—to return to the case at hand—with his rejection of his own suggestion that the Tudava myth might reflect repressed hostility between father and son.

If, then, as Malinowski claims, the Tudava myth is paradigmatic of Trobriand myths dealing with family relationships, it is entirely possible that in other myths of this type, as well, the father is absent from their manifest content only, and that he is present, as in the case of the Tudava myth, in their latent content. Since, then, the father is represented in the Tudava myth (according to Malinowski's second interpretation) as a cannibalistic ogre, and since myths of "ogres and their conquerors" are numerous in Trobriand mythology, especially in "Kultur" myths (Malinowski [1922] 1961:305), it is not implausible that all of the latter myths also conceal a theme of brutal fathers and patricidal sons.[3] If this theme were present in the manifest content of these myths, it would be an indication, Malinowski and I would both agree, that Trobriand boys unconsciously perceive their fathers as (among other things) aggressive and brutal ("cannibalistic ogres"), toward whom they harbor unconscious hostile (including patricidal) wishes. That except for the Kula legend, however, these perceptions and wishes are disguised, even when represented projectively in cultural forms, suggests (as I have already indicated) that they are too threatening to be permitted undisguised expression even in such indirect manifestations. Whether they are threatening because the unconscious fear of the father in the Trobriands is unusually strong, or because the guilt aroused by a conscious awareness of hostility to the benign and nurturant Trobriand father is especially painful, or both, makes no difference for our present purpose.

3. It might be noted in this connection that myths of ogre-killing sons are widespread in Melanesia, as well as in the adjacent islands of Micronesia and Indonesia (Lessa 1961:57–61, 220–37).

If we now turn to other matrilineal societies, we find yet again, as we have just found in the Trobriands, that Malinowski's claim that hostility to the father does not exist in such societies is simply not true, not at least if we use myths as our measure. Indeed, in a more recent investigation of the mythology of Oceania and Indonesia (referred to in an earlier chapter) it was discovered not only that myths of aggression toward the father, even including patricide, are found in matrilineal as well as patrilineal societies, but also—and perhaps more significantly for our present purpose—that the patricidal motive in both types is often Oedipal, i.e., it is based on rivalry with the father for the mother. A patricidal Oedipal myth from Ulithi, a matrilineal society in Micronesia, is especially instructive in this regard because it parallels the Dokonikan myth in one important feature. In this myth (Lessa 1961), a mother and son commit incest, and when the husband-father discovers their behavior, the son engages him in combat, and kills him by *cutting off his head*, following which mother and son live together in a permanent incestuous relationship.

If, then, undisguised patricidal myths are found in other matrilineal societies, the structural interpretation of the Tudava myth, according to which Tudava's slaying of Dokonikan—the disguised representation of the father—constitutes a patricidal act, poses no ethnographic problem. Indeed, the uncanny resemblance between the slaying of the father in the Ulithi myth and the slaying of Dokonikan—in both cases their heads were cut off—lends credence to this structural interpretation. That the patricide in the Ulithi myth (as well as in other patricidal myths that Lessa discovered in other matrilineal societies) is Oedipal in its motivation at least allows for the possibility that Tudava's motive was similarly Oedipal.[4] The fact, moreover, that Tudava and his mother, like the incestuous son and mother in Ulithi,

4. In accordance with psychoanalytic observations in which, at least in the West, decapitation is often an unconscious symbolic representation of castration, it might be suggested that the fact that Tudava (like the son in the Ulithi myth) kills Dokonikan by cutting off his head lends symbolic support to the Oedipal hypothesis. By adopting this suggestion, and the attendant symbolic equation (head = penis), the uncle's horror and dismay at seeing Dokonikan's severed head in his pudding would have yet another explanation (see footnote 1). Inasmuch, however, as we do not know whether these unconscious symbolic equations are applicable to the Trobriands, these suggestions remain speculative.

live together in a permanent relationship increases such a possibility.

Although admittedly no more than a possibility, the adoption of an Oedipal interpretation of this myth would go far in accounting for the popularity of Tudava and his elevation to a culture hero. Born of a virgin mother, and raised by her alone—so that he did not have to share her with either a father or siblings—Tudava is a son who achieves a double victory over the Oedipal father inasmuch as the latter is absent both as genitor and as mother's lover.[5]

We may now summarize this analysis of father-absence in family myths. Oedipal motives aside, the absence of the father from these myths—especially when the latter are juxtaposed with the Kula legend of attempted patricide and filicide, Trobriand attitudes toward actual patricide, and Trobriand beliefs concerning magical patricide—suggests that Trobriand boys have unconscious hostile feelings toward their fathers, and that father-absence is a defense against the conscious recognition of these feelings. This analysis, therefore, supports the speculation that father-absence in Trobriand dreams also reflects hostility toward the father and that it has a similar function. In addition, the replacement of the father by a cannibalistic ogre in the Tudava myth—and, by extension, in the Kultur myths—suggests that the son's hostility is aroused by the unconscious mental representation of the father as punitive and aggressive. If, finally, the comparative data on myths of this type, especially from other parts of Oceania, can serve as a guide, it may be further suggested that the boy's hostility to the father—and his unconscious mental representation of him as a cannibalistic ogre—is motivated by Oedipal rivalry with him. Indeed, since the Trobriand father is kindly and benevolent in his relationship with his son, it would be difficult to attribute any other motivational basis for his hostility.

We may now turn to the third domain of father-absence in the Trobriands—reproduction beliefs—for possible confirmation or discomfirmation of the above interpretations of the absent father

5. From an Oedipal point of view, therefore, the Tudava myth goes the Christ myth one better. Although the mother of Jesus, like the mother of Tudava, never had a lover, Jesus himself, unlike Tudava, did have a genitor (albeit a grandiose one), as well as a pater.

in the previous two domains. According to the Trobriand reproduction theory, it will be recalled, the father has no role in
reproduction, conception being caused not by sexual intercourse
but by the entry of a matrilineal ancestral spirit, in the form of
a "spirit child" (*baloma*), into the mother's womb. Unlike the
case of Trobriand family myths, in which—because of the composition of the Trobriand family—the absent father constitutes
a *sociological* anomaly, in the light of the cross-cultural distribution of reproduction theories, father-absence in the Trobriand
theory of reproduction constitutes a *cultural* anomaly.

Malinowski did not consider this theory anomalous. He argued that knowledge of the father's role in reproduction cannot
be expected in a people "on a very low level of culture" (*SR*:130).
In support of this argument, he disingenuously appealed to
"complicated physiological processes" and "certain aspects of
embryology" which people at a "low" cultural level could hardly
be expected to understand (*SR*:130).

Having posed the issue as consisting of a knowledge of embryology and physiology, Malinowski succeeded (however un-
intentionally) in befuddling the problem of father-absence in the
Trobriand theory of reproduction for more than fifty years, for
almost every anthropologist who has participated in the ensuing
debate over the spirit-child theory in the Trobriands and Australia has followed Malinowski's lead in taking the issue to be
one of biological knowledge—knowledge of what Malinowski
termed "physiological paternity"—when in fact it is nothing of
the kind. For if the ignorance of "certain aspects of embryology"
is what is at issue, then surely the Trobrianders are no more
ignorant of "physiological paternity" than any other people prior
to the development of the sciences of embryology and micro-
biology and to the invention of modern microscopy. Indeed, if
that is what is at issue, then the Trobrianders—and for that
matter all other peoples living in the age of prescientific biology—are ignorant not only of physiological *pa*ternity, but of
physiological *ma*ternity as well, for they are just as innocent of
the ova and their role in conception as of the spermatozoa and
their role in fertilization.[6]

6. In a recent discussion of the Trobriand theory of conception, Weiner
(1976:193) interprets this theory as a "protection for the innate value of women."
It gives them a "public position" of great power by conferring on them "the

What is rather at issue in the spirit-child theory of reproduction, as Malinowski's extensive discussion and compelling examples of the Trobrianders' "ignorance" of physiology indicate (*SLS*:179–95), is ignorance not of the facts of embryology and physiology, but of the relationship between pregnancy and coitus. A woman conceives, the Trobrianders insist, because a spirit-child enters her body, and not because a man has sexual intercourse with her. That being the case, to designate the ignorance of the latter relationship as ignorance of "physiological" paternity is clearly a misnomer; it should more properly be designated as ignorance of "sexually induced" paternity. Since, however, the former designation has become the standard one in the anthropological lexicon, I shall continue to use it here with the understanding that it is used in the latter sense only.

When we consider, then, that the theory that pregnancy is caused by sexual intercourse is a nearly universally held one even in cultures whose "level" is lower than that of the Trobriands,[7] Malinowski's explanation for the absence of the father from the Trobriand theory must surely lose most of its force. When we consider, moreover, that the absence of the father from their reproduction theory is not a singular phenomenon in the Trobriands, but is rather part of a larger pattern of father-absence, his explanation (which can in no way explain this pattern) loses its remaining force. I hasten to stress, however, that in rejecting Malinowski's explanation for the Trobrianders' ignorance of physiological paternity, I am in no way challenging its ethnographic reality, let alone contending that he was duped into accepting it because it "corresponded to his own private

---

ability to conceive alone." Aside from the other difficulties posed by this interpretation (which are implicit in the ensuing discussion), it rests on a false premise: inasmuch as the woman, according to Trobriand theory, conceives when a spirit-child enters her, it is hardly the case that she has the ability to conceive "alone." In short, this theory eliminates the father as an agent in conception, but it does not thereby confer much agency, let alone exclusive agency, on the mother, the latter serving primarily as a container in which the spirit-child grows and develops.

7. The notable recorded exceptions are found in some, but by no means all, regions of aboriginal Australia (Montagu 1974). Although scattered examples are reputed to be found elsewhere, in his survey of reproduction beliefs Hartland (1910:279) writes that the only "definite evidence that reproduction is held to be independent of coition" comes from Australia.

fantasy of the natural ignorance of childish savages" (Leach 1967:41). On the contrary, although, like Leach, I too find it "highly improbable" that "genuine 'ignorance' of the basic facts of physiological paternity should anywhere be a cultural fact" (ibid.), Malinowski's evidence for their "ignorance" seems to me entirely compelling.

To be sure, according to one account obtained by Powell in his restudy of the Trobriands, the father would seem to play a larger part in the Trobriand reproduction theory than Malinowski allowed. According to that account "the semen acts as a coagulant of the menstrual blood, producing a 'clot' which a spirit-child (*baloma*) enters . . . and which proceeds to grow after its 'quickening' by the entry of the *baloma*" (Powell 1957:277). Powell's informants explained that this account of conception and the one reported by Malinowski are both true, though "different." Malinowski's account, they said, is "men's talk," valid in formal situations, while the one they gave to Powell is "women's and children's talk"; it is what fathers and their sisters tell children when the latter are "old enough to take more than a childish sexual interest in the opposite sex" (ibid.:278). It might be observed, however, that this account not only is one among others reported by Powell, but was obtained almost forty years after Malinowski's when acculturative influences, including missionary pressure (*SLS*:186–87), may have begun to erode traditional beliefs. This suggestion is supported by the fact that the generation of Trobriand ethnographers following Malinowski but preceding Powell reported that Malinowski's account was entirely accurate. Thus, for example, on the basis of countless interviews conducted throughout the Trobriand Archipelago, Austin (1934:108) concluded that "there was no doubt that 'man's contribution toward the new life in the mother's body' was nil." Similarly, from his discussion with a group of Trobriand men, Fortune (1932:239) reported that their theory of conception, unlike that of the Dobuans whom Fortune had studied, was "just as Dr. Malinowski had reported it."

From these replications of Malinowski's finding, I believe that there is little ground to doubt that prior at least to the most recent period the Trobrianders were (as Malinowski claimed) ignorant of physiological paternity. That being so, we seem to have come to an impasse. For if on the one hand the accuracy of Malinowski's anomalous finding is not to be doubted, but if on the other hand the validity of his explanation is very much in doubt, how then *are* we to explain the Trobrianders' ignorance of physiological paternity?

The escape from this impasse, it seems to me, can be found in a careful scrutiny of the possible meanings of the word "ignorance." In its usual meaning "ignorance" denotes the *absence* of knowledge concerning some fact or event. Adopting this meaning, we would then say, as Malinowski says, that the Trobrianders believe in the spirit-child theory of reproduction in *default* of knowledge concerning the father's role in reproduction. Ignorance, however, may result not only from the absence of knowledge concerning some fact or event, but also from its banishment from conscious awareness; to employ the technical term, it may result from *denial*. Since, then, facts or events are "denied" because they are threatening or painful to the self, the adoption of this meaning of "ignorance" would suggest that although the Trobrianders are cognizant of the reproductive role of the father, they disavow this knowledge because it is threatening or painful. By this hypothesis, the Trobrianders believe in the spirit-child theory not in default of knowledge concerning the father's role in reproduction, but in *lieu* of such an explanation.

Although in an earlier essay on the spirit-child theory in Australia, I had proposed (Spiro 1968) that this theory could with equal plausibility reflect either an absence of knowledge concerning the reproductive role of the father or its denial, I am now convinced that the latter explanation is much the more probable. First, it resolves the impasse of accepting the accuracy of Malinowski's report concerning the Trobrianders' ignorance of physiological paternity and yet rejecting the validity of his explanation. Second, it resolves the anomaly which, in the light of the near-universal recognition of physiological paternity, is posed by Malinowski's explanation. Third, it is consistent with the axiom that any exception to a near-universal ethnographic belief or practice which cannot be explained as a response to ecological conditions, adaptive requirements, and other determinants of a "rational" type is most likely to find an explanation in motivational determinants of an "emotional" type. Finally, it is consistent with the explanation that has already been offered for father-absence in the two other domains making up the absent-fther pattern in the Trobriands.

Having detailed its theoretical advantages, we must now examine the evidence for the hypothesis that the spirit-child theory does not represent a lack of knowledge concerning the father's reproductive role, but its denial. In his study of the spirit-child theory in Central Australia, Róheim (1932) was able to demonstrate that although the adult members of the tribes of this area have no conscious awareness of physiological paternity, such knowledge is found in children prior to puberty, at which time it is then denied (Róheim, however, uses the term "repressed"). Since in the case of the Trobriands, however, we possess no data concerning the reproductive beliefs of children, we must rely on the indirect evidence afforded by social and cultural data.

That Trobrianders are aware—at some level—of physiological paternity is suggested in the first place in a paradoxical set of beliefs that Malinowski himself found bewildering. On the one hand, despite their twin beliefs that conception is caused by an ancestral spirit of the matriline and that matrikin are of the "same body," the Trobrianders nevertheless insist with "extremely strong social emphasis" that children never resemble their mother or any of their matrikin. Indeed, the latter being a "household dogma," it is "extremely bad form and a great offence" to even hint at such a resemblance. On the other hand, despite their insistence that father is not genitor, and moreover that he is a "stranger," they nevertheless insist with equal conviction that children always and only resemble their father, and that this resemblance is the "natural, right, and proper thing" (*SLS*:204). Now, since elsewhere Malinowski (1955:25–36) goes out of his way to comment on the "rationality" of Trobriand thought, and since, in any event, no one would maintain that the Trobrianders are "prelogical" in their thinking, the fact that they see no contradiction between two contradictory sets of beliefs (both of which, moreover, they hold with equal strength) suggests that despite their conscious "ignorance" of physiological paternity, the latter is "known" at some level of awareness.[8]

8. The people of Monteros, a township in Andalusia, maintain with the same urgency as the Trobrianders that whatever their actual appearance, newborn infants resemble their fathers. To suggest, rather, that a child resembles its mother arouses great anxiety because, given the males' fears concerning their

That this is so is suggested in the second place—and perhaps more convincingly—by an analysis of the symbolism of the Kula. In a detailed analysis McDougall (1975) convincingly demonstrates that knowledge of physiological paternity is unconsciously acknowledged and symbolically expressed by the Trobrianders in many of the prestations and rituals included in this elaborate ceremonial exchange system. She concludes her extended analysis by observing that, among its other symbolic meanings, the Kula "asserts, in a symbolic form, a fact necessary to the continuation of life itself: that men are indeed biological fathers" (ibid.:99). More, in performing its rituals, "the Kula enables men to act out [symbolically] the procreative role which is sociologically denied them" (ibid.:87). In brief, consciously "denied" physiological paternity is unconsciously recognized.

That the Trobrianders' "ignorance" of physiological paternity is a function of denial is suggested, again, by the vehemence with which they oppose this explanation for reproduction. Thus, Malinowski writes that he was "astonished at the fierce opposition evoked by my advocacy of physiological paternity" (*SLS*:186). Now, seeing as the theory of physiological paternity is a no less efficient explanation for reproduction than the spirit-child theory, such a strong reaction would hardly be expected in people whose "ignorance" of physiological paternity betokened merely a lack of knowledge concerning the father's reproductive role. On the contrary, it would only be expected in people whose "ignorance" betokened the denial of such knowledge, their "fierce opposition" to its advocacy being an index of the painful emotional feelings which the conscious recognition of the father's reproductive role aroused in them.

Put differently, it is unlikely that the strong emotional reaction of the Trobrianders to the physiological paternity theory of (ontogenetic) human creation, any more than that of Christian fundamentalists to the Darwinian challenge to the Biblical theory of (phylogenetic) human creation, can be entirely explained as

wives' infidelity, it is an indirect way of questioning the child's biological paternity (Brandes 1980:89). Since, as we shall see below, Trobriand males are jealous of their wives—like the Monteros they view women as highly sexual—one might speculate that the same (albeit unconscious) anxiety motivates the Trobriand belief, which would then lend greater credence to the suggestion that this belief implies an awareness of physiological paternity on some level.

intellectual disagreement with a competing theory for a biological phenomenon. Since, in both cases, it seems reasonable to
assume that there is more at stake than that in their opposition,
it is more likely that it is to be explained rather by the emotional
pain or threat that the competing theory causes them to suffer.
In the case of the Trobrianders this not only would explain their
emotional reaction to Malinowski's advocacy of physiological
paternity, but would constitute strong support for the hypothesis
that the "ignorance" of physiological paternity represents denial
rather than lack of knowledge of the father's role in reproduction. Unable to cope in a realistic fashion with the emotional
pain or threat that is aroused by their recognition of the reproductive role of the father, they attempt to cope instead in a
magical fashion—by eliminating the father as genitor and putting another genitor, a spirit-child, in his place. Why it is that
the recognition that father is genitor is so painful will be dealt
with below.

If this interpretation of father-absence in the reproductive domain is correct, it supports the hypothesis, suggested by the
analysis of father-absence in recalled dreams and myths, that
Trobriand males harbor strong unconscious hostility toward the
father. (So far as one can tell, all of Malinowski's descriptions
and reports concerning physiological paternity relate entirely to
males.) Moreover, it lends credence to the speculation, suggested by the analysis of myths, that this hostility is Oedipal in
its motivation. We shall begin with the first claim.

Although the Trobrianders are hardly the only society in
which awareness of the father's reproductive role is painful or
threatening, few others have gone so far as they in an attempt
to deny it. For make no mistake about it: the denial of physiological paternity, as Fox (1980:70) has observed, is

> a most extreme version of the father-denial ideology. It is not
> too much to call this, in a structural sense, the 'elimination'
> of the father. He is not killed, he is simply defined out of
> existence as far as his children are concerned. His role, as the
> sociologists would say, is reduced to the companion of the
> mother and children.

Put somewhat differently, the elimination of the father from his
role as genitor, a role in which (according to the cross-cultural

evidence) his presence is most expected and uniquely appropriate, is a qualified act of symbolic patricide (Jones 1925)—"qualified," because he is eliminated only as genitor, not as pater.

If, nevertheless, we might still be tempted to shrink from the notion that symbolic patricide as qualified and sublimated as this one is might be an expression of patricidal wishes, especially when the father is as benign as the Trobriand father seems to be, it need only be recalled that this is not the first time we have encountered patricide in the Trobriands. We encountered it in disguised form in the Tudava myth and in undisguised form in a Kula myth. More importantly, we encountered it in the Trobriand belief that the death of a male is almost always caused by either his wife or his children, by means of sorcery. If, then, to take the latter belief only, the Trobrianders impute to their fellows the wish to eliminate their father entirely, it is hardly startling to learn that these same Trobrianders might harbor the wish to eliminate their own father as genitor.

If, viewed as denial, the "ignorance" of physiological paternity is an expression of the son's hostility to the father, we may now return to my second claim that his hostility is "Oedipal" in its motivation. This claim is supported in the first instance by the previous observation that the symbolic patricide represented by the denial of physiological paternity is directed against the father in his role not as pater, but as genitor. If so, it may be inferred that the boy's hostility is motivated not so much by the pain aroused by the father's "authority," as by that aroused by his Oedipal rivalry with him, "Oedipal rivalry," however, in the restricted sense explained below.

The expression "ignorance of physiological paternity" is an elliptic misnomer, it will be recalled, for "ignorance of the relationship between conception and sexual intercourse." I submit, therefore, that the recognition that his father is genitor is painful for the Trobriand son either because it reminds him that his father enjoys the sexual possession of the mother whom he himself has desired, or because it reminds him that she, in turn, has betrayed him by preferring the father to him; after all, the awareness of parental intercourse, according at least to Oedipal theory, is always painful for the child for those reasons, and yet the Trobrianders do not deny that parents have sexual intercourse. More important than either of those, therefore, the recognition that father is genitor is painful for the son because, I suggest, it reminds him that his very existence was brought about by that hated sexual relationship that the father has with the mother. It is for that reason, it may now be suggested, that the Trobriand sons, at least, deny the "relationship between conception and sexual intercourse." (The fathers, as we shall see, have a complementary motive for denial.)

Startlingly enough, the logic behind that suggestion, as I discovered only after completing the first draft of this book, was suggested by Malinowski himself in the following remarkable passage in *Sex and Repression*. Commenting on the "educated boy" in the West who, so Malinowski claims, "fully realizes" only at puberty the "biological nature of the bond between his parents and himself," Malinowski writes:

> If he deeply loves and worships his mother, as is usually the case, and if he can continue to idealize his father, then the idea of his bodily origin from his parent's sexual intercourse, though at first making a rift in his mental world, can be dealt with. If on the other hand he scorns and hates his father, be it unavowedly as so often happens, the idea brings about a permanent defilement of the mother and a besmirching of things most dear to him (*SR*:62).

Here, then, is the kernel of the suggestion I myself have just offered for the "ignorance" of physiological paternity in the Trobriands: under certain circumstances (described so well in that passage), not only does the idea that he was conceived by the sexual intercourse of his parents make a "rift in [the boy's] mental world," but such an idea becomes extremely painful for him. It must be accounted as one of the central ironies in the history of the controversy over the Trobrianders' reproductive beliefs that Malinowski and his followers alike seem to have forgotten that passage—as presumably I did—when they came to interpret the meaning of the Trobrianders' "ignorance" of physiological paternity. Had they remembered it, that long, drawn-out controversy would probably never have occurred. For Malinowski had only to apply that passage to his Trobriand data to realize that the "ignorance" of physiological paternity is one means of coping with such pain, and from that realization it would have been an easy step to conceive the suggestion—

the one that I have proposed here—that perhaps that is the very motive for the Trobrianders' "ignorance".

Now if that suggestion seems rather farfetched (and if it would have seemed farfetched to Malinowski in spite of the fact that it is implicit in the passage I have just quoted), I would then point out that while the Trobrianders reject physiological paternity as an explanation for conception, they do not reject the principle that conception is caused by a genitor; they only reject the notion that father is the genitor. Having rejected the father, the Trobrianders replace him with another genitor, for according to their theory of conception, it will be recalled, it is the spirit-child who is genitor. Now the spirit-child theory is, of course, a culturally constituted rather than an individually created theory, one which is socially transmitted to each generation of Trobriand children as part of their cultural heritage. Whether the children independently create such a theory themselves we do not know; but although that question is of some theoretical interest, it is not germaine to the present issue. For having been taught with the full authority of his cultural heritage that conception is caused by the entry of a spirit-child into the mother's vagina,[9] each child who comes to believe in this theory—and why should he doubt it?—must *eo ipso* perceive himself to have been conceived in that very manner. Hence, since by this theory conception is caused by the entry of a spirit-child, not the father, into the mother's vagina, to believe in this theory is to believe that, although parents may engage in sexual intercourse, conception at least is not brought about by their sexual activity.

Trobrianders, as I have already observed, are hardly the only people for whom the awareness of physiological paternity is highly painful, nor are they (and the Australian aborigines) alone in attempting to cope with this painful cognition by denying

9. Actually, there are two Trobriand interpretations of the manner in which the spirit-child enters the woman (*SLS*:173–76). Although both agree that the spirit comes in the ocean and enters the woman when she is bathing, according to the less widely held interpretation, the spirit enters the woman's head, from which it gradually descends to the womb. (This is reminiscent of the impregnation of the Virgin Mary through the head, more particularly the ear.) According to the more widely held interpretation, however, the spirit-child enters the womb via the vagina. Since this occurs while she is bathing in the ocean, this interpretation not only makes better physical sense, but also, since it is analogous to the facts of biological impregnation, makes better symbolic sense.

that father is genitor and putting some other genitor in his place. The employment of such a defense mechanism is found in other societies as well, at both the individual and cultural levels. Motivated by hostility to the father, Western children, according to clinical data at any rate, have frequently been reported to deny that their father is genitor, and to replace him with a grandiose genitor—someone who is rich, famous, powerful, and the like (Freud [1908] 1968). At the cultural level this same phenomenon is found in "hero" myths; the substitution of a grandiose genitor—a king, a god, and the like—for an ordinary father is a worldwide theme in such myths (Campbell 1956; Raglan 1949; Rank 1964). Moreover, in addition to the fantasy of a grandiose genitor, it is not uncommon, to return to the individual level, for a Western boy to wish "to have by his mother a son who is like himself. . . . All his instincts, those of tenderness, gratitude, lustfulness [for the mother], defiance, and independence [toward the father] find satisfaction in the single wish *to be his own father*" (Freud [1910] 1968:173, italics in original). In sum, the son's wish is not only that the father be replaced as genitor, but that he (the son) himself be his father's replacement.

It should now be evident that the Trobriand spirit-child theory of conception constitutes at the cultural level a confluence of two fantasies which elsewhere exist separately not only at the cultural, but also at the individual level. As the spirit of a clan ancestor, the spirit-child (like the genitor in hero myths) is a *grandiose* genitor; and since, after entering the woman's womb, the spirit-child becomes the human-child-to-be, each child (like the child in the fantasies of Western children) is his *own* genitor. It is now clear why spirit-children, although genitors, do not arouse "Oedipal" hostility: by this theory of conception the spirit-child is the child himself, albeit in a different form. Hence, by his belief in this theory each child perceives himself to be his own genitor, and a grandiose one to boot.[10]

If cultural theories and doctrines are held not as clichés but as genuine beliefs, it is because they resonate with the needs,

10. The narcissism that is reflected in the belief that one is one's own genitor is of course obvious, as it is in other beliefs and practices in the Trobriands. Despite its importance, I do not discuss it here because, although consistent with pre-Oedipal issues to be discussed below, it is not a central problem for this book.

wishes, and fears of the social actors who hold them. That the Trobriand theory of conception is not a cliché, but a strong personal conviction, has already been evidenced by the powerful affect which is aroused in Trobriand actors when it is challenged. This is so, I would now suggest, because it resonates with and allows them to express and gratify powerful wishes—Oedipal wishes—regarding both parents. Thus, to believe that a spirit-child is genitor is to deny that father is genitor, a denial which (as has already been suggested) gratifies in fantasy the wish to eliminate the father, *qua* genitor, and to replace him in that role. Since, moreover, the spirit-child is none other than the child himself, to believe that conception is caused by the entry of the spirit-child, not the father, into the mother's vagina is to gratify in fantasy the wish to replace him as mother's lover (so far, at least, as conception is concerned). In short, to believe in the spirit-child theory, so I am suggesting, is to gratify simultaneously, albeit symbolically, the two wishes that constitute the Oedipus complex.

Thus far I have argued that the denial of physiological paternity, and its replacement by the spirit-child theory of conception, protects the son from the emotional pain that is aroused by his awareness that father is genitor. It must now be observed that it also protects him from the emotional pain that is aroused by his awareness of his hostility toward the father. According to the previous analysis, the awareness that father is genitor is so painful for the boy that it arouses hostile wishes of patricidal dimensions, the denial of physiological paternity being a symbolic expression of those wishes. But to harbor hostile, let alone homicidal, wishes against one's father may be presumed to be painful for any son—because, typically, even when the father is hated, he is also loved—especially sons whose fathers are as benign as Trobriand fathers seem to be. Hence, viewed as denial, the "ignorance" of physiological paternity not only gratifies in fantasy the son's wish to eliminate the father, but is a defense mechanism that protects him from the painful guilt feelings that are aroused in him by that wish. That is, since by denying that father is genitor, the son is now "ignorant" of physiological paternity, he is spared those feelings because (consciously) he no longer has that wish.

If, then, this analysis of Trobriand conception beliefs is valid, it can now be noted that the denial of physiological paternity has an important consequence for the father-son relationship in the Trobriands, as Jones (1925) pointed out some time ago. Since powerful wishes can escalate from fantasy to actuality, then insofar as "ignorance" of physiological paternity removes the Trobrianders' patricidal wishes from consciousness, it virtually eliminates any threat of their actualization. More than that, the removal of the principal grounds—i.e., the Oedipal grounds—for the boy's hostility to the father from consciousness permits him to maintain the cordial relationship with his father that Malinowski describes is actually the case. Since by this hypothesis, however, the boy's Oedipal hostility is not eliminated—only rendered unconscious—it is not surprising to find it displaced and projected in a variety of disguises in the cultural symbol systems that we have already described, as well as in others that will be described in later chapters. Nor would it be surprising if it were expressed in the boy's social relationships as well, which takes us back to the problem of the mother's brother, discussed in the previous chapter.

Although Malinowski claims that the hostility of the Trobriand boy is directed not to the father, but to the mother's brother, because the latter exercises jural authority over him, it was shown in chapter 2 that that claim cannot be sustained because his authority is manifested infrequently and not at all harshly. Moreover, Malinowski offers no evidence for the claim that the boy is hostile to the mother's brother. If, nevertheless, the boy is indeed hostile to him, then given that his hostility cannot be explained by the uncle's punitive authority, it is much more likely, as Jones observed, that it represents the displacement of his unconscious hostility to the father.[11]

11. Although it is apparent that this interpretation of the consequences of the "ignorance" of physiological paternity is indebted to Jones's pioneering work on the subject, I cannot accept his additional argument. From the thesis that the hostility to the mother's brother represents a displacement of the boy's hostility to the father, Jones argued that its displacement is the main function of matrilineal descent systems and, moreover, that they originated in order to serve that function. That a complex structural system should have been instituted for that purpose is hardly creditable.

Interestingly enough, McDougall (1975:94–95) offers almost a mirror-image interpretation of the relationship between matriliny and the "ignorance" of

Before drawing this discussion to a close, it must finally be observed that our interpretation of the Trobrianders' "ignorance" of physiological paternity is a two-way street. That is, since father and son alike are "ignorant" of physiological paternity, if the son's denial that father is genitor is an expression of his hostility to the father, then the father's denial that he is his son's genitor must be an expression of his hostility to the son. That fathers may have hostile wishes toward their sons may be a shocking, but hardly a surprising, suggestion. To realize how prevalent the antagonism of the father (and mother) to the child might be, we need only recall that child abuse is one of the most important social problems in our own country, that infanticide is a widespread human practice, that filicide is a far-ranging theme in myths and folktales, and that the ritual sacrifice of the son (especially the firstborn) has been practiced in many societies (Bakan 1971).

Although fathers may have many grounds for developing hostile feelings for their sons, one of them may derive from his "complementary Oedipus complex." Since the hostility of the adult, no less than that of the child, is aroused by anyone who is viewed as a rival for the possession of a love-object, to the extent that the father views the son as a rival for the love of the wife-mother, he would be expected to develop antagonistic feelings for him. Under such circumstances the son's Oedipal hostility toward and fear of the father might be aroused in the first instance by the latter's rivalrous hostility toward him, i.e., by his Laius complex, as it has been called.

---

physiological paternity. In her view the denial that father is genitor is not a defense against the child's hostility to the father but against the father's regard for the child. Since, so her argument goes, the Trobriand father feels affection for his own rather than his sister's children, were he to recognize a biological relationship to his own children, he would be unwilling to fulfill his financial obligations to his sister's. This argument, too, is less than convincing. First, since the denial of his genitorship does not reduce the father's affection for his children, as McDougall herself makes clear, it hardly protects him from the realization that the fulfillment of those obligations "runs precisely contrary to the course of his own desires" (ibid.). Second, McDougall's own analysis of the symbolism of the Kula shows that the more important psychological problem confronting the Trobrianders is their Oedipal problem, and that it is their denied Oedipal wishes that are symbolically gratified in the Kula exchanges.

Although, as we shall see in subsequent chapters, evidence from myths and folktales supports the deduction that the Trobriand father's "ignorance" of physiological paternity is an expression of his hostility to the son, there is less evidence to support the hypothesis that his hostility is a function specifically of a Laius complex. The most important evidence for the existence of the Laius complex in Trobriand fathers is found in two pregnancy customs.

In accordance with Trobriand custom the future mother leaves her husband's house to take up residence in the house of her parents or her maternal uncle no later than the eighth month of pregnancy. This custom "is associated with the strong fear of the dangers which surround a woman in childbed, and which are conceived to be due to a form of evil magic." (*SLS*:228). That being the case, the woman is guarded during this period by her male relatives who, armed with spears, sit up all night to protect her from prowling sorcerers. The important characteristic of this watch for our present concern is that although it is "primarily" the duty of the husband to protect his wife from the dangers surrounding her, "he is *never trusted alone*, and the male relatives of the pregnant woman not only assist but also *control him*" (*SLS*:229, italics mine).

Malinowski does not tell us why the husband is not trusted to be alone with his wife or why he must be controlled. But since no suspicion is directed toward him when the wife is not pregnant, it seems reasonable to conclude that the distrust and control are related to the potential danger that he poses not to the wife, but to the unborn child, which would also explain why it is that as her date of delivery approaches, the pregnant wife is moved to the home of her relatives. This suggests, then, that it is the husband's Laius complex that poses a danger for the unborn child—most especially if it is a first child—for the latter is his potential rival for the love of the wife-mother.

That suggestion is supported by the fact that following the birth of the child, the husband is prohibited from sleeping with his wife and child for the duration of the long post-partum sex taboo. The conjunction of these two prohibitions may then be interpreted as having the following functions. First, by reducing his opportunities for observing the intimate relationship between his wife and child, especially at night, it minimizes the chances for the arousal of rivalrous hostility to his son. Second, by reducing his opportunities for being alone with the child, it also minimizes the chances for his acting upon his hostility. In this sense these taboos serve the same function that is served by his being under the surveillance of his in-laws during the final months of his wife's pregnancy. Since the father's relationship with the child when these taboos are lifted is warm and cordial, it can only be assumed that his hostility has been repressed. Repressed, rather than eliminated, not only because of the evidence (to be presented below) for its expression in cultural symbol systems, but because the bonds of fatherhood (as we have already observed) are regarded by the Trobrianders themselves as "artificial and untrustworthy under any strain."

We may now summarize our analysis of the pattern of father-absence in the Trobriands and draw a conclusion. Since the father is absent from the three domains in which his presence would be most expected, and since, for all three, father-absence is plausibly explained as an indication of the son's hostility toward him, the fact that his hostility is coped with by repression, denial, and father banishment suggests that the son's hostility to the father in the Trobriands is of more than ordinary intensity. Moreover, that the analysis of father-absence in two of these domains—but most especially in the reproductive domain—suggests that the Trobriand son's hostility is Oedipal in its motivation would explain the apparent anomaly of hostility to a father who, far from being authoritarian and punitive, is rather kindly and nurturant. That is, the kindly father is pater, and toward him the son harbors kindly sentiments in return. The same father, however, is also genitor-cum-mother's lover, and it is toward him, as our analysis has suggested, that the son's hostility is directed. In short, this analysis suggests that, contrary to Malinowski's claim, "traces" of a repressed Oedipus complex *do* exist in the Trobriands.

The Hidden Mother

One swallow, however, does not a summer make. If we are to entertain the hypothesis that a repressed Oedipus complex exists in the Trobriands, we must be able to identify "traces" of unconscious incestuous desires for the mother independently of their inference from traces of Oedipal hostility to the father. Hence, before exploring the father-son relationship further (which we shall do in the next chapter), we must now confront Malinowski's contention that the "passionate" desires of the Trobriand boy for the mother are gradually and spontaneously dissipated in early childhood.

In fact there are, as we shall see, many traces of unconscious incestuous desires for the mother, but in view of Malinowski's contrary claim, it might be useful to first specify the kinds of traces we would not expect to find. Malinowski, it will be recalled, rejected the existence of such desires on the grounds, primarily, that there is no evidence of their manifestation where they would be most expected—in dreams and deeds of incest. That his informants accounted for the absence of such manifestations on the grounds that, inasmuch as she is an "old woman," only an "imbecile" would have sexual feelings for the mother clinched his argument so far as he was concerned.

This argument, however, as we observed in a previous chapter, is fallacious on two accounts. First, even in societies in which the Oedipus complex is known to exist, overt dreams of incest, let alone actual incest with the mother, are only found in cases of severe psychopathology (as, indeed, Oedipal theory would predict). The second reason—which, at the same time, provides an explanation for the first—is that in the normal case, the Oedipus complex disappears from consciousness in childhood, either by its dissolution or by repression. Even in the latter case, however, the repressed—i.e., unconscious—incestuous desire of the adult remains fixated on the mental representation of his childhood mother, rather than moving on to the contemporary mother of his maturity. In short, when Malinowski's informants explained that sexual feelings for the mother are precluded by the fact that she is an "old woman," they were only expressing standard Oedipal theory. On the assumption, then, that a repressed Oedipus complex existed in the Trobriands, one would hardly expect to find traces of an incestuous attraction to the mother either in actual incest or in dreams of overt incest with her (except, of course, in pathological cases).

This is not to say, however, that no traces of such an attraction would be expected in dreams, for the very opposite is the case. On the assumption that the Oedipus complex is repressed, dreams are one of the places in which incestuous desires for the mother—not, however, the contemporary mother, but the mother of childhood—would be most expected. Indeed, if they were absent, this would constitute compelling grounds for rejecting the hypothesis of a repressed Oedipus complex. Since, however, these desires are unconscious, we would no more expect their *overt* manifestation in dreams than in waking life. That is, if the unconscious incestuous desire for the mother breaks through the repression barrier in dreams, it does so—in normal adults at least—only in symbolic disguise, the mother being replaced by some other woman in the manifest dream content. This is the case in all societies for which relevant data are available, and we would not expect the Trobriands to be any different.

I will now suggest that the mother does appear in symbolic disguise in Trobriand incest dreams—in the disguise, that is, of the sister. Malinowski, it will be recalled, took the opposite tack. For him, the existence of dreams of (overt) sister incest in the Trobriands, coupled with the absence of dreams of (overt) mother incest, prove that although the sister is an incestuous object in the Trobriands, the mother is not. In the previous chapter, I observed that this is an invalid conclusion because— for motives expected by Oedipal theory—dreams of sister incest occur with no greater frequency in the Trobriands than in the West, in which, according to Malinowski, the mother is an incestuous object. Here, however, I wish to go beyond a mere refutation of Malinowski's argument, and argue that these dreams in fact support the hypothesis that the mother is a repressed incestuous object in the Trobriands.

There are at least four interrelated, and redundant, reasons why this might be so. Since dreams of sister incest require that incestuous desires for the sister break through the repression— and the incest—barrier, the absence of dreams of mother incest would then suggest that (1) the incestuous desire for the mother is strongly repressed, (2) the mother-son incest taboo is stronger than the taboo on brother-sister incest, (3) the moral repugnance for mother incest is stronger than for sister incest, (4) a strong reaction formation against the sexual attraction to the mother leads to a sexual aversion toward her. These redundant explanations almost certainly explain the relative incidence of overt brother-sister and mother-son incest dreams in other societies, including those of the West, and there is no a priori reason to assume that this might not be the case for the Trobriands. Of the four, however, only the cultural explanation—the greater strength of the mother-son incest taboo—can be empirically tested in the case of the Trobriands, and the test is positive. Thus, although Malinowski typically argues that the brother-sister taboo is the stronger, in at least one passage, it will be recalled, he does a remarkable volte-face: "The idea of mother incest is as repugnant to the native as sister incest, *probably even more*" (*SR*:100–101, italics mine).

Given, then, the not infrequent occurrence of overt dreams of sister incest, all four of the possible explanations for the manifest absence of the mother from dreams of overt incest entail the identical hypothesis: she is absent not because an incestuous attraction to the mother is weak, but rather because it is very strong—stronger by far, for example, than the incestuous attraction to the sister. This hypothesis is only apparently paradoxical. If an incestuous attraction is strong, then, given the strength of the incest taboo, the strength of the repression must be all the greater. Hence, the incestuous desire must remain altogether repressed or, if it breaks through the repression barrier, it must do so in a disguised form. This hypothesis, moreover, is supported by the finding, already discussed in the previous section, that the great majority of Trobriand dreams are not recalled. Unrecalled dreams, it will be remembered, are dreams which, because they are threatening, are repressed. If, then, many Trobriand dreams are repressed because of their poorly disguised aggressive wishes in regard to the father, as has already been suggested, I would now suggest that many others may be repressed because of their poorly disguised incestuous wishes in regard to the mother. (Since overt sister incest dreams, though they occur, are very disturbing to the Trobrianders, I would also suggest that still others may be repressed because of incestuous motives in regard to the sister.)

However plausible it might be theoretically, taken by itself this interpretation of the absence of mother incest dreams carries little empirical conviction. For it appears to claim—as critics of psychodynamic interpretations charge them, sometimes validly, with claiming—that *A* and non-*A* alike can both confirm a hypothesis, which means, of course, that no evidence could possibly disconfirm it. To be sure, the present interpretation is not susceptible of this kind of criticism because, according to Oedipal theory, the absence of overt mother incest dreams (non-*A*) is predicted for men with a normally repressed Oedipus complex, whereas the presence of such dreams (*A*) is predicted for men in which it is weakly repressed, if repressed at all. Nevertheless, since the proposed interpretation for the absence of dreams of overt mother incest is reminiscent of that vulnerable type of psychodynamic interpretation, I would prefer to take a conservative position with regard to its plausibility. In brief, I shall argue that this interpretation may be regarded as plausible if, but only if, the previously enunciated hypothesis—that Trobriand dreams of overt sister incest are a vehicle for the expression, in a disguised form, of unconscious incestuous desires for the mother—is supported.

According to that hypothesis, to make its logic explicit, the image of the sister in Trobriand dreams of sister incest not only represents the sister, but also is an unconscious symbolic representation of the mother, the sexual desire for the latter being displaced onto the former. This hypothesis is best investigated by applying to sister incest dreams the structuralist principle that was used in the analysis of the absent-father pattern, viz., that the clue to the identity of an absent, but expected, element in some cognitive structure is provided by its replacement. In order, however, to better understand the rationale for applying that principle here, I should like, even at the risk of redundancy, to reemphasize one characteristic of a repressed Oedipus complex that has already been emphasized before.

Let us recall, then, that if the Oedipus complex is repressed (rather than extinguished) in childhood, the son remains unconsciously fixated on the mental representation of his childhood mother, his first love-object. Let us recall, again, that the son would no more commit undisguised incest with his mother in his dreams than he would in waking life, because the same motives which led him to repress his incestuous desires for her in childhood (castration anxiety, moral anxiety, etc.) continue to operate in adulthood. This being so, his *conscious* sexual preference in both cases is displaced from the mother onto some other woman, usually, however, one who (on one or more dimensions) is reminiscent of her. Indeed, even when the Oedipus complex is extinguished, and not merely repressed, the mother is usually succeeded as a libidinal object for the son by a woman who "resembles her or is [psychologically] derived from her" (Freud [1931] 1968:228).

Bearing these observations in mind, it is not difficult to understand—the Trobrianders aside—why very often it is the sister who replaces the mother as the object of the boy's sexual desire. This is especially the case in postchildhood, for it is then that, on a displacement gradient, the sister, more than anyone else, most resembles the mother of childhood. In addition to their resemblance, there is sometimes yet another motive—one which, as we shall see in the next chapter, obtains in the Trobriands—for the sister's being the most likely choice for the mother's replacement. As stated by Freud, a brother "may take his sister as a love object by way of substitute for his faithless mother . . . [just as] a little girl finds in her elder brother a substitute for her father who no longer takes an affectionate interest in her as he did in her earliest years" (Freud [1916–17] 1966:334). To be sure, since sexual relations with the sister, like those with the mother, are interdicted by the incest taboo, sexual feelings for her are also repressed, but since the taboo on the sister is usually less powerful than the mother taboo, dreams of overt incest (as well as actual incest) with the sister are, relatively speaking, not infrequent, as we have seen in those societies for which we have the relevant data.

I would now suggest that the overt dreams of sister incest in the Trobriands are very often overdetermined. Since the Trobriand sister is a libidinal object for the brother in her own right (as Malinowski repeatedly emphasizes), it is fair to assume that the image of the sister in these dreams does indeed represent the sister; but, as suggested by the above discussion it may simultaneously represent, by the processes of displacement and of condensation, the childhood mother as well. From clinical evidence we know that these processes are often at work in dreams of overt sister incest in the West, and there is no reason why they may not occur in such dreams in the Trobriands as well, especially since Malinowski's classification of Trobriand dreams provides strong support for this hypothesis.

Malinowski classified Trobriand dreams into "free" (*SR*:89)—also "spontaneous" and "ordinary" (*SLS*:387)—dreams, on the one hand, and "official" (*SR*:89)—also "typical," "traditional" (*SR*:89), "stereotyped," "standardized" (*SLS*:387)—dreams, on the other. "Free" dreams are "spontaneous visions arising in sleep . . . which come to every human being" (*SLS*:387), and these comprise the rarely recalled (i.e., repressed) dreams, to which we have already referred. "Official" dreams, on the other hand, "are those which are prescribed and defined by custom" (*SLS*:387), and which "run on lines prescribed by tradition" (*SR*:89). Since dreams of the latter class are "expected of certain people," they are also "hoped for and awaited" (*SLS*:387). Not surprisingly, then, most of the recalled (i.e., nonrepressed) dreams belong to the latter class. What, perhaps, *is* surprising, however, is that dreams of sister incest are also included in this class. Since, therefore, sister incest dreams (by this classification) are expected, it is little wonder that they occur; and since they are prescribed by tradition, what better vehicle could there be for the displacement of mother incest wishes than in dreams in which, in any event, one incestuous prohibition is already violated. In short, the classification of sister incest dreams as "official" dreams makes it all the more plausible that the image of the sister is a condensed image, consciously representing the sister, but unconsciously the mother.

Since disguise in dreams (and elsewhere) is motivated by the wish to conceal forbidden (hence, anxiety arousing) wishes, this hypothesis regarding sister incest dreams explains the strong affect which, Malinowski reports, they arouse in the dreamer. For if the sister in these dreams also unconsciously represents the mother, it is little wonder that they "haunt and disturb" the dreamer. It also explains an otherwise unexplained paradox in Malinowski's report concerning the dysphoric affect which these dreams arouse. Since dreams of sister incest are members of the class of dreams that are "hoped for and awaited," it is hard to understand why they should arouse such affect. If, however, the image of the sister is a condensed image representing the mother as well as the sister, this apparent paradox may not be so paradoxical after all. Finally, this hypothesis is consistent with others of our arguments previously developed and which, together, constitute an integrated conceptual schema. Thus, it is

consistent with the argument that rather than disappearing gradually and spontaneously, as Malinowski contends, the "passionate" feelings of the young boy for the mother persist in a
repressed state in Trobriand men. It is consistent, too, with the
pattern of father-absence and the Oedipal hostility which, by
our interpretation, it manifests.

Although the dream is an important *private* place in which
"traces" of a repressed attachment to the mother is indicated,
it is not the only place. Traces of such an attachment are also
found in a *public* place, in the institution of the Kula, that complicated system of ceremonial exchange which (even more than
the "ignorance" of physiological paternity) has given the Trobriand Archipelago a prominent place on the ethnographic
map.

Requiring long ocean voyages, the Kula is an exchange system
in which food (fish and vegetables) and especially ceremonial
objects (shell necklaces and armshells) are traded in complicated
transactions between trading partners who inhabit different islands (Malinowski [1922] 1961). In an insightful analysis Mc-
Dougall has shown that the ritual of the Kula and the etiquette
that Kula partners display toward each other constitute a form
of ceremonial "courtship" (McDougall 1975:61) in which "the
Kula partner, like a spouse, must be wooed" (ibid.:87). In fact,
however, there is much more to it than that. Thus, for example,
after the armshells and necklaces have been exchanged, "it is
said that these two [objects] have married" (Malinowski [1922]
1961:356). In addition, the Trobrianders conceive of the armshells (bracelets worn on the upper arm) as feminine, and the
necklaces (which are in the form of pendants) as masculine.
Moreover, in one form of exchange the (feminine) bracelet is
said to "clinch" the (masculine) necklace, which, in turn, is said
to "pierce" the bracelet. Considering the manifest symbolism of
these ceremonial exchanges, it hardly requires an extended ex-
egesis for their meanings to be understood.

If, however, those meanings are not yet apparent, consider
the following additional feature of the Kula. If the (feminine)
armshell—in this form of exchange called "tooth" (*kudu*)—which
is given in exchange for the (masculine) necklace is not thought
to be its equivalent in value, the giver of the necklace will "vi-

olently complain" that the armshell is not a "proper 'tooth' " for his necklace, for since it has not been "properly 'bitten,' " it is not a "real 'marriage' " (ibid.:356–57). Now if it be remembered, as McDougall (1975:63) perceptively observes, that biting is also a prominent feature of Trobriand lovemaking, the symbolic meaning of this transaction should speak for itself.[12]

Granted, then, that the Kula exchange explicitly symbolizes sexual love and "marriage," it is nevertheless obvious that these meanings do not apply to the relationship between the Kula partners as such—both because the symbols are heterosexual, and because Malinowski ([1922] 1961:338) assures us that there is no homosexual dimension in their relationship—but rather to its symbolic representation. McDougall—who accepts Malinowski's contention that the sister is the primary object of the male's incestuous attraction in the Trobriands—speculates that the Kula partners represent brother and sister (McDougall 1975:89). This speculation, however, is confuted by the texts of Kula magic, which make it very clear that the partners stand to each other in the relationship not of sister and brother, but of mother and young son.

Consider, to take but one example, the features of the magical spell (Malinowski [1922] 1961:337) which is recited when the Kula expedition beaches its canoe (on the island of Dobu) and begins to prepare for the Kula exchange. Thus, in the passage

> They take me to their bosom; they hug me. The great woman befriends me, where the pots are boiling; the good woman befriends me, on the sitting platform,

the expressions, "great woman" and "good woman," so Malinowski ([1922] 1961:338) tells us, refer to the wife and sister of the exchange partner; and the expressions "take to their bosom," "hug," and "befriend" are ordinarily used "to describe the fondling and rocking and hugging of small children." That would explain why the spell continues with

12. We might speculate that the designation of the (feminine) bracelet as a "tooth" that "bites" the (masculine) necklace suggests that the Trobrianders, either consciously or unconsciously, have a vagina dentata fantasy. If so, this might account, among other reasons, for the males' fear of the vagina, to be discussed below.

No more it is my mother [i.e., I no longer need my real mother]; my mother art thou, O woman of Dobu! No more it is my father; my father art thou, O man of Dobu.

Then, in a passage that refers to the partner himself—the one to whom the voyager will propose a "marriage" between his own (masculine) necklace and the latter's (feminine) armshell—the spell continues with "an exaggerated description" of the voyager's "intimacy" with him (ibid.):

No more it is the high platform, the high platform are his arms . . . are his legs; no more it is my lime spoon, my lime spoon is his tongue; no more it is my lime pot, my lime pot is his gullet.

In short, the partner is one "on whose arms and legs he will sit, and from whose mouth he will partake of the betel chewing materials" (ibid.)—much like the Trobriand mother who, even prior to weaning him, holds the young child on her arms and legs, and feeds him boiled taro which she has chewed into a mash (*SLS*:234). Symbolically, then, the Kula voyager stands in the same relationship to his trading partner as a young boy to his nurturant (feeding) mother.

Lest, however, it be assumed that this feeding by the Kula "mother" is any less sexual than that by the biological mother (see below), it should again be emphasized that the ceremony resembles a "courtship," that it is consummated by a "marriage" between two valuables conceived of as opposite gender, and—something that has not yet been mentioned—that there is always an important "association between Kula magic and love magic" (Malinowski [1922] 1961:310). If that is not enough to establish the sexual element in the feeding, consider that, in yet another magical spell (ibid.:339), which is recited before commencing the Kula exchange, the feeding items referred to in the previous spell—the lime spoon, lime pot, and tongue—as well as the throat, larynx, mouth, and eyes are said to "flare up" and to "flash." These words, Malinowski (ibid.) explains, are normally used to refer to a "desire, a coveting, nascent in the eyes," which includes (among other things) a "wish and appetite in matters of sex." The sexual meaning of the feeding of the voyager by his Kula "mother" could hardly be more evident.

Now the Kula, as Malinowski emphasizes, is not just another ceremonial exchange; rather it is a (if not the) focus of Trobriand culture, involving much preparation, and entailing long and dangerous (natural and supernatural alike) voyages. To be sure, much of this effort is in the service of genuine economic exchange, for economic valuables are traded together with the ceremonial valuables (the necklaces and armbands); but as Malinowski makes abundantly clear, it is the exchange of the ceremonial valuables that—in the minds of the natives, if not of those anthropologists who have insisted upon seeing a "rational" explanation for the Kula—is the real object of these voyages. That this is so is underscored by the profound meanings that they possess for the Trobrianders.

Thus, these ceremonial valuables "form one of the leading interests in native life, and are one of the main items in the inventory of their culture" (ibid.:512). "Possessing high value" and arousing "emotional reaction," they are treated with "veneration and affection" (ibid.). They are the most "effective offering" that can be made to spirits because they put them "into a pleasant state of mind" (ibid.). When placed beside a dying man, they have a pleasant effect, "soothing and fortifying at the same time . . . to surround a man with them, even at his most evil moment, makes this moment less evil" (ibid.:513). And for the living Trobrianders, to possess one of these valuables is "exhilarating, comforting, soothing in itself. They will look at [it] and handle it for hours" (ibid.:514).

Given, then, the deeply affective meanings that are associated with the possession of these ceremonial objects; given, moreover, the explicitly sexual meanings of these objects when they enter into the symbolic marriage that is effected between them in the Kula exchange; and given that the symbolic relationship between the voyager and the partner with whom he exchanges these objects recapitulates the feeding relationship, including its sexual overtones, between a young boy and his mother—given all of this I would suggest that a repressed incestuous longing for the childhood mother is evidenced in the institution of the Kula.

We may now conclude this chapter by observing that contrary to Malinowski's contention, important "traces" of a "repressed Oedipus complex"—and an unusually strong one at that—are present in the Trobriands in regard to both its aggressive and its incestuous dimensions. These traces are sufficiently important, I would suggest, to warrant the hypothesis that a repressed Oedipus complex exists in the Trobriands. In the following two chapters we shall present the methods employed for testing this hypothesis as well as the results of the tests.

4

Testing the Trobriand
Oedipal Hypothesis:
Predicted Ontogenetic Determinants

In the preceding chapter I argued that there are sufficient "traces" of an unconscious incestuous attachment to the mother and Oedipal hostility for the father to suggest as a hypothesis that a repressed, unusually strong Oedipus complex exists in the Trobriands. In this and the following chapter, in which we pass from the context of discovery to the context of validation, we report the results arrived at from testing that hypothesis. Employing the hypothetico-deductive method, the confirmation of this hypothesis requires (*a*) evidence for the existence in Trobriand males of those psychological characteristics which, according to Oedipal theory, are predictably associated with—and are, therefore, indexical of—a repressed and unusually strong Oedipus complex, and (*b*) evidence for the existence of those conditions in the Trobriand family system which, according to the theory, predictably produce such an Oedipus complex. In this chapter we shall deal with the latter prediction, reserving the former for the following chapter.

The Oedipus complex, regardless of its strength, is brought into existence in the first instance by the boy's incestuous attraction to the mother. Hence, an unusually strong Oedipus complex would be expected in males with an especially intense incestuous attachment to her. Such an attachment is brought about, according to Oedipal theory, by a highly "seductive" mother who, wittingly or unwittingly, arouses in her son unusually strong sexual feelings. Here, then, is another example of the thesis that the "complementary Oedipus complex" of the parent may serve to initiate the Oedipus complex of the child. If, then, to return to my argument, the son is more or less in exclusive possession of the mother—because the father is prominent by his absence, either physically or psychologically—her seductiveness and his attraction would be expected to be all the stronger. Such a condition is most likely to occur if the mother's seductiveness commences during the *pre-Oedipal* period of psychosexual development—the period in which, even if he is present, the father is not yet a salient figure, either cognitively or affectively, for the child. This same condition would be expected to bring about especially strong hostility to the father, for when—during the Oedipal period—the father finally becomes a salient figure for the boy, the latter's rivalry with him for the love of the wife-mother (whose love he had heretofore monopolized) is all the more intense.

In accordance with these theoretical expectations regarding the ontogenesis of a strong Oedipus complex, the acceptance of the Trobriand Oedipal hypothesis requires (among other conditions) that the following ontogenetic prediction be confirmed: during the pre-Oedipal period of development the Trobriand boy experiences a highly seductive mother and a father who is remote either physically or psychologically.

That the Trobriand child might experience such a state of affairs is hinted at in the "absent-father" pattern discussed in the previous chapter. In two of the elements present in that pattern—family myths and reproduction beliefs—the father is nonexistent from the very beginning of the child's life, which suggests that these collective representations express not only the son's hostility to the father—as was previously suggested— but also his wish for the return of a golden age of early childhood in which he enjoyed exclusive possession of the mother. That the idyllic early mother-child dyad portrayed in Trobriand family myths is later disrupted by the arrival of a cannibalistic ogre supports this suggestion, for the ogre (as we suggested in the previous chapter) may be viewed as the projection of the mental representation of the "bad"—i.e., Oedipal—father, who breaks up the mother-child dyad.

Since myths, however, represent fantasy, what can we say about the reality of the early parent-child relationship in the Trobriands? Although we do not have a large number of hard data, it is possible nevertheless to gain some clues about their relationship from social structural and other kinds of information.

The most important social structural clue regarding the parent-child relationship in the Trobriands during the pre-Oedipal period consists of Malinowski's report that the Trobrianders practice a long postpartum sex taboo, during which the child sleeps with the mother while the father sleeps elsewhere, usually in a different house. In reading about these practices, I recalled the cross-cultural findings of John Whiting regarding their Oedipal implications. Nevertheless, I did not pursue this clue until, taken by surprise by Malinowski's claim that no traces of the Oedipus complex were to be found in Trobriand culture, I also recalled some Trobriand folktales and myths which are described in the following chapter, and which, in hindsight, seemed to support Whiting's findings—or, more accurately, my reinterpretation of them.

It was almost twenty-five years ago that Whiting, Kluckhohn, and Anthony (1958) suggested that the conjunction of a long postpartum sex taboo and exclusive mother-child sleeping arrangements produces strong dependency feelings in the child in respect to the mother because, as the exclusive focus of his emotional attachment, he looks to her as the main source for the gratification of his needs. These customs, they further suggested, intensify the boy's hostility to the father, because when the latter returns to the marriage bed at the end of the postpartum taboo, he replaces the son in the special relationship with the wife-mother. Willy-nilly, then, the boy comes to perceive the father as a hated rival for the love and attention of the mother. If then, they reasoned, his hostility to the father were to persist into puberty, the boy might express it in overt acts of aggression which, at that age, could be highly dangerous. Hence, they predicted, painful male puberty rites are more likely to be performed in societies that practice these customs than in those that do not, because (so they reasoned) by arousing the son's fear of the father these rites have the function of preventing filial aggression.

This prediction was tested and confirmed in a statistical analysis of a sample of fifty-five societies. Moreover, in examining those few societies that did not conform to their prediction, it was discovered that, rather than painful puberty rites, they practiced another custom instead—male extrusion from the household. Inasmuch as this custom also precludes the expression of aggression to the father—by removing the son from his presence—it may be viewed, so they reasoned, as a functional alternative to puberty rites.

Although Whiting et al. explicitly rejected the universality of the Oedipus complex (1958: 361), they viewed their findings as having identified the postpartum sex taboo and mother-son joint sleeping as one set of sufficient (but not necessary) antecedent conditions for its existence. It should be noted, however, that theirs is a rather idiosyncratic interpretation of the Oedipus complex, so far as the mother-son relationship is concerned, for in their view these customs produce not a libidinal, but a dependent attachment of the son to the mother, which they take to be an "Oedipal"attachment.[1] It is my view, however (for reasons to be explained below), that these customs do not intensify the boy's dependent attachment to the mother so much as his libidinal attachment to her, and that in doing so they produce not merely an Oedipus complex but rather an unusually strong one. Hence, I view painful male puberty rites and male extrusion as cultural means for coping not only with the hostility dimension of the Oedipus complex, but with its incestuous dimension as well. That is, I view them as having the function (among others) of preventing the expression not only of the son's hostile feelings for the father, but also of his incestuous feelings for the mother.

With these preliminary observations concerning the possible Oedipal consequences of a long postpartum sex taboo and joint mother-child sleeping, let us return to the Trobriands. So far as the first custom—the postpartum sex taboo—is concerned, sexual intercourse between spouses is prohibited in the Trobriands at least until the child can walk, but preferably until he is weaned, the latter occurring at the age of two at the earliest (*SLS*:233). Either age, however, satisfies Whiting's criterion for

---

1. In a later paper (Burton and Whiting 1961), Whiting changed his view concerning the relationship between these childhood customs and painful male puberty rites, which he now interpreted as related not to the boy's hostility to the father, but to his attachment to the mother. These customs, he now argued, produce an identification of the son with the mother, so that the function of puberty rites is to replace his feminine identity with a masculine one.

a "long" postpartum sex taboo. With respect to the second custom—exclusive mother-child sleeping arrangements—the Trobriand child sleeps with the mother, while the father usually
sleeps in a different house until the child is weaned (*SLS*:235).
Moreover, even following weaning, the child remains pretty
much within the orbit of the mother until the age of three (Powell
1957:138). We may now examine in detail the ways in which
each of these customs might contribute to an unusually strong
Oedipus complex, beginning with its incestuous dimension.

According to the epigenetic theory of psychosexual development (Erikson 1963:chapter 2), the boy does not normally enter
the "phallic" stage of psychosexual development until sometime
in the third year of life. Since, however, genital arousal can and
does occur even in the "oral" stage, when the genitals are still
a subsidiary erogenous zone, the attainment of phallic primacy
may be accelerated by any number of external social conditions
that affect the epigenetic timetable. In the case of the Trobriands,
I would suggest, such an acceleration is brought about by the
boy's intimate and continuous physical contact with the pre-
Oedipal mother which results, first, from the prolonged period
of exclusive mother-child sleeping and, second, from late
weaning. Let us begin with the latter.

Male infants, as is well known, may display genital as well
as oral arousal while nursing, as is indicated by penile erection
(Kaufman 1970:33). Since in the Trobriands, weaning is sometimes not completed until the age of four—so that the boy continues to nurse even after attaining phallic primacy—nursing
may consequently not only satisfy his oral needs, but also arouse
his genital urges, thereby intensifying the boy's libidinal feelings
for the mother. When we consider, in addition, that throughout
the nursing period the boy sleeps with the mother, it can be
fairly assumed that the sexual stimulation of nursing is only one
source of his heightened sexual feelings for her. This assumption
is supported by two recent studies, using large-scale cross-cultural samples (Ember 1978; Kitahara 1976), which show that joint
mother-child sleeping intensifies the son's attraction to the
mother.

Childhood sexuality, however, is not a one-way, but a two-
way street in that the child's sexual feelings for the parent, as
was noted in an earlier chapter, can be aroused not only en-

dogenously, but also exogenously, i.e., by the parent's sexual feelings for the child. Such feelings, usually unconscious, are likely to be especially strong when the parent's sexual needs are frustrated. In the latter event, the parent may behave "seductively" toward the child, who, experiencing the parent's "love" as a sexual temptation, is then sexually aroused in return (Fenichel 1945:93). This, I would suggest, is the main reason that mother-child sleeping in the Trobriands intensifies the boy's attraction to the mother. Deprived of all sexual gratification for the duration of the long postpartum sex taboo, the only outlet available to the mother for her libidinal needs is found in her relationship with her child, and it would not be surprising, therefore, if she were to behave more seductively with him than is usually the case in the "complementary Oedipus complex." When it is remembered, moreover, that this prolonged taboo takes effect after each birth, so that during her childbearing years the woman experiences long periods of sexual deprivation, this reaction becomes all the more expectable.

This expectation is abundantly supported by studies of sexually deprived mothers in other societies. For example, in a study of cognitive and social development in Latin American infants raised in a prison by their consort-less mothers, Spitz (1945) found that the mothers' frustrated libidinal needs were focused on their children. Kakar (1978:chapter 3) arrived at a similar conclusion in his psychocultural study of male character development in India where, for entirely different reasons, mothers are sexually frustrated; in addition, Kakar found that the son responds with heightened sexual feeling to the mother's "seductive" behavior. Similar findings are reported by Slater (1966) in a psychohistorical study of ancient Greece, and by Slavin (1972) in a psychological study of American male college students. Again, in her fine-grained clinical investigations, Bibring (1953) discovered that in (American) families in which the husband-father, though physically present, is yet psychologically distant from the wife and son, the "mother is as much in need of a husband as the son is of a father." Hence, focusing her love on the son, and behaving seductively toward him, she arouses his incestuous desires. Finally, in a cross-cultural study of sexual deprivation resulting specifically from the postpartum sex taboo, Stephens (1962), basing his conclusions on a sample of forty primitive societies, found a high correlation between this taboo and the intensification of the boy's sexual feelings for the mother.[2]

On the basis of these and many similar studies, it seems reasonable to assume that the long postpartum sex taboo has similar sexual consequences in the mother-son relationship in the Trobriands, more especially because during the entire period in which her husband is absent from the marriage bed, the mother not only sleeps with the child, but feeds him at the breast. That breast-feeding is often a sexually stimulating experience for the mother is a well-established finding (Kaufman 1970:32), its sexual quality, according to the findings of Masters and Johnson, ranging from plateau tension levels to orgasm (Weisskopf 1980:779). Indeed, in the case of the (American) women making up the Masters and Johnson sample, at least one-fourth of those who did not breast-feed their children were motivated by guilt and fear concerning sexual arousal (ibid.). When we then consider that the nursing mothers in their sample resumed marital sexual relations earlier than nonnursing mothers (ibid.), it may

2. More speculative, but most intriguing, is a suggestion of Jonas and Jonas (1975) which was stimulated by Sade's (1968) research on mother-son incest in rhesus monkeys. In this research Sade discovered that mother-son incest is inhibited by the mother's dominance, but if, for various reasons, the son achieves dominance, mother-son incest is then consummated. Stimulated by this work, and drawing upon their clinical experience, Jonas and Jonas suggest that in humans, too, the son's incestuous attraction to the mother is intensified if he becomes the dominant partner in their relationship, a reversal which may occur if the mother suffers a loss of confidence and self-esteem. In such a case, they point out, the following pattern can be observed in humans: (1) The mother is inconsistent in her relationship with her son, oscillating between cajolery and punishment, (2) argues with the son as if he were an equal, (3) treats him as a playmate, and (4) manifests an attitude of helplessness in his presence. Given this pattern, the son senses that his rank is equal, if not superior, to that of his mother, so that she is then perceived by him as a possible sexual object.

It is not implausible to suggest that the behavioral characteristics displayed by the mothers described by Jonas and Jonas might also be displayed by Trobriand mothers as a result, however, of sexual frustration, rather than a loss of self-esteem. If so, this would be another contributing factor to the development of a heightened desire for the mother in Trobriand boys induced by the long postpartum sex taboo. (For a different application of this dominance hypothesis to the Trobriands, see also the paper by Abernethy 1974, who, however, accepts Malinowski's report that the Trobriand son has no incestuous desires for the mother.)

be assumed that the sexual needs aroused by the nursing experience were the important motive for their doing so.[3]

If, then, breast-feeding is as stimulating for Trobriand as for American women, it might be expected that the sexually deprived Trobriand mother, whose sexual needs are aroused by her nursing child, would behave seductively toward him. That throughout this prolonged period of sexual stimulation and deprivation the mother also sleeps with the child makes this expectation all the more likely, for it provides her with the opportunity, as well as the incentive, for acting seductively toward him. On both accounts, therefore, we would expect the child to be stimulated by the seductiveness of the mother and to respond with heightened sexual feelings for her. It is perhaps because of these reciprocal interactions between mother and child, leading to an intensification of the child's sexual feelings, that Malinowski characterized his feelings for the mother as "passionate."

On the basis, then, of findings from a wide range of human societies it can now be concluded, I believe, that the prediction that the Trobriand boy experiences a highly seductive mother during the pre-Oedipal period has been supported in part, albeit indirectly. Since, moreover, it is a mother of that type who, according to theoretical expectations, produces a strong incestuous attachment in her son, this conclusion provides ontogenetic support for our hypothesis that a strong Oedipus complex—so far at least as its libidinal dimension is concerned—exists in the Trobriands.

According to our stipulation, support for the aggressive dimension of the postulated Trobriand Oedipus complex requires that during the pre-Oedipal period the boy experience not only a highly seductive mother, but also a physically or emotionally remote father. It should be apparent by now that the same Trobriand conditions—a long postpartum sex taboo and exclusive mother-child sleeping arrangements—that create the seductive pre-Oedipal mother also create a remote pre-Oedipal father. It

3. Masters and Johnson interpret this finding as a function of the mother's guilt. I find this interpretation less than convincing since the guilt could more easily be reduced by weaning. That the mothers returned to marital sexual relations while, however, continuing to nurse, suggests that it was heightened sexuality, rather than guilt, that motivated their earlier return.

will be remembered that for the duration of the postpartum sex taboo it is the mother who is primarily attendant upon the boy, and although the father may spend time with him during the day, he is physically separated from him at night, when the boy and his mother sleep together. Since, then, during the pre-Oedipal period the father is not very prominent in the boy's life, he cannot be a salient figure in either his thoughts or his feelings. In sum, since the pre-Oedipal Trobriand boy experiences a father who is relatively remote, both physically and psychologically, the second part of the ontogenetic prediction is also supported.

Briefly, we may now elucidate the expected relationship between the remoteness of the Trobriand father during the pre-Oedipal period and the son's subsequent development of Oedipal hostility toward him. For the duration of the postpartum sex taboo, when the father is a relatively remote figure and the child is the focus of the mother's emotional life, it can be assumed that the son feels little hostility (or any other affect) for the father. When, therefore, following the termination of that taboo, the father replaces the son in the mother's bed and displaces him from his exclusive possession of her, it may be assumed that he becomes an especially salient figure for the son, and that hostility—Oedipal hostility—is not the least of the affects that the son develops for the father at that time.

In short, given his premature incestuous attachment to the mother, the boy's Oedipal hostility to the father is aroused not by a rival who is already in possession of a love-object he himself desires, as is the case in the typical system of early child care, but by one who is a threat to his own possession of her. In the former case, the "Oedipal" mother is one whose love the boy would like to possess, and whose fulfillment is blocked by the "Oedipal" father. In the Trobriand case she is one whose love he already possesses but is in danger of losing to the father. And not only her love. For when the father replaces him in the mother's bed, the boy is also deprived of his nearly exclusive possession of his mother's body, and it may also coincide with the loss of her breasts as well. In the Trobriand case, therefore, the boy's perception of the father as a hated Oedipal rival, and his consequent hostility to him, would be expected to be all the stronger, as has already been suggested by the absent-father pattern.

Inasmuch, then, as both conditions of our ontogenetic prediction—"during the pre-Oedipal period of development the Trobriand boy experiences a highly seductive mother and a father who is remote either physically or psychologically"—have now been supported, if only indirectly, it may be concluded that the first of the two stipulated requirements for the acceptance of the Trobriand Oedipal hypothesis has now been at least partially satisfied. The presentation of the required evidence for its more complete satisfaction, for reasons explained below, must wait until we discuss the second prediction.

Before turning to the second prediction, however, it might be mentioned that in addition to the predicted contribution of the boy's pre-Oedipal experience to the development of the postulated Trobriand Oedipus complex, there is a condition in his Oedipal experience which, although not predicted, might be said to intensify the pre-Oedipal contribution. I am referring to his witnessing of the primal scene.

That Trobriand children are permitted to witness parental intercourse following the father's return to the mother's bed is explicitly remarked upon by Malinowski—who, however, takes this as a measure of Trobriand permissiveness in the sexual training of children. Thus, "within the house, where parents have no possibility of finding privacy, a child has opportunities of acquiring practical information concerning the sexual act. I was told that no special precautions are taken to prevent children from witnessing their parents' sexual enjoyment. The child would merely be scolded and told to cover its head with a mat" (*SLS*:54). This permissiveness, it will be recalled, ends only at puberty, when, so that he not observe their sexual behavior, the boy must leave the parental home.

Insofar as the observation of parental intercourse—the so-called "primal scene"—is sexually exciting for the boy, it arouses his sexual feeling for the mother, according, at least, to clinical findings remarked upon in chapter 2. This being the case, the sexual excitement unwittingly aroused in the Trobriand boy by the Oedipal mother, following his premature sexual stimulation by the seductive pre-Oedipal mother, could only be expected to intensify his incestuous attachment to her. Similarly, since according to the same findings the witnessing of the primal scene also arouses rivalrous rage toward the father, the Oedipal hostility aroused in the Trobriand boy by his displacement by the father from the maternal bed could only be intensified by his continuous witnessing of a scene which underscores the fact that the father has indeed replaced him.

Since the witnessing of the primal scene, though it adds additional support to the Trobriand Oedipus hypothesis, was not one of our predictions, let us return to the two predictions whose support, according to our stipulation, is required for its confirmation. In evaluating the first prediction, I observed that the evidence presented in its support is primarily indirect, and that the additional evidence required to strengthen its support will be presented in connection with the testing of the second prediction. The latter prediction—actually a set of predictions—is important therefore not only for the testing of the existence of the postulated Oedipus complex itself, but also for completing the testing of its postulated ontogenesis.

5

Testing the Trobriand
Oedipal Hypothesis:
Predicted Psychological Concomitants

Characteristics Related to the Oedipal Triangle

The following characteristics, though not exhaustive, are the key psychological characteristics which, according to Oedipal theory, are associated with a repressed and unusually strong Oedipus complex. (1) Strong incestuous desires for sister and adolescent daughter, (2) strong rivalry with siblings, especially male siblings, (3) a strong unconscious wish to reconstitute the Oedipal triangle in relationships with women attached to other males, and the corresponding wish to avoid its recapitulation in relationships with women to whom the actor himself is attached, (4) avoidance of parents in certain situations, but especially those related to or reminiscent of their sexuality, (5) unconscious castration anxiety, including the unconscious belief that sexual transgression is punished by castration, (6) a "splitting" of the mental representation of the mother into a conscious "good mother" and an unconscious "bad mother."

Since, then, these constitute the set of psychological characteristics that are predictably associated with a strong Oedipus complex, the acceptance of the Trobriand Oedipus hypothesis requires that this entire set of psychological characteristics be found in Trobriand males. This prediction will be treated in the following manner. For each of the predicted characteristics, we shall first explicate the theoretical or empirical basis for its derivation from Oedipal theory, following which we shall present the Trobriand data that are available for testing the prediction. Inasmuch, however, as few psychological data are available for the Trobriands, the data will again consist of those social and cultural forms within which, in accordance with our discussion in the previous chapter, the predicted psychological characteristics are manifested.

Let us begin, then, with the first prediction, the expectation of a strong, unconscious incestuous desire for the sister as well as the adolescent daughter. According to Oedipal theory, if the son has an unconscious libidinal fixation on the childhood mother, then, in addition to the libidinal desires which sister and adolescent daughter arouse in their own right, his incestuous attraction to them is intensified because, on a displacement gradient, they are most reminiscent of—and hence the unconscious symbolic representations for—the childhood mother. We shall restrict our present test, however, to the daughter since the Trobriander's powerful incestuous attachment to the sister—the cornerpiece of Malinowski's argument—has already been abundantly demonstrated in dreams, myths, and actuality.

That the daughter may serve as a symbolic representation for the mother has been demonstrated not only in the West, but elsewhere. In India, to offer but one example, the Bengali daughter, who is often called "mother," is treated "as a substitute sexual object by her father and father-figures during her later childhood and in adolescence, even after puberty" (Roy 1975:125). Moreover, the high goddess, Durga, is represented simultaneously as daughter, wife, and mother, and as Roy (1975:127) interprets it, her worship is "the outcome of the sublimated libidinal wishes of father toward daughter and son toward mother."

In the West, this unconscious symbolic equation of mother and daughter has been demonstrated by numerous empirical studies of actual daughter incest. In one of the more recent studies—an investigation of a large sample of sex offenders—Gebhard and his associates found the mother fixation of incestuous fathers striking. "The combination of incest with a young person and the youthful partiality for the mother," they wrote, "suggests an Oedipal phenomenon that we are not equipped to analyze" (Gebhard et al. 1965:209). Studies of incestuous fathers which are more psychologically oriented (Cavallin 1966; Cormier, Kennedy, and Sangowicz 1962; Lustig et al. 1966) also found the daughter to be the unconscious substitute for the childhood mother, and these investigations suggest that the father committed incest with the daughter either because of his repressed incestuous desires for the mother, or because of his vengeful feelings for her for having rejected his sexual advances.[1]

Let us now see how this first prediction fares when put to the empirical test in the Trobriands. Although there are no reported dreams of overt daughter incest, it is reported that any intimacy between a man and his adolescent daughter "is fraught with temptation" (*SR*:69). More important are the reported cases of actual father-daughter incest, which, significantly, are always instigated by the father (*SR*:95). Despite the fact, moreover, that Malinowski claims that father-daughter incest does not have even "an echo in folklore" (*SR*:70), incestuous desire for the daughter is evidenced in a folktale, as well, as he himself indicates in another place. This is the tale of Momovala (*SLS*:411–12) who, while accompanying his daughter to the gardens, sends her up a tree. Seeing her genitals, he experiences "intense emotional excitement," and when she comes down from the tree, Momovala, who has already discarded his pubic leaf in anticipation, seizes her and "copulates and copulates." In short, three types of data—behavioral, psychological, and cultural—constitute evidence in support of the first prediction.

Let us, then, turn to the second prediction, the expectation of strong male sibling rivalry. According to Oedipal theory, rivalry with male siblings is associated with a repressed Oedipus complex of special strength because if the boy has a strong incestuous desire for the mother, his siblings—as well as his father—are perceived by him as rivalrous obstacles to his wish to gain exclusive possession of her. If, therefore, the male remains unconsciously fixated on his childhood mother, it would be expected that his hostility to his siblings would also persist as an unconscious motivational disposition. In the Trobriands rivalrous feelings would be especially expected in the elder sibling because, as we shall see, his earlier privileged relationship

1. From a psychodynamic point of view, the processes by which the daughter, in cases of actual incest, comes to unconsciously represent the mother may be rather complex. Thus, Cormier et al. (1962) found five stages in this process. First, the daughter is a substitute for the wife. Second, she is a substitute for the wife whom the male had courted in his youth. Third, he (the father) is the young man wooing that young wife. Fourth, the present wife symbolizes the forbidden mother. Fifth, the daughter symbolizes the early, giving mother.

with the mother is taken over by his younger sibling. Since there are no data concerning the relationship between Trobriand brothers in childhood, we shall test our prediction by proceeding directly to the evidence for sibling rivalry in adults.

"In tribal law," Malinowski observes, brothers "should be at one in common interests and reciprocal duties as well as in affection" (*SR*:110). In contrast to this normative expectation, however, in reality "there is always a feeling of uncertainty, always a mutual suspicion" between brothers (*SR*:110). More than that, in myth—but even "in real life to a certain degree"— brothers are "enemies, cheat each other, murder each other, and suspicion and hostility obtain rather than love and union" (*SR*:111). In support of this claim Malinowski cites two myths of fratricide.

In one myth two brothers quarrel over a garden plot, in the course of which the elder kills the younger brother. The former, moreover, not only shows no "compunction" about his fratricide, but goes so far as to cook his brother and to hawk his baked flesh from village to village. As a result, cannibalism itself "is traced to a fratricidal act" (*SR*:105–6). In the second myth the fratricide is reversed, the younger killing the elder brother. In this myth, a certain man possesses powerful magic which not only enables him to fly his canoe through the air, but also enables his garden to survive a drought, whereas the gardens of the other men die. As a consequence all the men, including his younger brother, "are jealous and full of hatred," and determine that he must die. It is his brother, however, who actually kills him (*SR*:108–9). It should be noted, moreover, that quarreling over garden plots, far from being confined to myths, "often happens in real life" as well (*SR*:106).[2]

Recognizing that this relentless record of sibling hostility— whose expression ranges from quarreling to cannibalism—might be interpreted as an expression of a repressed Oedipus complex,

2. Given what we now know about the intensity of sibling rivalry in the Trobriands, we may now venture to interpret Malinowski's finding—one that greatly perplexed him—that even to hint that siblings resemble each other, although each is held to resemble the father, is "extremely bad form and a great offense" (*SLS*:204). That is, if siblings are as hostile to each other as Malinowski claims, it is understandable that one would be strongly averse to being reminded that he resembled his hated sibling. Indeed, how else would one explain the following reaction of a group of men to Malinowski's admitted faux pas in

Malinowski—who was constrained from drawing such an inference because it contradicted his claim that the Oedipus complex does not exist in a matrilineal society—claimed that sibling rivalry in the Trobriands reflects a distinctively "matrilineal imprint" (*SR*:106). As projected in myths, their rivalry, so he claimed, conforms to the expectation that "in a matriarchal [i.e., matrilineal] society myths will contain conflicts of a specifically matrilineal nature" (*SR*:107). Even for the second myth, however, the claim that "the matrilineal complex comes powerfully to the fore" (*SR*:109) by the elder brother's refusal to share his magic with the younger males of his matriclan is confusing. In the patriarchal family, too, sibling conflict is often instigated by the breach of the expected solidarity of the males of the patriclan, for in either type of descent system that is what the interdiction of sibling rivalry means from a normative point of view. In neither case, however, does the interdiction speak to the motivational sources of the rivalry, or why it so often is aroused by petty quarreling and escalates into such extreme forms as fratricide.

In any event, Malinowski's claim that the conflict that characterizes the relationship between siblings in Trobriand myths can only be understood in terms of the "principle of matriliny" (*SR*:97) is simply mind-boggling. Nor does the mind stop boggling when he admits that these conflicts "correspond roughly to analogous conflicts within a patriarchal family," for he immediately qualifies this admission by remarking that in families of the latter type they are associated not with brothers, but with a "different"—but an unspecified—cast of characters. It is as if, to take some obvious examples from our own culture, the Biblical myths of Jacob and Esau, of Joseph and his brothers, or of Cain and Abel did not exist. These myths, it is worth remembering, arose in a patrilineal and patriarchal society, and persist with

---

mentioning a man's resemblance to his brother. "There came such a hush over the audience that I was startled by it at once." The man in question promptly left the group, and others, "half-embarrassed, half-offended," left soon after. "What astonished me in this discussion," Malinowski continues, "was that, in spite of the striking resemblance between the two brothers, my informants refused to admit it," and "in arguing the point" with them, they became "quite angry and displeased" (*SLS*:205).

undiminished interest in our own bilateral and nonpatriarchal one.[3]

When, then, Malinowski warns the "attentive reader" that any intimations of the Oedipus complex that might be discerned in the sibling conflicts found in the "matrilineal" myths of the Trobriands could only be based on an "artificial and symbolic rehandling" of these conflicts, the only prudent course is to drop the whole thing. In short, despite Malinowski's expressed "hope" that the "extreme importance" of these last two observations "has been made sufficiently clear," I must say that this hope has not been realized—not, at any rate, for me. In my view it seems fair to conclude that if, both in behavioral and cultural forms, Trobriand brothers are "enemies, cheat each other, murder each other, and suspicion and hostility obtain [between them]" (*SR*:111), there is abundant evidence to support our second prediction.[4]

We may now turn to the third prediction, the expectation that men would wish to possess women attached to other men and

3. Malinowski, as we have often observed, persistently sees as uniquely matrilineal a variety of features of Trobriand society and behavior which are just as frequently found in patrilineal and bilateral societies. In this context we might offer one more example. That a mother in a Trobriand myth favors her younger over her elder son is seen by Malinowski as a "distinctly matrilineal feature" (*SR*:112), although the same theme—to take another example from our own culture—is found in the Biblical myth in which Rachel, favoring Jacob over Esau, goes so far as to incite him to steal the latter's birthright. This myth, like the other Biblical myths referred to above, originated in a patrilineal (indeed, in a patriarchal) society, and persists to this day in our own bilateral society.

4. Sibling aggression, which ranges from simple quarrels to fratricide and cannibalism, is sufficient evidence to support this prediction, whether or not its unconscious Oedipal motivation can be explicitly documented. Such motivation *can* be documented, however, if this aggression can be shown to express certain unconscious motives. Hence, although I have consistently refrained from offering interpretations whose validity depends on the acceptance of debatable universal *unconscious* symbols, such caution is not required in regard to culturally specific *conscious* symbols. When we consider, then, that in the Trobriands, in which gardens are inherited in the matriline, there is a conscious, structurally based association of earth and mother, and when we consider, further, that the earth is consciously perceived by the Trobriander as "the real mother earth who brought forth his lineage in the person of the first ancestress, who nourished him and will receive him again in her womb" (Malinowski 1935:vol. 1, p. 350), it seems fairly evident that in the Trobriands the garden is a conscious maternal symbol. If so, it seems plausible to assume that Trobriand myths of fratricide

would be jealously possessive of the women to whom they them-selves are attached. The Oedipus complex, as I have often stressed, consists of a triangular relationship in which the son's wish for an exclusive relationship with his mother is frustrated by his powerful father, the victor in their rivalry for her affection. Hence, a repressed Oedipus complex, according to Oedipal the-ory, promotes attempts to undo this defeat, by reconstituting such a triangle in adulthood. These attempts are achieved by establishing a relationship with a woman who is associated (as wife or mistress) with another man: structurally corresponding to the mother in the original Oedipal triangle, such a woman is psychologically an unconscious symbolic representation of her. If she is an older woman, so much the better, for she then not only is the structural equivalent of the mother, but is isomorphic with her. In either event, since the cuckolded husband or lover in this triangle is the structural equivalent, and therefore the unconscious symbolic representation, of the father, if a man is successful in his attempts to woo the woman, he achieves his Oedipal triumph: he not only possesses the symbolic mother, but defeats the symbolic father.

A repressed Oedipus complex similarly promotes a strong wish to retain exclusive possession—hence jealousy—of a woman (wife or mistress) to whom the man is attached because any potential rival for her affection, not excluding his son, is uncon-sciously perceived as symbolic of his childhood rival—father or brother—for the possession of his mother. Since, then, if his rival were to be successful in winning the woman, this would be a symbolic recapitulation of his Oedipal defeat, he is strongly jealous of her. In short, if the first part of the prediction consists of a wish to achieve a symbolic Oedipal victory, the second part consists of a fear of a symbolic Oedipal defeat.[5]

---

and fraternal aggression found in real life are overdetermined. In both cases the conscious motivation for fraternal conflict relates to rivalry over garden plots. But if, as now seems plausible, the garden is a maternal symbol, then, in addition to its conscious motivation, it might be suggested that unconsciously the conflict is motivated by rivalry for the love of the mother.

5. Since, as we have suggested, the strong Trobriand Oedipus complex is caused at least in part by the long postpartum sex taboo, and since cross-cultural investigations have shown that strong jealousy of the mother is especially as-sociated with this custom (Broude 1980:196–200), the second part of the predic-tion is all the more expected to hold in the Trobriands.

So far as the first part of the prediction is concerned, evidence for the wish to reconstitute the Oedipal triangle in the Trobriands is found in both folktales and real life. Take, for example, the following tale of a man's adulterous relationship with an older, married woman. In this tale, the younger of two brothers seduces the wife of a chief of a distant place. Her husband captures the adulterer and places him on a high platform to die, but his elder brother rescues him, and subsequently causes all the men of that village to disappear (by magic). Following their victory, the two brothers take all the women of these men in marriage. In short, every boy's Oedipal fantasy—the killing of the father(s) and the marrying of the mother(s)—is carried out with a vengeance!

Adulterous affairs occur not only in folktales, but in actuality, for despite the fact that there are strict norms prohibiting infidelity, "deviations from them are frequent" (*SLS*:115). Moreover, in accordance with our predictions, almost all the examples recounted by Malinowski, which take up five pages of description, involve a man and a *married* woman, despite the fact that not only are younger, unmarried women, as well as divorcées and widows, available and less prohibited, but an affair with them would be far less dangerous. According to Malinowski, the frequency of adultery shows that the Trobrianders are a people of "strong passions and complex sentiments" (*SLS*:119), though he does not explain why this might be so. Oedipal theory, however, as we have just seen, offers a different interpretation for this finding, as well as an explanation for it.

In formulating this prediction, I did not anticipate the extreme degree to which the wish to recapitulate the Oedipal triangle in the Trobriands would extend. Almost all marriages in the Trobriands are monogamous, polygyny—a mark of wealth, power, and prestige—being practiced only by the chiefs. That the sons of chiefs are as adulterous as the sons of commoners is not surprising. What is surprising, however, is that they typically seek (and find) their paramours from among their fathers' wives (excepting, of course, their own mothers). This, surely, is a most extreme example of a son's fulfillment of his Oedipal wishes. To be sure, since his lover is only his stepmother, their affair does not, in the literal sense, constitute mother-son incest. Since, however, she is his father's wife, and therefore the structural equivalent of his mother, she is certainly, psychologically viewed, her symbolic representation. The woman's husband, however, far from being a symbolic representation of the father, is the son's actual father. Hence, the Oedipal triumph over the father that is inherent in such an affair is actual rather than symbolic. In short, if the adulterous folktale recounted above is about as far as a son can go in fulfilling his Oedipal wishes in fantasy, an adulterous affair with his father's wife is about as far as he can go in fulfilling them in actuality. No wonder that such affairs are "the point on which village gossip centers its most eager and malicious interest" (*SLS*:138).

Malinowski's failure to recognize the Oedipal dimension of these affairs is perhaps the most serious example of his more general failure to perceive "traces" of the Oedipus complex in the Trobriand data. The Trobrianders, he says, do not take such an affair as seriously as we would: at most it arouses "their interest by its piquancy" because a "bodily tie between father and son is not recognized" (*SLS*:138). And yet he also tells us that the couple was traditionally punished by death—by either spearing, sorcery, or poison—a practice since abolished by the European administration. If death is the punishment for an act which at most arouses "piquancy," we can only wonder what the punishment might have been had such acts been taken seriously! Malinowski also writes that the fact that a young wife in a polygynous marriage might, if it were done with discretion, carry out such an affair with impunity is evidence that Trobriand polygyny "was never a cruel and inhuman institution" (*SLS*:141). That such an affair might also, however, have Oedipal implications of the kind suggested here—especially since today, with the abolition of the traditional punishment, "all these inter-family adulteries are committed much more openly and shamelessly" (*SLS*:140)—is a possibility he did not consider.

The second part of this prediction is supported as strongly as the first. "In law, custom and public opinion," Malinowski writes, "sexual appropriation is exclusive" (*SLS*:114–15). Moreover, not only is adultery as severely condemned in the Trobriands as it is in Christendom, but "the most puritanical public opinion among ourselves is not more strict" (*SLS*:115). Jealousy of a sexual rival—whether the rivalry concerns a mistress, a wife, or a temporary lover—is powerful, and even a suspicion of infidelity leads to quarrels and fights with the suspected rival. Indeed, the cuckolded husband or lover was so severely aggrieved, that the adulterer was traditionally speared to death and the adulteress was expected to commit suicide by jumping from a tree.

These data present us, however, with two anomalies. First, despite the puritanical attitudes toward, and severe penalties for, the commission of adultery its incidence is nevertheless very high. Second, despite the almost complete license which is found in regard to premarital sexuality, there is nevertheless passionate jealousy of a sexual rival. From the perspective of Oedipal theory, however, these anomalies are more apparent than real, for if the Oedipus complex is repressed, the desire for exclusive possession of one's own woman is exceeded only by the wish to possess another man's woman, in both cases victory over the sexual rival being the lure. In a passage of striking psychological insight, Malinowski himself perceived such a motive in Trobriand men (without, however, recognizing its Oedipal roots). The passage is worth quoting in its entirety, not only for its clinical penetration, but also for the (unwitting) support it offers for an Oedipal explanation for these apparently anomalous findings. Commenting on the Trobriand requirement that males must offer their sweetheart to a visiting Kula stranger, Malinowski writes:

I was impressed by what might be called the reverse side of jealousy. The way in which boys would complain to me about [this] custom-sanctioned sexual hospitality; the way in which they dwelt on the subject and described it with apparent depression, but not without some morbid curiosity; and the insistence with which they would return to it, gave me the impression that there was for them some element of sexual excitement in the situation. Whether jealousy among the Trobrianders is an emotion with two almost contradictory feeling-tones which alternate, the one strongly unpleasant, and the other somewhat pleasurable and sexually stimulating, it is difficult to say (*SLS*:323).

Having now discovered abundant support for the third prediction, we can now turn to the fourth prediction, the expectation of parent-child avoidance in situations related to or
reminiscent of parental sexuality. Since, according to Oedipal
theory, the confrontation of one's parents in situations of that
type might arouse the unconscious hostile and libidinal wishes
of a repressed Oedipus complex, parent-child avoidance is predictable as a defense against the threat that those wishes might
be not only aroused, but acted upon. If, then, a repressed Oedipus complex is a typical personality characteristic of the members of a society, and more especially if it is incompletely
repressed (as we shall argue is the case in the Trobriands), one
would expect such an avoidance pattern to be institutionalized
in some custom or taboo (an "avoidance taboo") that mandates
parent-child avoidance.

In the Trobriands, this fourth prediction is supported by the
custom (described in the previous chapter) of extruding the adolescent son from the parental home. To be sure, Malinowski
(as we have already observed), offers contradictory explanations
for this custom, as well as different ages for when it is put into
practice; moreover, he is not clear whether it applies to both
sexes or to males alone. In one source (*SR*:58) he writes that
both boys and girls (of unspecified age) must leave the parental
home, and in that source he writes that this custom is a function
of the brother-sister incest taboo. He repeats this explanation for
the custom in a second source (*SLS*:519–20), though there he
says that the boy alone is extruded and that his departure does
not occur until he "grows up." In the same source (*SLS*:61–62)
he again affirms that it is the boys alone who are extruded (and
only "sometimes" do the girls also leave), and here he specifies
that this occurs between the ages of twelve and fourteen. The
latter claim is supported by the recent observations of Weiner
(1976:141), who reports that boys alone leave the parental home
and that their departure occurs between the ages of twelve and
fifteen. More important, however, is the explanation that Malinowski offers for the boys' extrusion at that time—that they
should not "hamper by their embarrassing presence the sexual
life of their parents" (*SLS*:62).

In one sense, it makes little difference which of these conflicting reports is correct because whatever the age of extrusion, and

whatever the explanation for its practice, its consequence is the separation of the son from his parents, which confirms our prediction. In another sense, however, it would be important to resolve these conflicting reports because if, for example, the correct explanation for son extrusion is the one offered in the last quotation, this would indicate that even in their *conscious* motivation the Trobrianders attend to the very reason that is suggested by Oedipal theory. A simple solution is to credit both reports, especially since they are not mutually exclusive. Accepting that solution, there are at least three reasons, however, for assigning primary importance to the second explanation for the sons' extrusion—that they not "hamper by their embarrassing presence the sexual life of their parents." First, unlike the first explanation, which was offered in support of a polemical argument, the second was offered in a nonpolemical context. Second, the latter explanation is the one offered by the Trobrianders themselves. Third, it is also the explanation offered by other peoples who practice this custom, peoples who are as geographically and culturally remote both from the Trobrianders and from each other as the Muria of India and the Nyakyusa of East Africa.

If we now turn to that second report, I would suggest that the reason offered by the Trobrianders for the extrusion of the boys at puberty—that their "embarrassing presence" hampers the sexual life of their parents—may conceal yet another (and more important) reason, one that is remarked upon by Malinowski himself. Boys are extruded at puberty, he writes, because that is the age that the boy "attains that physical vigor which comes with sexual maturity" (*SLS*:520). If that is the case, then the explanation that was previously offered for the psychological extrusion of the father from myths, dreams, and reproduction may serve to explain the physical extrusion of the adolescent son from the parental household. These two types of extrusion, as we shall see, sustain a complementary relationship to each other.

If, as I previously suggested, the absent-father pattern reflects the boy's hostility to him for thwarting his incestuous wishes for the mother, it may now be suggested that if the boy is extruded from the family household at puberty because he has attained the "physical vigor which comes with sexual maturity," that is because it is only then that both of those Oedipal wishes can be seriously—and dangerously—actualized. In short, I am suggesting that it is not so much their "embarrassing presence" that accounts for the extrusion of the boys from the site (and sight) of parental sexual activity at puberty, as the fact that their presence at that time poses a potential Oedipal threat to the parents. That the one-room Trobriand house assures the son's continuous witnessing of their sex life should he remain in the household, thereby exacerbating his Oedipal wishes and strengthening the pressure for acting upon them, renders his extrusion all the more "functional" for parents and son alike.

It might now be observed, as I noted above, that this explanation for the extrusion of the Trobriand son from the parental household is the explicit explanation that is offered by the Nyakyusa (Wilson 1949) for the practice of son extrusion, and the implicit reason offered by the Muria (Elwin 1968:26–28) for this practice.Since in these societies, just as in the Trobriands, children experiment with sex when they leave the parental home, Elwin's explication of the counter-Oedipal consequences of (if not the motives for) this practice applies without change, so I would suggest, to the Trobriands. Child extrusion, Elwin (1968:28) explains, "alters the entire parent-child complex by putting in the father's place a new disciplinarian [in the case of the Muria and the Nyakyusa the head of the dormitory and of the boys' village, respectively; in the case of the Trobriands, the mother's brother], and in the place of the mother a new object of sensual attraction."[6]

6. Elwin's hypothesis is supported by Cohen's statistical studies of extrusion and initiation, although Cohen himself offers another interpretation for his findings. Thus, in a cross-cultural sample of sixty-five societies, Cohen (1964:65–67) found that child extrusion is overwhelmingly practiced in those societies in which the child is socialized by his parents and close kin, while it is almost never practiced in societies in which the parents and nonkin are the socializers. He also found (ibid.:114) that initiation rites at puberty are practiced much more frequently in societies in which children are socialized by parents and close kin than in those in which they are socialized by parents and nonkin (in which they are almost never practiced). Consistent with the above interpretation of son extrusion in the Trobriands, I would interpret Cohen's findings as suggesting that when the child's relationships primarily involve parents and kin, his libidinal and hostile feelings, which are then focused on them, are handled by extrusion and initiation. Where nonkin, however, participate in his socialization, the child's feelings toward the parents are diluted, and therefore such drastic measures are not required to preclude the possibility of their eruption in overt action.

It need only be added that in the Trobriands, in which the rivalry between father and son for the possession of the wife-mother is exacerbated by their rivalry for the sister-daughter, this serves to increase the functional advantage of the son's extrusion at puberty. In any event, this custom fully supports our fourth prediction.[7]

We may now turn to our fifth prediction, the existence of unconscious castration anxiety, including the unconscious expectation that castration is the punishment for sexual transgression. According to Oedipal theory, it will be recalled, the boy's incestuous wish for the mother arouses castration anxiety for at least three reasons: (*a*) because of actual castration threats, which are often made in connection with masturbation (and since the mother is often the sexual object, consciously or unconsciously, of the boy's masturbation fantasies, the relationship between castration anxiety and the Oedipus complex is a close one); (*b*) because of the operation in the boy of the talion principle, according to which the offending organ—in this case, of course, the penis—is the object of anticipated punishment; (*c*) because of the boy's observation of the female genitalia, the absence of the penis in females being interpreted by him as resulting from castration, a fate which he fears might befall him should he challenge his father's possession of the mother. But whatever the reasons for its development, castration anxiety (according to Oedipal theory) leads to the repression, if not the dissolution, of the Oedipus complex; and if the former is the case, castration persists as the unconsciously anticipated punishment for incestuous wishes, as well as for other forms of sexual transgression. Here we shall examine the evidence for the first two reasons for castration anxiety in the Trobriands, while in the next section we shall examine the evidence for the third reason.

7. It might also be noted in this connection that the Trobrianders also practice childhood adoption, and that (like many peoples throughout Oceania) the incidence of adoption is extraordinarily high: according to Powell (1957:374), the adoption rate for the period of his study was 46 percent. In some cases, children are adopted because of the termination of marriage, either through death or divorce; in others, because a couple who have no children want a child, or because a couple that have too many children want to be relieved of their heavy burden. In either case, one of the consequences of widespread adoption is the same as son extrusion: the separation of children from their parents precludes the overt expression of their Oedipal wishes.

Unfortunately, Malinowski (despite his interest in testing psychoanalytic theory) did not explore the question of castration anxiety in the Trobriands, nor did he investigate childhood masturbation. So far as the latter, however, is concerned, we can perhaps make some educated guesses concerning its practice from his brief discussion of adult masturbation. For adults, Malinowski writes, sexual "aberrations" (in which category he includes masturbation) are considered "bad and only worthy of fools," and they are practiced only by abnormal persons, but not by the "ordinary man or woman." Hence, to ask an "ordinary" man if he masturbates would "shock his natural inclination" (*SLS*:469–70). Since "natural inclination," in this case, can only mean "culturally acquired inclination," it seems reasonable to infer that these adult attitudes toward masturbation must derive from childhood experience in which, either in fantasy or in actuality, they are punished for this practice.

That castration is included among the threatened punishments is suggested by the castration theme—and self-castration at that!—which is found in Trobriand legends and folktales. Since Malinowski was not interested in castration narratives as such—the two castration tales summarized below are recounted by him as examples of various types of sexual behavior, whose castration theme he rather surprisingly ignores—we do not know the incidence of castration tales in the Trobriands. Nevertheless, even one tale—and here we have two—would be sufficient to make the point, as Stephens's (1962:116) cross-cultural study of the theme of genital injury in folktales and myths indicates. In Stephens's study not only was that theme absent in 62 percent of the societies in his sample of 42 societies, but the Trobriands was the *only* society in which the theme reached the level that, by his criteria, could be labeled "fairly frequent." Let us, then, examine the tales that are available to us.

In the tale of Momovala, castration is the result of daughter incest. After forcing his daughter to have intercourse with him, Momovala was informed by his wife that the daughter, out of remorse for this deed, had died by inviting a shark to kill her. Upon receiving this information, Momovala committed sadistic coitus with his wife, thereby causing her death, following which he cut off his penis and he himself died (*SLS*:411–12).

The second tale is about Inuvayla'u, the headman of both his clan and his village. Inuvayla'u had an enormously long penis, and whenever the wives of his younger brothers and maternal nephews proceeded to the gardens or the lagoon, he would direct his penis through a hole in his thatched house and would thereby have intercourse with them. Eventually his deeds were discovered by the women's husbands, and, according to one version, they ducked him in a pool of water; according to a second version, however, they banished him from the village.[8] According to both versions, Inuvayla'u became "full of shame and of sorrow," and he reacted by castrating himself, cutting off his penis with his knife, bit by bit, as he walked, slowly, toward the ocean, wailing all the way. Finally, when nothing was left of his penis, he cut off his testicles as well (*SLS*:413–22).

There are a number of features about these tales, and the Trobrianders' reaction to them, that support the castration anxiety prediction. First, in both tales castration is a punishment for transgression and, specifically, for sexual transgression. This is all the more significant in the light of Stephens's finding that in only ten societies in a sample of forty-two was punishment for sexual transgression in folktales and myths (whether by castration or any other form) more frequent than nonpunishment, the Trobriands being one of those ten (Stephens 1962:116). Second, that these tales are reflections of the Trobrianders' own castration anxiety is evidenced by Malinowski's classifying the Momovala tale in a category which he terms "Sex in Folklore: Facetiae," for the tales in this category are told in order to "raise a ribald laugh" (*SLS*:403). When we consider, then, that the tales in this category were ordered by Malinowski in a sequence of "increasing ribaldry," and that the Momovala tale is the last in the sequence, the Trobrianders' reaction of ribald laughter is, I would suggest, a measure of their own intense castration anxiety. For how else might their reaction be interpreted except as a counterphobic response to a tale which Malinowski himself characterizes as "perhaps the cruelest story in my collection" (*SLS*:412).

The third feature of these tales that supports the castration anxiety prediction is that the castration in these tales is a pun-

8. Of this version Malinowski writes: "I prefer to discard this tragic version, partly because Anglo-Saxons do not like sad endings" (*SLS*:419)!

ishment for sexual transgression, and that the transgression is of a specifically "Oedipal" type, a feature which is central to the prediction. In the Momovala tale, it will be recalled, the transgression is with a daughter, in the second, with sisters-in-law. In accordance with two of our previously supported predictions, daughter and sister are symbolic representations of the mother, and the husbands of women with whom one has sexual relations—even more so if the husbands are one's brothers—are symbolic representations of the father. In short, the castration anxiety projected in these tales is specifically associated with Oedipal wishes.

The fourth and last feature of these tales that supports the castration anxiety prediction is that the punishment for sexual transgression is not ordinary castration, but rather self-castration. That the transgressor himself is his own punitive agent suggests that the moral and castration anxiety evoked by unconscious Oedipal wishes, and therefore the strength of the wishes themselves, is especially intense. Now when it is recalled that in the Oedipus myth Oedipus also inflicts punishment upon himself for his transgressions, but that its form—tearing out of his eyes—is at the most *symbolic* castration,[9] the fact that in the Inuvayla'u tale the self-punishment is *actual* castration suggests not only that castration anxiety in the Trobriands is as strong as was predicted, but that it is close to the surface of conscious awareness.

We may now turn to our sixth and final prediction, the "splitting" of the mental representation of the mother into a "good mother" and a "bad mother." This prediction is especially important because more than any of the other predicted characteristics, the splitting of the maternal representation—and most especially the prominence of the "bad mother"—is most directly related to the predicted ontogenesis of the Trobriand Oedipus complex, viz., the boy's experience with a highly seductive pre-Oedipal mother. In the previous chapter I observed that the support for that ontogenetic prediction, though positive, was indirect, and that additional evidence would be presented in this

9. That the blinding of Oedipus symbolizes castration, although first suggested by Freud on the basis of unconscious dream symbolism, is richly documented by Devereux (1973) in a remarkable linguistic, ethnographic, and literary analysis.

chapter. The support to which I was referring consists of the evidence, to be presented below, for the predicted splitting of the maternal representation. That being the case the latter prediction is a pivotal one because its confirmation is required for the acceptance not only of the postulated Trobriand Oedipus complex, but also of its postulated ontogenetic determinants. Given, then, the importance of this prediction, as well as its complex theoretical derivation, it is treated separately in the following section.

Characteristics Related to the Pre-Oedipal Mother

Briefly, the "good mother" is a highly idealized mental representation of the mother comprising images and fantasies of a loving, generous, and altogether desirable figure. The "bad mother," on the other hand, is an equally extreme, but polar opposite representation of the mother comprising images and fantasies of a frustrating, dangerous, and altogether hateful figure. Why, it may now be asked, should such splitting of the maternal representation—or, for that matter, the mental representation of anyone—occur?

We might begin with the observation that until a child has reached the cognitive developmental stage of "object constancy," the integration of the many different (and often conflicting) images and fantasies that he has of any person into a single mental representation of him is all but impossible to achieve. In some cases, however, and in regard to certain persons it is never achieved. The integration into a single mental representation of their conflicting images and fantasies of the mother, for example, is often much too painful for children—and sometimes adults—to sustain. Hence, by "splitting" the maternal representation into a "good mother," by which they consciously represent her, and a "bad mother," which is repressed and by which they represent her unconsciously, they avoid both the threatening perception of her "bad mother" characteristics, as well as the emotionally painful consequence of hating a person whom they simultaneously love.

If so, it may finally be asked, why would we possibly predict the "splitting" of the maternal representation in the Trobriands? If, as in some societies, the Trobriand mother were inconsistent in her treatment of the child—nurturant under certain conditions, punitive under others—it might then be "logical" to assume that he would develop two separate mental representations of her, one loving and nurturant, the other hostile and rejecting. This hardly seems likely, however, in the Trobriands, in which according to all evidence, she is uniformly loving and nurturant. In the early years, especially, she not only gives the child a great deal of love and attention, but attends to his needs with care and affection. Indeed, even if she were not disposed to behave in such a manner, when we consider that during the long postpartum sex taboo the mother can devote herself exclusively to the child, that he has the warmth and security of her body every night when he sleeps with her, and that he has access to her breast whenever he wants it—when we consider all of this, the expectation that in the Trobriands, of all places, the boy would come to view his mother not only as "good" but also as "bad," and that he would develop hostile and fearful as well as loving and affectionate feelings for her is on the face of it patently "illogical."

To be sure, despite Malinowski's idyllic portrayal of the Trobriand mother, there are more than a few features of maternal care in the Trobriands that might be expected to arouse the child's rage. First, when, at the conclusion of the postpartum sex taboo, the boy is replaced by the father in the mother's bed, we would expect him to perceive the mother as having rejected him in favor of the father. This "rejection," especially since she is seen as preferring someone over him, would be expected to arouse strong hostility to her.[10] The fact, then, that he later witnesses her sexual behavior with the father could only be expected to strengthen his belief that she prefers the father to him, and therefore to intensify his hostility for her. A reaction of this type is hardly restricted to the Trobriands. In Japan, for example, it is sufficiently prevalent to be dubbed the "Ajase complex," after the mythological Buddhist hero Ajase, who kills his mother because of her sexual preference for his father.

His replacement by the father is not the only "rejection" that the Trobriand boy suffers at the hand of the mother. Although

10. After completing the first draft of this book, I discovered that John Whiting (no date) proposed this hypothesis many years ago in an unpublished cross-cultural study of the postpartum sex taboo (Fox 1980:74).

she may continue to nurse him even after the return of the father, the arrival of a sibling means not only that the latter receives whatever residual attention he himself had received from the mother, but that he experiences a second "rejection" by her in favor of yet another apparent favorite—the new sibling, who replaces him at the mother's breast, as well as in her bed. This, of course, not only would explain the origin of the intense sibling rivalry which we have already observed in the Trobriands, but also would be expected to further exacerbate the boy's hostile feelings for the mother.[11]

As a consequence of these "rejections," then, it would certainly be "logical" to expect the Trobriand boy to view part of his mother as "bad," and to develop strong hostile feelings for her, more especially because they follow a long pre-Oedipal period in which he had been her favorite, and during which he had enjoyed exclusive possession of her body, her affection, and her attention. To view part of the mother, however, as "bad" is one thing, and to form a mental representation of her as a "bad mother" is another. If part of the mother is "bad," she may arouse hatred in her son, but its intensity is usually of a magnitude that allows it to remain consciously recognized and consciously coped with, and the mother's "bad" characteristics are integrated with the "good" to form a single, integrated maternal representation. When, however, the "bad" characteristics of the mother are perceived to be relentlessly dangerous and threatening, the child cannot cope with them, and they are split off from his mental representation of the mother to constitute a separate "bad mother" representation. Again, then, although it would seem entirely "logical" to expect the Trobriand boy to view part of his mother as "bad," it seems "illogical" to expect him to form a "bad mother" representation.

"Logical" or not, however, there are important theoretical grounds for such a prediction, for this type of maternal representation is formed not in the Oedipal period (the period in which the Trobriand boy suffers maternal "rejection"), but in the earlier pre-Oedipal period, in connection with a "seductive" pre-Oedipal mother. That such a pre-Oedipal mother is found

11. If adoption is experienced by Trobriand children as "rejection," it might then be added that as many as one-fourth of all boys suffer yet another rejection, not, however, in favor of a perceived rival.

in the Trobriands was, of course, the brunt of the argument in the previous chapter. Let us, then, address the theoretical grounds for the expectation that it is the son's experience with his pre-Oedipal mother that leads to the formation of a "bad mother" representation in the Trobriands.

As a result of the conjunction of three pre-Oedipal conditions—a long postpartum sex taboo, exclusive mother-child sleeping, and prolonged breast feeding—the Trobriand mother—so at least we attempted to establish in the previous chapter—is highly seductive with her son, which, in turn, prematurely arouses strong sexual feelings in him. Such feelings, according to Oedipal theory, should produce an ambivalent attitude to the mother, for although on the one hand, being strongly attracted to her, the son comes to love her, on the other hand these same feelings lead him to perceive her as fiercely aggressive, which, in turn, arouses feelings of fear and rage toward her. This somewhat startling prediction is based on the following assumptions. First, the premature arousal of his sexual feelings (for many reasons explained below) is extremely painful for the boy. Second, his pain is attributed by him to the aggressive sexuality of the mother (which is how he perceives her "seductiveness"). Since these assumptions are hardly self-evident, it is perhaps important to explicate them in some detail.

If a child is sexually aroused prematurely by seductive parents, clinical evidence suggests that, because of his physiological and emotional immaturity, "the intensity of this excitement may be beyond the child's power of control; this creates traumatic states which connect the realms of 'genitality' and 'threat' with each other" (Fenichel 1945:91). Unable to discharge or to understand his sexual excitement, the child places the blame for his painful physiological and emotional condition on the parent. If, moreover, such parents are aware of their sexual feelings for their children, they may overcompensate by "sudden threats or frustrations, so that frequently the same children are excited and then frustrated by the same parents" (ibid.:93). On both counts, therefore, children of seductive parents might be expected to become hostile to them.[12]

12. Fox has proposed a similar hypothesis in connection with his analysis of brother-sister incest. If, according to his analysis, brothers and sisters are permitted relatively free physical contact in childhood, their physical stimulation

But that is not all. If the seductive parent is the mother, and if her seductiveness is brought about by the absence of the husband-father—in the Trobriands he is absent only at night, when, however, sleeping in one bed with the son, the mother's seductiveness would be expected to be most manifest—the boy cannot rely upon the husband-father to protect him either from the mother's seductiveness or from the painful and frightening sexual desires which it arouses in him. Then, the longer the father is absent, the more sexually frustrated and (therefore) seductive the mother becomes; and the more seductive the mother is, the more intense are the sexual feelings of the son and his conflict concerning those feelings expected to be. One way by which he might resolve this conflict—between the wish for and the fear of the mother—is to project his frightening wishes onto her (Slavin 1972:5), thereby transforming one part of her into a "dangerous temptress" (Bibring 1953:281).

Perceived as a temptress, the mother is dangerous both sexually and aggressively. She is dangerous sexually because, having projected his sexual feelings onto the mother, the son exaggerates her seductiveness and thereby comes to view her sexual demands as insatiable. Incapable of handling these demands, he develops terrifying fantasies of being sexually overwhelmed and devoured by her (Slater 1966:314). Moreover, should he respond sexually to her seductiveness, he is then (in his eyes) placed in dangerous rivalry with his father, who, as a punishment, might castrate him, just as (in his view) the mother has been castrated (Slavin 1972:6; Bibring 1953:282). As a temptress, the mother is also perceived to be a dangerous aggressor because the son's hostile, as well as his sexual, feelings, are projected onto her. His hostility is aroused in the first instance by both the emotional frustration and the dangerous situation (vis-à-vis the father) in which she has placed him, and in the second instance by her humiliating rejection of him in favor of his rival, the husband-father (Horney 1932). In sum,

---

results in heightened sexual excitement, which, since it cannot be discharged, often leads to "anger and aggression." If, he argues, this happens "very often," they will develop for each other "a strange mixture of love and hate, of approach and avoidance, of promise and disappointment" (Fox 1980:25). Such a condition, he then concludes, leads to sexual aversion between siblings, a conclusion, however, which I do not accept.

since the seductive mother arouses the boy's sexual and hostile feelings, and since he then projects these feelings onto her, one part of the boy's mental representation of her makes her into a *dangerous* temptress, someone who is attractive and fearful alike.

In addition, however, to his distortion of her psychological characteristics, the son of a seductive pre-Oedipal mother might also distort her physical characteristics: he may endow her with a fantasized penis. Even if the mother is not seductive, it is frequently the case that the pre-Oedipal boy develops a fantasy of the "phallic mother," the fantasy that the mother has a penis (Brunswick 1940). This fantasy is usually interpreted as a defense against the castration anxiety that is aroused in the boy by his awareness of the absence of a maternal penis (Greenacre 1968). Although it was formerly assumed by psychoanalytic theorists that castration anxiety does not develop in the boy until the Oedipal period, recent studies of psychosexual development in children have shown that, as a result of their awareness of the anatomical differences between the sexes, pre-Oedipal boys also can develop castration anxiety, as early as their second year of life (Galenson and Roiphe 1980).

If the boy, then, is aware that his mother has no penis, he may, as a defense against the resultant castration anxiety, develop a fantasy of the "phallic mother." If, moreover, the mother is also seductive, his need to endow her with a penis is all the more urgent. This urgency has been variously interpreted as stemming either from his anxiety that his attraction to the mother's vagina will actually result in his castration by the father (Slavin 1972:6; Bibring 1953:282), or from his belief that his humiliating rejection by the mother is a reflection on his small penis, which is incapable of satisfying her (Horney 1932). Whether the one or the other, both interpretations agree that the boy develops (as Horney put it) a "dread" of the maternal vagina which he may defend himself against by denial in fantasy, i.e., by endowing the mother with a penis.[13]

That the mother, however, should be perceived to possess such sexually threatening and fiercely aggressive characteristics is, understandably enough, painful and frightening for any child. Given the psychological capacities of a very young boy,

13. For an existentialist view of the "phallic mother," see Becker (1973:221–30).

there are few ways available to him for coping with the painful and frightening feelings that are aroused by a mother who is perceived to possess such dangerous characteristics. One way, however, is to psychologically segregate these characteristics and to split them off from the mother's other—loving and benevolent—characteristics, thereby forming two separate mental representations of her: a "good mother" and a "bad mother." If, then, the "bad mother" is projected onto other women, or in the form of mythical and supernatural figures—as it usually is— the "good mother" is the primary mental representation that the son has of his mother. Hence, the splitting of the maternal representation not only permits the son to love his mother unqualifiedly, but also spares him from both the painful feelings of fear and hatred for his mother, as well as the guilt that is aroused by harboring those feelings toward a person whom he also loves, for they are, instead, displaced onto the projected "bad mother" figures.

With this rather extended theoretical discussion, we may now return to the Trobriands and the prediction that, as a result of the Trobriand child's experience with the pre-Oedipal mother, and the consequent splitting of the maternal representation, there are prominent projected manifestations of the "bad mother" in the Trobriands. After describing some Trobriand myths which provide projective evidence for splitting, we shall present detailed descriptions of the "bad mother" in a variety of social, cultural, and behavioral forms.

The Tudava myth, to advert to a myth we already know (see chapter 3), provides our example of maternal splitting. Tudava's mother is an idealized, nonsexual mother who, having no attachment to husband, brother, or children, lovingly administers to Tudava's needs exclusively, without, however, even a hint that her love for him is contaminated by erotic elements, frightening or otherwise. In short, she is an ideal-typic "good mother"! The projection of such an idealized mother—loving and virginal—can only be formed by the segregation and splitting off of the negative characteristics of the mother, for only in that fashion can her positive characteristics, uncontaminated by the negative, be exaggerated and idealized.

Still, although the "good mother" may be represented in the Tudava myth, because of the absence of a "bad mother", the myth does not constitute an explicit example of the splitting of the maternal representation. For an explicit example, I am indebted to Edwin Hutchins. While reading this discussion of maternal splitting in manuscript, Hutchins was reminded of a myth that he had collected in the course of his research in the Trobriands in 1975–76. Recognizing it as a paradigmatic example, he kindly translated it into English from Trobriand, in which he had recorded and transcribed it. The following summary is based on his translation.

A certain chief, Tomakawala guyau, was married to Karawata. Near the end of her pregnancy, Karawata asked her husband to take her to a particular water hole where she wanted to bathe. After arriving in a small canoe, Tomakawala guyau went to gather firewood, and Karawata went to the waterhole to bathe. While she was bathing, a female ogre, Bokaikukuna, put on Karawata's clothes and jewelry, and swallowed much of the wood that Tomakawala guyau had collected. Pretending to be his pregnant wife, the ogre demanded that Tomakawala guyau take her back with him to the village. Although he did not entirely believe her, he obeyed her from fear. When Karawata discovered that her husband was abandoning her, she implored him to take her with him, but instead he beat her with his canoe pole until she fell to the ground unconscious, and he returned to the village with the ogre.

A sea eagle, Muluveka, saw Karawata, and took her to his nest on the top of a tree. Four days later she gave birth to a boy, and they both lived with Muluveka, who fed and cared for them. Karawata thought of him as her father, and the boy called him "grandfather."

When, as an adolescent, the boy descended to the village to participate in a model canoe race, he was seized by the villagers, who did not know his identity, and brought before Tomakawala guyau. The boy revealed his identity to him, and told him about the ogre's ruse and his mother's rescue by Muluveka. Tomakawala guyau ordered the ogre to appear before him. By this time, however, she had swallowed so many wooden bowls, cups, and other household possessions that when she tried to emerge from the house, the step broke under her weight and she split open as she fell to the ground. Her split body was buried, and Tomakawala guyau proclaimed the boy his son.

This myth not only exemplifies the splitting of the maternal (and the paternal) representation, but also highlights most of the pre-Oedipal and Oedipal themes that have been emphasized throughout the previous chapters, as well as the defenses by which they are resolved. The splitting of the maternal representation between the sexual and aggressive ogre, on the one hand, and the asexual and nonaggressive biological mother, on the other, is paradigmatic. In her "bad mother" aspect the mother is an ogre, the symbol of aggressive female sexuality. That she represents a split-off representation of the mother is reflected in the fact that she is the father's consort. Since, then, the mother's "bad" characteristics are split off and segregated in the figure of the ogre, the boy's mater—who is also his genetrix—is the "good" mother. Hence, in her "good mother" aspect, the mother is neither aggressive nor sexual. Unlike the "bad mother" who rejects (abandons) the son in favor of the husband-father, the "good mother" is nurturant toward him. Moreover, although she has a consort—the eagle—their relationship is entirely asexual; she thinks of him as father. And although she loves her son, her love for him is devoid of sexual overtones. In effect she is a nonseductive pre-Oedipal mother.

The father representation is similarly split between the sexual and aggressive biological father, on the one hand, and the asexual and nurturant eagle, on the other. In his "bad father" aspect, the father is the sexual partner of the "bad mother" and attempts to kill his son even when he is in the womb. In his "good father" aspect, however, his relationship with the mother is asexual, and toward the son he is a provider, one who cares for him, makes him toys, etc.

That the splitting of the parental representations in the myth reflects the pre-Oedipal and Oedipal fears, hatreds, and wishes that have concerned us throughout this chapter seems rather apparent. (1) The Trobriand words for "bathe" and "coitus"—so Hutchins informs me—are near homonyms, ordinarily distinguishable only by context. Since, then, the ogre—the "bad mother"—first appears when the mother is bathing, it is not wildly speculative to suggest that this episode portrays maternal sexuality as dangerous to the child even while it is still in the womb. (2) The "bad" father who beats his wife while she is with child until she falls to the ground unconscious, and presumably dead—the eagle does not attempt to rescue her until he notices a sign of life in her—is portrayed as a dangerous filicide. (3) The abandonment of mother and child by the "bad" parents, I would suggest, is an expression of the Trobriand son's hatred of and wish to be rid of the father in his genitor-cum-mother's lover aspect—the absent-father theme—as well as the mother in her aggressive sexuality aspect. That the hatred of the "bad mother" is the stronger, however, is reflected in the fact that when the son finally encounters her when he is an adolescent, she falls dead—an expression of the son's death wish regarding this aspect of the mother. (4) That the mutual hostility between father and son is Oedipal in its motivation is indicated by the fact that when the ogre—the sexual mother—drops dead, and the "good" mother alone survives, father and son are reconciled. (5) Hence, the triangular relationship between the boy, his biological mother, and the eagle, I would suggest, reflects the wish of the Trobriand son that in his family of orientation the mother not be sexually attracted to the father—that she view her husband as her asexual "father"—and that the father, reciprocally, be like a "grandfather" to him—nurturant and protective, but in no sense a rival for his mother's affection.

With this explicit support for the predicted splitting of the maternal representation in the Trobriands, we must now consider to what extent, if any, the "bad mother" plays the prominent role in the thought and behavior of the Trobrianders that our prediction requires. Since, as was observed above, this maternal representation is highly threatening to the child, it is usually projected. According to clinical evidence, it may be projected both in the male's perception of women, as well as in his fantasies, and the affects aroused by the "bad mother" are then displaced onto these "bad mother" figures. Thus, if, according to clinical findings, the boy had acquired a dread of his mother's genitals, this fear may be experienced in regard to the female genitals in general; and if this initial dread was acquired as a function of the castration anxiety aroused by the seductive mother, he may develop a generalized fear of the female genitalia "as threatening his very existence" (Slater 1966:68). Such fears, it is reported, have important consequences for male sexual behavior, ranging from psychological impotence to sadomasochistic behavior (Greenacre 1968:56–59); in the latter case, the male welcomes, if he does not actively seek out, aggressive lovers. If, moreover, he has also developed a fantasy of the "phallic mother," he usually exhibits some form of fetishism in his sexual behavior (Bak 1968; Greenacre 1968).

According to anthropological evidence, in societies in which the "bad mother" is a fairly typical maternal representation, as we have predicted for the Trobriands, the fear of women is reported to be widespread; moreover, this fear is expressed not only in sexual behavior of the type described above, but also in culturally constituted beliefs and fantasies. As examples, one might point to the culturally constituted beliefs concerning the dangerous female genitalia that are found, for example, in India (Kakar 1978:93–95), Burma (Spiro 1977:235–43, 259–71), and ancient Greece (Slater 1966:parts 1 and 2). Even more important, so far as their relevance for the Trobriands is concerned, are the findings of three large-scale, cross-cultural studies (Ember 1978; Kitahara 1976; Stephens 1962). According to these findings, a variety of sexual fears regarding women are aroused in males by beliefs concerning the dangerous female genitalia which are specifically related to the postpartum sex taboo and exclusive mother-child sleeping. It might also be observed that in some societies these fears are used to advantage in confronting enemies, both internal and external. In ancient Greece, for example, the vulva had the power to frighten evil spirits, and its representation on a shield could turnaway the enemies' sword in battle (Slater 1966:323). In Burma, too, an adversary could be conquered by a woman's exposure of her genitals (Spiro 1977:236).

In addition, however, to the culturally constituted beliefs and fears which are derived from and reflect selected aspects of the "bad mother," this maternal representation may also be projectively represented, as such, in various collective representations. One need only point to the highly sexual and aggressive female witches of the Western tradition for appropriate examples. Less parochially, such collective representations of the "bad mother" have a very wide cross-cultural distribution, as Neumann (1963)—from whom I have borrowed the term—has shown in abundant detail in his historical and comparative study of its projection in myth, religion, folklore, and art. Among the great religions, of course, one thinks especially of the projection of the "bad mother" in the terrifying (both sexually and aggressively) mother goddesses of Hindu India (Zimmer 1962:chapters 4–5) and Buddhist Tibet (Sierksma 1966).

We may now examine whether, and to what extent, any of these manifestations of the "bad mother" are present in the Trobriands.

The "Bad Mother" Maternal Representation

The "bad mother" is found in the Trobriands in many manifestations which correspond to those that have just been described. For clarity of exposition, I shall classify them into "behavioral" and "cultural" manifestations. Moreover, starting with the latter type, I shall place them along a continuum, proceeding from the least threatening manifestations of the "bad mother" to the most threatening.

For the least threatening, I would point to the cultural theme, pervasive both in myth and in the Trobriand interpretation of a certain class of dreams, of the sexually aggressive female and the sexually passive or submissive male. So far as the dream interpretation is concerned, there exists in the Trobriands a class of dreams that Malinowski calls "official" or "expected" dreams which includes a subclass in which a woman acquaintance of a man visits him in order to have sexual intercourse. Trobrianders interpret such dreams as a sign that the woman has sexual designs on the man in real life, and that in order to carry out her designs she has already worked love magic on him (*SR*:91; *SLS*:392–93). So far as myths are concerned, Malinowski reports that "in most mythological and legendary incidents, the man remains passive and the woman is the aggressor"(*SLS*:547). In the critical brother-sister incest myth, for example (see chapter 2), it is the sister who aggressively pursues the brother, and only after numerous futile attempts to elude her does he finally succumb to her sexual importunities.

It will be noted, then, that the passivity of the male in sexual dreams and his belief that he is helpless to escape his dream-visitor's sexual designs in real life are paralleled by the submissiveness of the male in myths in which, though he attempts to resist the female's sexual aggressiveness, he finally submits to her sexual demands. In short, not only do the sexually aggressive females in these myths and dream interpretations exhibit one of the characteristics of the "bad mother" representation, but the sexually submissive males conform to the defenseless self-representation expected in sons of "bad"—i.e., "seductive"—mothers.

Much more threatening characteristics of the "bad mother" are manifested in other cultural forms, most especially in folklore. If the previous two manifestations of the "bad mother" may be said to be the projection, at a cultural level, of the *sexually aggressive* attribute of such a maternal representation, it is its *aggressively sexual* attribute that may be said to be projected, in all its terrifying dimensions, in folklore.

Consider, as a starter, the attributes which men of the northern villages impute to the women of certain southern villages—"impute" because, although the men take the beliefs concerning these women to be veridical, Malinowski says they are a "standing myth" (*SLS*:277). Should a stranger, according to this "myth," pass these women while they are engaged in communal weeding, they not only have the right to attack him, but they subject him to every kind of "sexual violence, obscene cruelty, and rough handling" (*SLS*:274). For example, after pulling off and tearing up his pubic leaf—"the symbol of his manly dignity"—they then proceed to gang-rape him. In addition, if their insatiable sexual needs are not satisfied by means of his penis, these "furies" will use his fingers, toes, and any other projecting part of his body for their sexual gratification, following which they will rub their genitals against his nose and mouth. Having had their fill, they then defecate and urinate over his entire body, but especially over his face, causing him to vomit continuously. When they are finally through with him, they tear his hair from his head, and lacerate and beat his body "till he [is] too weak to get up and move away" (*SLS*:275).

It would be difficult, I submit, to find a more graphic cultural manifestation of the aggressively sexual attributes of the "bad mother" (but see below). Equally graphic, however, are the men's reported reactions to this "myth." According to Malinowski they repeatedly reacted to any description of the *yausa* (as the account of the women's sexual brutality is called) with "derisive laughter and amused exaggeration." In his view, this is "a clear indication of how superior they felt to the benighted heathen [the southern villagers] who practiced it" (*SLS*:279). I would suggest, however, that one does not need a practiced clinical eye to view their reaction as, on the contrary, a "clear indication" of a counterphobic response to an acutely threatening cultural fantasy, one which arouses repressed memories of a correspondingly threatening personal fantasy, the fantasy of the "bad mother."

Although Malinowski describes the men's *attitude* in rather bland prose—"[they] are interested in this custom and amused by it" (*SLS*:277)—his description of their *behavior* indicates that, in fact, they are obsessed by it, in the true sense of "obsession." Thus, in a rather telling example, he recounts one of those afternoons (so well known to every field worker) in which his research was not going anywhere, his informants were bored, and he could not get them to talk about anything. Suddenly, the *yausa* happened to be mentioned, and "immediately the natives became voluble and dramatic; their laughter and animation attracted other people, and soon I was attracted by a group of men" (*SLS*:278). From then on Malinowski discovered that the mere mention of the *yausa* would unfailingly arouse intense interest in these men. Moreover, they would with compulsive regularity use any opportunity to raise this topic, and when doing so they would "love to enter into details, and to demonstrate [them] by convincing mimicry" (*SLS*:275). Indeed, the *yausa*, Malinowski complained, was so frequently "dragged" into any conversation, and then gone into in such "detailed and graphic descriptions" that it became for him "the anthropologist's bugbear" (*SLS*:278).

This compulsive recounting of, and obsessive concern with, a myth of such unmitigated sexual brutality and violence can only be interpreted—so far, at least, as dynamic personality theory is concerned—as an attempt on the part of the actors to master a repressed memory of an emotionally traumatic fantasy by reexperiencing it through a cultural—and therefore psychologically distant—fantasy. Since, as we have already seen, this myth of the aggressively sexual women of the *yausa* corresponds to similar cultural manifestations of the "bad mother" found in other societies, it is their repressed childhood memory of a "bad mother" that constitutes, I would suggest, the traumatic fantasy that the Trobrianders are attempting to master in their obsessive preoccupation with the *yausa*.

Evidence for the correctness of this interpretation is provided by the "legend" of Kaytalugi, the island of "sexually rabid women" (*SLS*:183). Except for their young sons, these women are the sole inhabitants of the island, their only contact with men being with strangers who, from time to time, chance to visit their island. These women are not only very beautiful, but, like the mythic women of the southern villages, "very bad, very fierce . . . because of their insatiable [sexual] desire" (*SLS*:422–23). Thus, when a man arrives in Kaytalugi, the women throw themselves upon him, and one after another they proceed to rape him. If, however, intercourse is impossible, they use the man's nose, ears, fingers, and toes (in lieu of his penis) to satisfy their lust. When they have finished with him, he usually dies from their rapacious treatment. The lust of these women is so strong that, as mothers, they mete out the same treatment to their own sons. Constantly using them sexually, mothers spare neither the penises, fingers, toes, nor hands of the boys to satisfy their lust until the latter fall ill and die from this constant sexual abuse.

Here, then, we have a cultural fantasy of mothers whose lust is so powerful that they rape their own sons, and so fierce that they kill them in the process. Nevertheless, so Malinowski writes, the Trobrianders "believe absolutely in the reality of this island and in the truth of every detail of their account" (*SLS*:423). But why, it is only reasonable to ask, should anyone "believe absolutely" in the reality of a cultural fantasy of such relentless sexual brutality, let alone in the truth of its "every" grizzly detail, unless it resonates with a personal fantasy which, corresponding to it, gives it credibility? And why, it may be further asked, should anyone construct such a terrifying personal fantasy unless it, in turn, corresponds to—and therefore represents—an experiential or phenomenological reality? The fantasy, of course, is the fantasy of the aggressively sexual "bad mother," a maternal representation which, as we have come to know, corresponds to and represents the phenomenological reality of young sons whose incestuous desires are aroused by highly seductive pre-Oedipal mothers. When it is remembered, then, that the cultural fantasy regarding the Kaytalugi boys corresponds to the social reality of the pre-Oedipal Trobriand boys—in both cases the boys live with mothers who, deprived of husbands, must turn to their sons for libidinal gratification—it is not difficult to understand how the "bad mother" in the Trobriands is projected and represented in the cultural fantasy of the Kaytalugi mothers.[14]

If this were not enough, additional cultural evidence for the existence of an aggressively sexual "bad mother" in the Trobriands is found in folktales and legends. These, moreover, contain two other projected manifestations of this maternal representation—fear and hatred of the dreaded female genitalia and the fantasy of the "phallic mother." At least four tales and legends of this type were published by Malinowski. I shall briefly summarize all four before commenting on them.

Consider (*a*) the tale of the reef heron (*SLS*:404–6) who insults the old woman Ilakavetega by charging that her vagina is "full of sores." When, later, he becomes tangled in some reef coral, the woman and her granddaughters avenge this insult by killing and eating him. Subsequently, his death, in turn, is avenged by a sorcerer who first rapes and then kills the woman and her granddaughters.

Consider again (*b*) the tale of the woman with five clitorises (*SLS*:405–8). When a stingaree sees these clitorises he sings a ditty in which he vows to saw off one of them "till it snaps and is gone." First, however, he copulates with her, and then he cuts off the clitoris. When the woman's five sons return to the house, she complains to them of the stingaree's action, and the eldest son promises to protect her. Nevertheless, on the following day the stingaree finds her again, and after singing his ditty, he again copulates with her, and cuts off a second clitoris. This is repeated on successive days until the woman is left with only one clitoris, which, were it cut off, would cause her death. She is saved from

14. In his study of the fear of the mother's genitalia in ancient Greece, Slater (1966:12 ff.) suggests that the preference of the males for immature females and their insistence on the pubic depilation of females represented an avoidance of the threatening maternal genital. In the light of this interpretation, it is significant (as Slater himself observed) that, like the Trobrianders (*SLS*:299–300), not only do the terrifying women of Kaytalugi not remove their body hair, but their pubic hair "grows so long that it makes something like a *doba* (grass petticoat) in front of them" (*SLS*:422).

this fate, however, by her youngest son, who manages to kill the stingaree before he can carry out his vow.

Consider too (c) the legend of Digawina ("filled out vulva") (*SLS*: 408), who steals all kinds of food—yams, taro, bananas, etc.—by packing them into her vagina. Determined to put a stop to this behavior, a certain man conceals a large crab in the food that Diwagina hopes to steal. The crab cuts through her clitoris and there by kills her.

Consider finally (d) the legend of Karawata (*SLS*:408–9), a woman who gave birth to a cockatoo. On three different occasions she tells her clitoris to guard her cooking oven while she goes to work in the garden, and each time her son, the cockatoo, swoops down, strikes the clitoris, and eats the contents of the oven. By this time no food is left in the oven, and both Karawata and her clitoris die of hunger.

Here, then, we have a series of legends and tales in which the female genitalia—either the vagina, the vulva, or the clitoris—are variously denigrated, feared, hated, and attacked by a male; in which, nevertheless, a male rapes the female, or sometimes kills or is killed by her; in which the clitoris is cut off by a male; or in which the male (the woman's own son) kills the mother's anthropomorphized clitoris as well as the mother herself. Although, unlike the previous evidence for the "bad mother," these folktales do not speak for themselves, it seems fairly clear that, if nothing else, they represent the projection of the Trobriander's fear and hatred of the dreaded vagina (tales a and b). Moreover, they suggest—but here I am speculating—that this affective reaction is evoked by the boy's narcissistic humiliation at being unable to sexually satisfy the mother (tale a) or by a fear of castration which he defends himself against by denying that women have a vagina, endowing them instead with a fantasy penis (tales b and d). This interpretation is speculative because it is based on the assumption that the clitoris in these tales is a phallic symbol, an assumption which is suggested by both the size and the detachability of the clitoris in the tales. If this speculation is sound, then inasmuch as in one tale the woman is endowed with five clitorises, the postulated castration anxiety might be inferred to be intense. Finally, these tales also suggest that the rage induced in the boy by the mother's se-

ductiveness exposing him to the danger of castration is revenged
in fantasy by his castrating her instead (tales *b, c,* and *d*).[15]

Although the last two interpretations are speculative, the first
is merely a restatement in abstract terms of the tales themselves.
Hence, on the basis of that interpretation alone, it seems clear
that these tales constitute cultural manifestations of the dread
of the dangerous female genitalia, which, it will be recalled, is
an important attribute of the aggressively sexual "bad mother."

This attribute of the "bad mother" is manifested yet again in
the culturally constituted belief that the dreaded Trobriand flying
witches (of which more below) are especially dangerous because
of the poisonous emanations that are emitted from their vulva
and anus.[16] In this regard Leach (1954) has suggested, in a highly
ingenious analysis, that the abstract designs engraved on the
shields of Trobriand warriors represent these flying witches.
That is why, he argued, these shields were carried into battle:
by turning the dreaded power of the witches' vulva and anus
against their enemies, the warriors used them as lethal weapons
to their own advantage. This is exactly what the Burmese and
ancient Greeks did, as we observed above.

It might be added, in this connection, that evidence for the
fear of the vagina exists not only at the cultural, but at the
behavioral level, as well. Thus, in their sexual behavior cunnilingus is scrupulously avoided in the Trobriands: no Trobriand
male, Malinowski writes, "would touch the female genitals in
this manner" (*SLS*:475). The Trobriand opposition to cunnilingus

15. It might be suggested, then, that castration anxiety in the Trobriands has
two motivational sources. One source consists of the boy's fear that he will be
castrated as a result of the mother's incestuous "seduction" of him, in retaliation
for which he "castrates" her; this is reflected in the tales and legends summarized
here. The other source consists of the boy's fear that his father will castrate him
for his incestuous wishes in regard to the Oedipal mother; this is reflected in
the folktales of self-castration as a punishment for incest, which were summarized above.

16. Since this attribute of the "bad mother" is, in theory, generated by the
castration anxiety evoked by the mother's seductiveness, the juxtaposition of
anus and vulva in the Trobriand belief is reminiscent of Greenacre's findings
that severe castration anxiety is associated with two opposing conceptions of
the female genitals. One conception consists of the fantasy that women possess
a penis. The other views the female genitals as "degraded, *dirty*—and mutilated
(*essentially anal*)" (Greenacre 1968:49, italics mine).

cannot be attributed, as one might otherwise suggest, to an opposition to oral sex because fellatio is widely practiced in the Trobriands.

Having mentioned one of its less important behavioral manifestations, we may now examine some of the more important behavioral manifestations of the aggressively sexual "bad mother" in the Trobriands.

We have already observed that in a certain class of Trobriand myths and in the cultural interpretation of a certain class of dreams, women are invariably portrayed as sexually aggressive in their pursuit of men, while the latter submissively acquiesce in their demands. We have also observed that in Trobriand myths, legends, and tales of aggressively sexual women, their male victims never defend themselves against their sexual brutality. It may now be observed that in Trobriand sexual behavior, this pattern of submissiveness is repeated by the males once again. Indeed, the reaction of Trobriand males to a pervasive pattern of aggressively sexual and sexually aggressive female partners constitutes a textbook example of the sadomasochistic orientation which, as we have seen, is expected of males with a "bad mother" maternal representation.

Consider the following description which typifies the Trobriand male's sadomasochistic reaction to female aggression.

> If a boy from Kwaibwaga begins to sleep with someone from another village, and a girl in Kwaibwaga wants that boy for herself, then Kwaibwaga unmarried girls organize and wait for the unsuspecting villain to walk along the paths between the villages. The village girls spring out of their hiding places along the path and attack the boy with knives. I bandaged several boys who had been attacked in this manner by Kwaibwaga girls, *and shortly after such incidents the boy was sleeping with a Kwaibwaga girl* (Weiner 1976:171, italics mine).

Even more important, however, than their unprotesting acceptance of a lover imposed on them by female physical brutality is the fact that Trobriand males actually welcome aggressively sexual females as their lovers. Thus, it is a "general rule," so Malinowski informs us, that if a young man is sexually attracted to a young woman, "before their passion is satisfied" he allows her to "inflict considerable bodily pain" on him, including

"scratching, thrashing, or even wounding with a sharp instru-
ment" (*SLS*:257). If that were not enough, it should also be
observed that prior to the arrival of the missionaries (who apparently stamped it out) certain Trobriand villages regularly
practiced collective sexual orgies (*kamali*) in which the males
were attacked by females with shells, knives, pieces of obsidian,
and even small axes. In response to the females' aggression,
however, the males neither counterattacked, nor did they defend
themselves by escaping from their assailants—not, at any rate,
if they were attracted to them. These, remember, were sexual
orgies—some orgies!—which means, so Malinowski reports,
that if a male was sexually attracted to an aggressive female,
"he would, *naturally*, not run away but take her attack as an
invitation" (ibid.: italics mine). I shall return to that curious
adverb "naturally" below.

Although these three examples of Trobriand sadomasochistic
behavior were recorded by the ethnographers without comment,
I would submit that at least some comment is called for. Thus,
it is surely more than a little curious that, following a brutal
attack by the friends of a girl who wishes to sleep with him, a
boy should not only not defend himself, but acquiesce in her
demands. And it is no less curious, surely, that during lovemaking a young man should voluntarily submit to the infliction
of severe pain by his lover, or that during a group orgy he should
"naturally" view the brutal attack of his female assailant as an
"invitation."[17] "Naturally" hardly seems the appropriate term

17. That the sexual gratification of the female requires that she inflict pain on
her partner, whether he be lover or stranger, is no less curious of course than
the male's submission to her aggression. Hence, although this book is concerned
with the male Oedipus complex exclusively, it would nevertheless be tempting
to speculate about the meaning of the sexual behavior of the females, if only we
had some data which could provide us with a handle on this problem. Since,
however, such data are lacking, I would only suggest that inasmuch as the
Trobriand girl, according to Malinowski, has an Oedipus complex, her aggressive
sexuality (like the boy's submissiveness) might also be instigated by unconscious
Oedipal motives. In short, if (according to Oedipal theory) the sex partner is to
some extent an unconscious substitute for the original love-object, and if the
girl does not resolve her hostility to her father which is induced by her perception
of his having rejected her love for him, her sexual aggressiveness might then
be interpreted as a displacement of this hostility onto her sexual partner.

for such a view, whether—and this is not clear—it is the natives' or the anthropologist's.

Appropriate or not, however, it is consistent with still other attitudes of Trobriand males to the aggressive sexuality of the females. In the case of a boy and his sweetheart, for example, Malinowski (*SLS*:257) writes: "However severely he is handled, such treatment is accepted in good part by the boy, as a sign of love and a symptom of temperament in his sweetheart." As a "typical" example of such an attitude Malinowski offers the reaction of a boy whose sweetheart had inflicted a deep cut across his back during lovemaking, creating a wound which required dressing. Although the boy "was evidently in great pain," he "did not appear to mind," perhaps because "he reaped his reward that same night." Similarly, males submitted to the even more brutal forms of female aggression in the collective orgies because they viewed their brutality as "a form of feminine wooing" and a "compliment." Indeed, since it was "a sign of manliness and a proof of [his sexual] success to be properly slashed about," it was actually "the ambition of a man to carry away as many cuts as he could stand, and to reap the reward in each case" (*SLS*:258).

It might be noted, however, that he does not "reap the reward" that easily, because in addition to the physical pain it costs him, his "reward" must be paid for with actual gifts. In the Trobriand view sexual intercourse is a "service" which the female renders to the male (*SLS*:319–21). In exchange for this service, which is seen as a "sexual gift," the male is required to offer a gift to the female, if not for every sexual act, then at least for a continuous sexual relationship (Malinowski 1935:vol. 1, p. 203). More specifically, the gift is viewed as payment for her "scarlet" (as the female genitalia are called). This requirement, moreover, continues even after marriage, when, however, the gift consists of services which the husband performs for the wife, most especially taking care of her children (ibid.:204). In brief, in order to gratify his sexual desires, the male not only submits to the female's aggressivity, but also compensates her with a gift.

Returning, however, to the physical pain not only to which the males submit, but which they actually welcome in their sexual behavior, I would suggest that this sadomasochistic attitude to their female partners is best interpreted as counterphobic.[18] To be sure, pain thresholds are culturally variable, but since Malinowski explicitly reports that the males suffer acutely from these attacks, the fact that they not only submit to them, but positively welcome them, strongly supports the counterphobic interpretation. Such a defensive maneuver is best explained, I would suggest, by viewing it ontogenetically, for it is the defense mechanism that a little boy might develop in attempting to cope with a sexually seductive pre-Oedipal mother. For reasons explained above, this type of pre-Oedipal mother arouses great fear in her son. Since, however, he has no way of avoiding her— this is especially the case in the Trobriands because the son is in the constant presence of the mother during the day and sleeps with her at night, when, it might be expected, she is most "seductive"—the only way to overcome his fear is to put a positive construction on her behavior, to view it, for example, as a "form of feminine wooing" and as a "sign of love." Viewing it in that manner, he will not be frightened by her behavior, but will rather take it as a "compliment." To be sure, her behavior may nevertheless cause him pain, but it is worth it because, in exchange, he stands to "reap the reward."

In sum, I am suggesting that in submitting to and even welcoming the aggressive sexuality of the females, Trobriand males are recapitulating in this sadomasochistic relationship an adaptive response that they had first established as young boys in their relationship with their sexually seductive pre-Oedipal mothers. Because, however, the mental representation of the aggressively sexual "bad mother" that is formed in the latter relationship is highly threatening, they project this representation onto other females—which, since Trobriand females *are* aggressively sexual, is easy to do—and they then respond to the

18. Sadomasochistic sexuality is not, of course, restricted to theTrobrianders, as the ethnographic record abundantly indicates. In the Micronesian atoll of Truk, to offer but one example, men submit to being cut, beaten, burned with cigarettes, and urinated on by their sweethearts (Swartz 1958). In interpreting the sadomasochistic reactions of Trobriand males as counterphobic, I am not suggesting that this interpretation would hold for other societies, as well, unless of course the latter were characterized by the same antecedent sociocultural conditions as I have delineated for the Trobriands.

latters' aggressive sexuality in the counterphobic, sadomasochistic fashion they had first devised in that early paradigmatic relationship with the mother. This interpretation also accounts for the curious fact (which I have commented on more than once) that the males, both in myths and in real life, make no attempt to defend themselves against the females, either by counterattack or by escape. For if the aggressiveness of the "bad mother" is projected onto other females, the aggressive power with which they are imputed would evoke such fear in the males that any defense would be viewed as hopeless. It would be better by far to merely capitulate.

Considering all of the evidence that has been marshaled on its behalf thus far—from myths, legends, folktales, dreams, and behavior—I would suggest that the "bad mother" prediction, so far at least as its aggressively sexual dimension is concerned, has been abundantly supported. We have not yet, however, established the existence of the nonsexual aggressiveness of this maternal representation. In fact, however, this dimension of the "bad mother" also exists in the Trobriands, as is evidenced by its cultural manifestation in the fiercely malevolent and cannibalistic flying witches to which we have already referred, but which we have not yet described.

Although wizards and witches alike are believed to abound in the Trobriands, the power of the wizards, according to Malinowski, is "extremely poor" when compared to that of the witches. Thus, whereas a wizard can, at best, inflict a lingering disease, which is easily cured by counter magic, there is "little chance" of combating the malevolent activities of a witch (*SLS*:45–46). Witches—called *mulukuausi* (Malinowski 1955), or *mulukwausi* (Malinowski [1922] 1961)—are "actual living women who may be known and talked with in ordinary life," but who, in a disembodied form, "are extremely virulent, powerful, and also ubiquitous. Anyone who chances to be exposed to them is sure to be attacked" (Malinowski 1955:152–53). Dangerous on land, these "terrible women" are even more dangerous on sea, where they destroy shipwrecked sailors (Malinowski [1922] 1961:chapter 10). Although, on land, witches may sometimes cause such ailments as toothaches, swelling of the testicles, tumors, and genital discharge (*SLS*:47), more typically they kill and eat their unfortunate victims. Pouncing on them from some hidden—usually high—place, the invisible witch removes their insides, together with their eyes and tongue, before eating them (*SLS*:45). Possessed of "ghoulish instincts," witches not only eat their living victims, but also devour entire corpses, thereby becoming "more than ever dangerous to the living" (Malinowski 1955:153). That is why, following a death, Trobrianders refuse to walk about the village or to enter the surrounding cultivated land. Although they are especially dangerous at that time, witches are "objects of real terror" at all times (ibid.).

Despite the fact that they view them with "fear" and "dread," the men are nevertheless sexually attracted to witches, and although a "marriageable young witch" is especially desirable, an old witch is "no less desirable sexually than other women" (*SLS*:46). Nevertheless, a witch, unlike a wizard, does not practice her powers openly; indeed, even when she is reputed to be a witch, a woman will not admit to being one. In this regard witches are different from wizards because, according to Malinowski, wizards actually exist while witches exist "only in folklore and in the imagination of the native . . . [that is] in legend and fiction" (*SLS*:46).

The existence "in the imagination of the native" of females of such extreme malevolence, who at the same time arouse his sexual desire, is of course precisely what might be expected in the case of men who have formed a maternal representation of a "bad mother." Such a representation, as we have seen, is constructed by a son who, on the one hand, is sexually attracted by a seductive pre-Oedipal mother (as the Trobrianders are by witches), but who, on the other hand, reacts to her (as the Trobrianders react to witches) with fear and dread because he copes with the rage which her seductiveness arouses in him by projecting it onto her. Since, however, the resulting "bad mother" representation is much too threatening, he represses it and projects it in a disguised form in various collective representations, including cannibalistic witches.[19]

19. Since all of the characteristics of the witch are imputed to her by the child's projections, it may be assumed that her cannibalism, too, represents the projection of the boy's own cannibalistic fantasies regarding the mother which he had previously projected onto the "bad mother." Since, according to clinical findings, these fantasies are usually developed by the infant at the breast, this would support the assumption that the "bad mother" is a construction, primarily, of the pre-Oedipal child. Primarily, but not necessarily entirely. For the

That the Trobriand witch represents the "bad" characteristics of the seductive pre-Oedipal mother, which are split off from the maternal representation to form a separate "bad mother," is given powerful support by the fact that the Kula, the institution in which the mother's "good" characteristics are most prominently displayed (chapter 3), is the very place in which the witch is also especially prominent. Although the Kula voyage is filled with many dangers, real and fantasied, the most important danger by far—"the most unpleasant, the best known and most dreaded" (Malinowski [1922] 1961:236)—is posed by witches who carry out their maleficent designs by causing shipwreck. That they might succeed is always on the voyagers' minds, and numerous magical spells are used as protection against their intentions. Indeed, Malinowski ([1922] 1961:244–66) devotes the greater part of a chapter to their description. Here then, I submit, is a paradigmatic cultural expression of the splitting of the mental representation of the seductive pre-Oedipal mother: although the Kula, among its other latent functions, permits the male to symbolically recapitulate the pleasure received from the "good" characteristics of the pre-Oedipal mother, this pleasure can only be obtained (as it was originally obtained in actuality) by bringing on (in the form of a witch) her destructive "bad" characteristics.

If, after all this, there are still any lingering doubts about the splitting of the maternal representation in the Trobriands, it may now be observed that in addition to the projection of the "bad mother" in the various disguised forms which we have been at pains to describe, the latter representation is also projected onto a class of actual mothers. That is shown in Trobriand beliefs concerning sorcery. Malinowski ([1922] 1961:74) tells us, it may be remembered from the discussion in chapter 3, that "it is a firm and definite belief among all the natives that if a man's sorcery has to be any good, it must first be practiced on his mother, or sister, or any of his maternal kindred." That it is the mother, however, who takes the pride of place is indicated in the very next sentence, where Malinowski characterizes this putative practice as a "matricidal act." In sum, the Trobrianders

Oedipal child, who is "rejected" by his mother following his pre-Oedipal monopoly of her, may also have fantasies of attacking and devouring her, a type of retaliation, however, which has its prototype in the cannibalistic fantasies of the earlier pre-Oedipal period.

themselves believe that some individuals (those who become sorcerers) hate their mothers enough that, in order to attain a personal goal, they are willing, if not motivated, to kill them. Here, then, is a cultural belief according to which some few mothers are viewed and treated by their own sons as "bad mothers."

Like all the other cultural manifestations of the "bad mother," however, this cultural belief concerning sorcerers tells us more about the believers than about the sorcerers. For, in fact, we do not know whether there are few or many sorcerers in the Trobriands—Malinowski says that there are a "number" in each district and "one or two" in every village—or whether in fact they attempt to kill their mothers or not. The only thing we know—and for our present purpose all that we need to know—is that "all the natives" *believe* this to be the case. Since, then, no sorcerer has ever been observed attempting to commit matricide, the latter can only be an act which Trobrianders *attribute* to sorcerers; and since the mothers of sorcerers are no different from other Trobriand mothers, such an attribution tells us about the Trobrianders' *feelings* regarding their own mothers rather than about the sorcerers' *actions* regarding theirs. In summary, in holding a "firm and definite belief" that sorcerers kill their mothers, Trobrianders only reflect a matricidal wish regarding their own mothers (in their "bad mother" aspect). In order to defend themselves against this belief, which is ego-alien, they project it (as an accomplished act) onto the sorcerers.[20]

That, it will be recalled, was the (implicit) logic of Malinowski's argument regarding the Trobrianders' hatred of the maternal uncle when he (erroneously) contended that the Trobrianders believe that the sorcerer's first victim is his mother's brother, and the same logic applies when (as it now turns out) it is his mother who is believed to be his homicidal target. It must be emphasized again, however, that the matricidal hatred that is reflected in that belief is directed not toward the mother as such, but at the split-off "bad mother" maternal representation.

20. It is interesting to note, then, that while in the Trobriands it is the mother who must be chosen by the sorcerer as his first victim, among the Navajo (who are also a matrilineal people) it is a sibling who must be chosen (Kluckhohn 1967:102–3).

With this we have completed the summary of our findings regarding the predicted splitting of the maternal representation in the Trobriands. On the basis of these findings, it seems reasonable to conclude that the prediction has been confirmed. That being the case, since all six predictions whose support was required for the acceptance of the Trobriand Oedipal hypothesis have now been supported, it seems reasonable to conclude that that hypothesis can now be accepted with a reasonable degree of confidence.

The confirmation of the predicted splitting of the maternal representation has an important consequence for the predicted ontogenetic determinant of the Trobriand Oedipus complex. According to our hypothesis, it will be recalled, an Oedipus complex of the postulated strength of the Trobriand Oedipus complex is initiated by the boy's experience with a highly seductive pre-Oedipal mother. Although the supporting evidence for that hypothesis, as reported in chapter 4, was not inconsiderable, it was mostly indirect. The additional, but required evidence—the existence of a "bad mother" representation—could not be presented in that chapter because its prediction was an indivisible part of the set of predictions that had first to be tested in this chapter. Now, however, that this crucial evidence can be added to that already presented in chapter 4, we can conclude that the ontogenetic hypothesis can now be accepted with a reasonable degree of confidence.

Not surprisingly, this crucial evidence in support of the ontogenetic hypothesis serves to underscore the postulated strength of the Trobriand Oedipus complex. In accordance with our theoretical expectations, it was found that the Trobriand "bad mother" is manifested in such phenomena as cannibalistic witches and unconscious matricidal wishes. If, then, the early sexual arousal by the pre-Oedipal mother is powerful enough to produce a "bad mother" of such threatening dimensions, the Trobrianders' repressed incestuous attachment to the childhood mother must be very strong. Since, moreover, Trobriand unconscious patricidal wishes are more widespread than matricidal ones—the Trobrianders believe, it will be recalled, that with some few exceptions the death of the father is caused by the sorcery of his son or wife—and since these wishes have now been shown to arise from the son's rivalry with him for the love of the mother, that attachment must be very strong indeed. By the same token, if the Oedipal rivalry with the father is powerful enough to lead to unconscious patricidal wishes, the repressed hostility to the father must be equally strong.

Summary and Conclusions

Since the path which we followed in the last three chapters, first in arriving at, and then in the testing of the Trobriand Oedipal hypothesis, has taken us through a veritable jungle of ethnographic data, speculations, theories, and cross-cultural and clinical findings, it may perhaps be useful to briefly retrace our steps, omitting the many detours which we were required to take along the way.

On the basis of the Trobriand absent-father pattern, and of the cultural belief that the death of adult males is caused by magical patricide, it was inferred that Trobriand males have very strong, unconscious hostile wishes in regard to the father. From two types of data it was also inferred that these wishes are Oedipal in motivation. First, two of the three elements constituting the absent-father pattern suggested that the hostility to the father is motivated by rivalrous conflict with him for the love of the wife-mother; second, Malinowski's description of the nurturant and nonauthoritarian father precluded the tenability of a non-Oedipal interpretation. Since, however, the Oedipal basis for the son's hostility was inferential, this hypothesis could not be seriously entertained unless it was supported by independent evidence of a strong, unconscious incestuous attraction to the childhood mother. An analysis of Trobriand dreams and of the symbolism of the Kula provided that support. The former suggested that the image of the sister in dreams of overt sister incest is a condensed symbol representing both the sister and the mother. The latter suggested that the ceremonial exchange in the Kula unconsciously represented the gratification of incestuous longings for the early childhood mother.

On the basis of that inferential evidence it was concluded that there were sufficient grounds to entertain the hypothesis that a repressed Oedipus complex of more than ordinary intensity exists in the Trobriands. This hypothesis was then tested by means of two sets of predictions derived from Oedipal theory.

One set consisted of predictions regarding the ontogenesis of an Oedipus complex of this type, the other of the psychological characteristics that are associated with it. All the predictions were confirmed.

The confirmation of the second set of predictions suggests that the following indications of a repressed and strong Oedipus complex are reliably found in the Trobriands. First, Oedipal hostility is sufficiently intense that in order to preclude its overt expression, the adolescent son is extruded from the household. Second, although hostility to the father is not expressed in aggressive behavior, the persistence of the son's need to avenge his Oedipal defeat is sufficiently strong to motivate both symbolic and—when the father is polygynous—actual attempts to accomplish this aim. Third, the son's incestuous desire for the mother is sufficiently strong that its direct expression must also be precluded by extruding him from the household during the period—puberty—when his sexual needs are especially powerful. Fourth, the incestuous desire for the mother is sufficiently threatening that it is displaced onto the adolescent daughter, but most especially the sister. Fifth, the early incestuous attachment to the mother leaves permanent residues in a "bad mother" representation, and a consequent sadomasochistic sexual orientation, as well as in strong castration anxiety.

The confirmation of the first set of predictions suggests that the following indicated conditions for the ontogenesis of an Oedipus complex of that type are reliably found in the Trobriands. In the pre-Oedipal period of child development the boy experiences a highly "seductive" mother and a physically and emotionally remote father which, in a psychological chain reaction, leads to a strong incestuous attachment to the mother and an equally strong Oedipal rivalry with the father. On the basis of both sets of predicted findings it was concluded that the Trobriand Oedipal hypothesis can be accepted with a reasonable degree of confidence.

Before turning to the wider ramifications of this conclusion, it is worth pointing out that it has an important unintended consequence for the understanding of the integration of the Trobriand sociocultural system and, by implication, of sociocultural systems in general.

That social and cultural variables exhibit some degree of integration—that to a greater or smaller degree they sustain certain "functional" relationships with each other—is one of the characteristics of sociocultural systems to which, I take it, most social scientists would subscribe. Indeed, this characteristic is entailed by the very notion of "system." It will perhaps have been noted, then, that the Trobriand Oedipal hypothesis served to organize a wide array of social and cultural variables which (whether found in the Trobriands or elsewhere) are usually treated as so many separate and discrete items in an ethnographic catalogue. These variables—including, for example, the ignorance of physiological paternity, the belief in flying witches, the infrequency of (recalled) dreams, the myth of Kaytalugi, the extrusion of males at adolescence, folktales concerning attacks on the clitoris, the postpartum sex taboo, household sleeping arrangements, female sexual violence, Kula exchange, and so on—are typically viewed as unrelated ethnographic "facts" which sustain little relationship to one another. Indeed, Malinowski himself, the founder and most eloquent proponent of functionalism, viewed them in precisely that manner. In his writings on the Trobriands, each of these social and cultural variables was dealt with separately under such standard ethnographic rubrics as sex, myth, household composition, and the like. In short, for Malinowski the relationship of these variables to each other was the relationship of beads strung on a necklace, or (to employ yet another metaphor) of the entries in an encyclopedia.

That kind of relationship, however, is far from the relationship that they can now be perceived to sustain as a result of the strong support that was found for the Trobriand Oedipus hypothesis. In the process of testing that hypothesis, their relationship was shown to be that of the pieces of a jigsaw puzzle which, although not immediately apparent, constitute one integrated and interlocking structure. That is, each of those variables was shown to be related to each of the others as either an expression, a consequence, or an antecedent of the Oedipus complex. In sum, the support for the Trobriand Oedipal hypothesis enables us to discern in an array of social and cultural variables a degree of order, pattern, structure, functional relationships, causal chains—whichever term one prefers—which heretofore had not been perceived to exist.

But if we can now discern a high degree of *empirical* integration among these ethnographic variables, it is because Oedipal theory provided the analytic schema for their *conceptual* integration. That is, instead of explaining each variable by means of a separate and ad hoc theory (as is frequently the case), the Oedipal hypothesis subsumed them all under a single and a generative (predictive) theory. Hence, it not only succeeded in bringing unexpected order out of an ethnographic miscellany, but did so while satisfying the scientific principle of explanatory parsimony. In my view a hypothesis that integrates, both empirically and conceptually, a wide array of (otherwise unintegrated) social and cultural variables is more likely to be correct, ceteris paribus, than any alternative hypothesis, including of course Malinowski's hypothesis of a Trobriand matrilineal complex.

6

Is the Oedipus Complex Universal?

The Motivational Disposition to Incest

In the previous chapters I attempted to achieve two separate, but related, goals. First, I attempted to demonstrate that its empirical foundation is too weak to support Malinowski's argument that a matrilineal complex exists in the Trobriands. Second, I attempted to show that the evidence indicates to the contrary that an unusually strong Oedipus complex exists in the Trobriands. In this (the final) chapter I wish to examine the implications of these Trobriand findings for human societies in general.

Malinowski and those who follow his lead have argued that the male Oedipus complex is culturally relative because it is produced not by the boy's experience in the family in general, but by his experience in the "patriarchal" family uniquely. Since, so they argue, it is the authoritarian father—the nineteenth-century European father being paradigmatic of the class—who arouses filial hostility, matrilineal societies whose family structure does not conform to the "patriarchal" type—the Trobriands being paradigmatic of the class—would not be expected to produce an Oedipus complex.

In a sophisticated and perceptive explication of that argument, Campbell and Naroll (1972:437) quite properly observe that in principle the boy's hostility to the father may be motivated either by his rivalry with him for the love of the mother (as Freud claimed) or by the father's punitive authority (as Malinowski claimed). Freud, they argue, confounded these two motives in

144

his construction of the Oedipus complex because, in his European patient population, the father was both the authority figure and the mother's lover. Since in the Trobriands, however, these roles are performed by different persons rather than by one and the same person, and since the boy's hostility, according to Malinowski, is directed to the authority figure (mother's brother) rather than the mother's lover (father), the hostility dimension of the Western Oedipus complex is brought about not by the son's sexual rivalry with the father, they argue, but by his resentment of the latter's authority.

That argument can now be faulted on three grounds. First, there are no a priori grounds for assuming that hostility to the father cannot be motivated by both sexual rivalry and resentment against his authority. Indeed, that is the view I have adopted here in distinguishing between Oedipal and non-Oedipal grounds for filial hostility. Second, there are no evidential grounds, as we observed in chapter 2, for claiming that in the Trobriands the jural authority of the mother's brother is exercised either frequently or punitively. Hence, even if the boy's *conscious* hostility is directed toward the mother's brother, it cannot be a function of the latter's punitive authority. Third, the findings presented in the last two chapters demonstrate rather conclusively that in fact it is the father who is the prime target of the boy's hostility in the Trobriands, and moreover his hostility is Oedipal in motivation, i.e., it is motivated by his rivalry with him for the love of the wife-mother.

Even, however, without that empirical demonstration, the claim that the male Oedipus complex would not be expected in matrilineal societies because the father is not an authority figure can be faulted on theoretical grounds alone. In order to sustain that claim, it would have to be demonstrated that in matrilineal societies it is the case not only that the father is not an authority figure for the son (however important that might be for the non-Oedipal dimensions of the father-son relationship), but that the mother is not a love-object for him. For if it is the case that the son has a libidinal attachment to the mother in matrilineal as well as in "patriarchal" societies, the contention that he would nevertheless not be hostile to the father—or anyone else that he perceived to be the rival for her love—would be warranted only on the assumption that hostility to a rival is a phenomenon which is restricted to patriarchal societies. That assumption, however, is easily refuted, if only by the abundant evidence to the contrary reported by Malinowski for the Trobriands. That being the case, unless it were demonstrated that a libidinal attachment to the mother is restricted to boys in patriarchal societies, then, all things being equal, it would be no less likely for the Oedipus complex to be found in matrilineal societies than in patriarchal ones.

Malinowski, who waffled on this issue of the boy's relationship to the mother—on the one hand he claimed that in the Trobriands the young boy has a "passionate" attachment to his mother, on the other that this attachment disappears spontaneously prior to the normally expected onset of the Oedipus complex, a point to which we shall return—nowhere adduced any structural feature(s) peculiar to matriliny that might account for the absence of a libidinal attachment to the mother in matrilineal societies. Unless such a feature can be identified, it seems judicious to go along with the large body of evidence which suggests that a motivational disposition to nuclear family incest in general, and to mother-son incest in particular, is a pan-human characteristic. Since Lindzey (1967) has brought together much of the evidence pertaining to incest in general, our discussion of that topic will take its departure from his excellent paper, following which we shall turn to mother-son incest, which is our primary concern here.

The evidence marshaled by Lindzey can be classified into two categories, indirect and direct. Beginning with the former, we might mention in the first place the abundant social-psychological findings which suggest that "personal attractiveness and interpersonal choice are mediated, or determined, by similarity in attitudes, values, needs, and background factors," and that "positive social choice is strongly facilitated by physical or geographic proximity" (Lindzey 1967:1056). When these social-psychological findings are combined with the sociological findings concerning homogeneity of mate selection and the demographic findings concerning assortative mating (which indicate that the grounds for preferential choice in nonsexual domains apply to the sexual domain as well), their cumulative force suggests that in the absence of countervailing factors (most notably, incest taboos) sexual choice within—but not restricted to—the nuclear family would be a likely outcome.

That suggestion is supported by the direct evidence regarding the motivational disposition to nuclear family incest. Consider, first, the psychiatric findings concerning the existence of incestuous wishes at least in clinical populations. Consider, again, the psychological findings concerning the frequency of incestuous wishes, both overt and covert, in the dreams of normal populations. Consider, moreover, the anthropological findings concerning the near-universal incidence of the incest motif in myths, legends, and folktales, as well as the universality of nuclear family incest taboos. Consider, in addition, the sociological findings concerning the prevalence of incestuous behavior: in the United States, for example, one out of every twenty persons questioned in 1970, according to an authoritative estimate, had had an incestuous experience (Justice and Justice 1979:17). Consider, finally, the ethological findings (Bischof 1975) which indicate a near-universal motivation to incest in infrahuman mammalian societies.[1] If, then, we consider the cumulative force of these various kinds of evidence, it is hard to avoid the conclusion that the existence of a pan-human motivational disposition to incest is a highly probable hypothesis. This hypothesis, I hasten to add, does not entail the conclusion that nuclear family members are the strongest objects of sexual desire—though that too may sometimes occur—but only that they, among others, are members of that class.

Although almost all anthropologists, representing the entire range of anthropological thought, accept this conclusion, it has always had its opponents. If, so their counterargument goes, incest behavior is rare in human societies, it is not because of

---

1. Despite their motivational disposition, incestuous behavior is infrequent in mammals because of a variety of structural constraints—most notably the formation of all-male adolescent groupings, adolescent extrusion, and dominance structures—which are summarized by Bischof (1975) in his admirable survey of the mammalian evidence. Although Bischof, a zoologist, shows that in the absence of these structural arrangements incest would be prevalent in mammalian societies, and although he argues that these arrangements are the evolutionary result of a selection process to constrain its occurrence, he then, strangely, concludes that the infrequency of mammalian incest indicates the absence of motivation to incest. It is hard to account for this non sequitur in an otherwise exemplary study.

social or cultural pressures, most notably the implementation of incest taboos, which lead to its inhibition (as the proponents of the incest hypothesis argue), but because (to quote a recent statement of a distinguished critic) "human beings are 'naturally' non-incestuous" (Fox 1980:14). (Fox's view is much more complex than this quotation suggests, as will become apparent when we return to it below.) Hence, before turning to the motivational disposition to incest in the mother-son dyad, which is our concern in this book, it is necessary to examine this counterargument especially since prominent findings from China and Israel have been recently adduced on its behalf.

Various of its proponents base the counterargument to the incest hypothesis on different theoretical grounds, but they all agree with Westermarck (who first proposed it) that sexual indifference or aversion, rather than attraction, develops between any persons (including family members) who live together from an early age. It is this naturally developing aversion that then accounts for the relative infrequency of incestuous behavior (Westermarck 1906–8:vol. 2, p. 368). In order to fully grasp this counterargument it must be emphasized that none of the proponents of the incest hypothesis argue that—except for young children—members of the nuclear family have a conscious wish to take one another as sexual partners. They, no less than Westermarck, are fully aware that, consciously, most individuals are either indifferent or aversive to having sexual relations with family members. For them, however, sexual indifference or aversion is a consequence not of childhood propinquity but, rather, of the internalization of incest taboos and the consequent repression or extinction of the incestuous wishes.

Although Westermarck's theory has been persistently rejected by social scientists, most particularly on the grounds—first adduced by Frazer ([1887] 1910:vol. 4, p. 97 ff.)—that the universality of nuclear family incest taboos implies that the motivational disposition to incest is also universal, it has recently been defended on the basis of two sets of findings, one from China, the other from Israel. Since these findings, both confined to the question of sibling incest, have been widely heralded as constituting conclusive support (cf. Bischof 1975; Demarest 1977; Fox 1980:chapter 2; Money 1980; Wilson 1978) for Westermarck's theory, it is important to examine them rather carefully.

The Chinese case, which has been extensively studied by Wolf (1966, 1968, 1970) and by Wolf and Huang (1980), concerns a type of marriage known as *simpua* marriage. In this marriage type, a boy's parents choose as his future bride a young girl, often orphaned or from a poor and socially inferior family, who is adopted as a daughter, who lives in the family household throughout childhood, and whom he subsequently marries at the appropriate age. In short, prior to their marriage the structural relationship between the boy and his chosen bride is little different from that of biological siblings raised in the same family. According to Wolf's findings, the adultery and divorce rates found in *simpua* marriages are higher and the fertility rate is lower than those found in regular Chinese marriages. Taking these rates as a measure of sexual dissatisfaction, Wolf argues that the greater sexual dissatisfaction in *simpua* marriages is a consequence of the sexual aversion that develops between the boy and girl in childhood, which supports Westermarck's theory that propinquity leads to sexual aversion.

Convincing as it might seem, Wolf's argument, I believe, is invalid on both empirical and theoretical grounds. Empirically, Wolf's findings regarding *simpua* marriage do not sustain the conclusion that children who live together typically develop a sexual aversion for each other, for although these marriages are characterized by higher rates of divorce and adultery and a lower rate of fertility than regular marriages, it is nevertheless the case that the great majority of them do not display these characteristics. If it is then claimed that these findings indicate that there is a greater likelihood for childhood propinquity to lead to sexual aversion, even this lesser claim can be sustained only on the dubious assumption that adultery, divorce, and low fertility are necessarily (as Wolf takes them to be) measures of sexual dissatisfaction. Surely, other factors also contribute to these forms of behavior in China—in regular and *simpua* marriages alike—as we know to be the case elsewhere.

But even accepting the assumption that sexual dissatisfaction is the sole determinant of divorce, adultery, and low fertility, Wolf's ethnographic data cast considerable doubt on his contention that the postulated sexual dissatisfaction found in *simpua* marriages is primarily determined by the sexual aversion that putatively, the couple develop as a result of their living together in childhood.

Consider in the first place that the boy, according to Wolf, feels cheated and frustrated by a *simpua* marriage because it deprives him not only of honor and prestige—these marriages are viewed as "vulgar and inferior" and are therefore "socially despised"—but of a dowry, affinal alliances, and other advantages of a regular marriage, as well. Considering all of these disadvantages, it is hard to credit Wolf's contention that although the boys "resent their having their best interests sacrificed by their parents," their resentment is nevertheless "not likely to disrupt permanently their relationship as husband and wife" (Wolf 1970:506). I would assume, on the contrary, that their resentment would have that effect precisely.

Consider, again, that a girl adopted for a *simpua* marriage is an object of "abuse" by her adoptive family; indeed, such girls are treated so badly that they are the very "symbol of the life of misery." Consider, too, that (presumably as a result of this treatment) the girl is hostile to the members of her adoptive family, including her "brother" (and future husband), of whom she is jealous and toward whom she displays "sibling" rivalry. It is again hard to credit Wolf's contention that these factors do not importantly affect the girl's subsequent relationship with the boy when she becomes his wife. It is also difficult to believe that the girl's abusive treatment by his parents does not affect the boy's perception of her as an inferior person, one who is unworthy of esteem and affection. Indeed, since the main reason for a *simpua* marriage is the wish of the boy's mother to have a subordinate daughter-in-law, one who will not be a rival for her son's affection (as is the case in regular marriages), it would seem not unlikely that she goes out of her way to prevent her son from establishing an affectionate relationship with his "sister."

In short, given all of these considerations, it is hard to credit Wolf's claim that the boy's "resentment" and the girl's "misery" have no influence on their feelings for each other, and that these feelings, in turn, have no effect on their subsequent relationship as husband and wife, most especially their sexual relationship. Indeed, everything that we know about the influence of emotional attitudes on sexual desire and performance supports the contrary assumption. Hence, even if it were the case that the differences in the rates of fertility, divorce, and adultery in regular and *simpua* marriages are exclusively determined by a higher incidence of sexual dissatisfaction in the latter marriages, it is hard to believe that all of these social and cultural factors have no influence on that dissatisfaction. Indeed, given those factors it is a wonder that these marriages do not display a much greater degree of dissatisfaction.

When, then, to these social and cultural impediments to a satisfactory sexual relationship that are contained in Wolf's data we add the observation that in *simpua* marriage the boy and girl must marry each other even if, being sexually unattractive, they would not have married had they been raised separately; and when to that we add the additional observation that almost everywhere divorce in early marriages is higher than in later ones, so that the higher divorce rate of *simpua* marriages (in which twice as many couples marry before seventeen than in regular marriages [44 as against 22 percent]) would be expected as a function of the couple's age at marriage—when these observations are also taken into account, I would then submit that Wolf's contention that the case of *simpua* marriage proves Westermarck's theory that childhood propinquity leads to sexual aversion rests on a very shaky foundation.

Let us then turn to the second ethnographic case that allegedly proves Westermarck's theory, the Israeli kibbutz movement. In 1958 I reported that in the kibbutz I had studied none of the children who had been reared together from birth had married each other, and that to the best of my knowledge none had had sexual intercourse with each other (Spiro 1958:347–48). These findings were replicated in a later study by Talmon (1964) in three kibbutzim. Still later, based on a study of the marriage records of kibbutz children in all kibbutzim—2,769 marriages in all—Shepher (1971) reported that in not one case had there been a marriage between children reared together from birth through the age of six years. Shepher also reported that so far as he was able to ascertain, this finding also applied to love affairs, those at least that were publicly known.

Now what makes these three reports of considerable interest is that no marriages (and probably no love affairs) have taken place among members of the same peer groups *despite the fact*

that such marriages are not prohibited. It is understandable, therefore, that these findings have aroused a great deal of attention.

I interpreted my own findings as indicating that members of
the kibbutz peer group repress their sexual feelings for each
other. This interpretation was based on two sets of data. First,
with one exception they themselves attributed the absence of
marriage within the peer group to the sexual indifference which,
they explained, arose from their perception of each other as
"siblings." Second, the data regarding sexual behavior and socialization in these peer groups, to which I shall advert below,
suggested rather strongly that their sexual indifference did not
develop spontaneously.

Some (but hardly all) incest theorists, especially those ac-
quainted with Shepher's subsequent large-scale report, interpreted the kibbutz findings, as did Shepher himself, as supporting
Westermarck's theory that children reared together in childhood
(whether or not they are siblings) develop a sexual aversion for
each other. Since the latter interpretation, however, was offered
without giving any consideration to (what I believe to be) the
crucial data on sexual socialization, in order to evaluate these
competing interpretations it is necessary to summarize those
data for the particular historical period—because much has
changed since then—for which the marriage findings were reported (for details see Spiro 1958:chapters 9, 11, 13, 14).

In that period, consistent with the kibbutz ideology of sexual
freedom, young children were almost entirely free to engage in
sexual play without interference or punishment by their care-
takers. Since, therefore, boys and girls of the same age not only
lived together in one dormitory, but also slept and showered
together and had frequent other opportunities to see each other
in the nude, it is not surprising that they also engaged in (child-
like) sexual behavior and that they displayed little sexual shame
(Spiro 1958:219–28). An important change in their behavior occurred, however, around eleven or twelve, when girls, who were
beginning to show the first signs of puberty, refused to shower
together with the boys, and in general began to display overt
signs of sexual shame. At the same time, sexual behavior no
longer occurred, and was replaced by a great deal of bickering
and hostility between the sexes. Although the bickering and
hostility gradually disappeared, sexual shame, including the

avoidance of mixed showers, persisted throughout high school, and there was no return to the sexual play that characterized early childhood, nor was there an assumption of sexual behavior of a more mature form.

With this brief behavioral description, we may now examine the cultural and structural factors associated with these behavioral changes. First, despite their differential physical maturation at puberty, boys and girls of the same peer groups continued to live and sleep together. This meant that physically immature boys continued to be the roommates of girls who may have begun to menstruate, and whose secondary sexual characteristics—the development of breasts, the growth of pubic hair, and the like—were becoming prominent. Hence, although the girls were beginning to experience the sexual tensions of puberty and a concern with the physical changes in their bodies, the boys remained physically immature. It is not surprising, then, that the girls displayed no interest in the boys, and that in some cases the latter were put off—even frightened—by the girls, while others (outsiders) were sexually aroused by them.

Even at a later age, however, when the boys' maturation caught up with the girls', two other factors intervened. First, in the case of the older children—beginning around prepuberty and continuing until the end of high school—the permissive ideology of the kibbutz regarding the sexual play of young children was replaced by a strong prohibition on sexual behavior. The introduction of such prohibitions at this age was not based— not, at least, officially—on sexual puritanism, but on the assumptions that sexual behavior disrupts the learning process, that intellectual development is enhanced when the sex drive is sublimated in intellectual pursuits, and that pair bonding, which often results from sexual behavior, interferes with the intensive group interaction and group identification that the kibbutz viewed as paramount values. Hence, at this age strong pressure was exerted on the children to defer all sexual encounters until graduation from high school, and especially to avoid the formation of permanent liaisons. The latter in particular were the object of strong social sanctions.

Second, despite these sexual prohibitions and their attendant sanctions, kibbutz educators believed that to encourage children to develop a wholesome attitude to sex and a "natural" attitude to the body and its functions, it was important that boys and girls live together not only in early childhood but throughout their educational careers until graduation from high school. Beginning, however, in the seventh grade the group of approximately sixteen age peers, who had previously shared one barrack-like dormitory room, was divided into groups of four—two males and two females—each group sharing one bedroom.

Here, then, I would submit, is a classic example of incompatible demands. On the one hand, we have a group of teenagers, at a physiological developmental stage of maximum sexual tension, who are exposed to persistent sexual stimulation induced by living in close quarters with members of the opposite sex, who dress and undress in one another's presence—though it was expected that they avert their eyes during this process—and who sleep in adjacent beds. At the same time, these same teenagers are expected to comply with a cultural norm which prohibits sexual behavior between them on pain of serious social sanctions. Such a contradiction, I would submit, can only result in intolerable conflict and unbearable sexual frustration. Edith Buxbaum, a child therapist, highlights this contradiction in her discussion of a fifteen-year-old kibbutz boy who could not sleep because of his urge to touch a girl, and who was advised to seek psychiatric help for his "problem." It seems paradoxical, Buxbaum (1970:286) writes,

> that people should consider it abnormal for a fifteen-year-old boy to want to touch a girl with whom he sleeps in the same room. Indeed, it would be extraordinary if he did not want to. Yet, this is what kibbutz educators expect and the children expect of themselves. They are not supposed to have these feelings, or if they have them, they are not supposed to act on them.

That, however, only a small percentage of these teenagers required professional help to cope with the tensions induced by this contradiction suggests that the majority managed to erect strong psychological barriers against them. These barriers, as I suggested above—and as Buxbaum (1970:285–90) and Bettelheim (1969:235–40) have suggested elsewhere—could only have consisted in the repression of their sexual wishes (which would explain how they might have consciously become sexually indifferent to each other) and, if that were not sufficient, in the formation of a reaction against them (which would explain how they might have consciously developed a sexual aversion for each other).[2]

There are three reasons, I would submit, for preferring this interpretation of these kibbutz findings to that of Westermarck's followers. First, the early sexual play of kibbutz children for the period under discussion was replaced by sexual abstinence only after the sexual permissiveness of childhood was replaced by the sexual prohibitions of adolescence. This suggests, pace Westermarck, that their sexual aversion for each other—if that is what it was—did not develop endogenously. Second, the sexual abstinence of the adolescents applied not only in regard to the members of their peer group—the group with whom they lived as children—but to other groups as well—those with whom they did not live as children. Third, and most important, this interpretation is supported by the recent findings of Kaffman (1977), a psychiatrist employed by the kibbutz movement, regarding sexual behavior in the kibbutz.

Although Kaffman's findings regarding peer-group marriage do not disagree with the early findings reported above, those regarding love affairs are at variance with them. "There is hardly a kibbutz," Kaffman writes, "without its report of heterosexual relationships between adolescents brought up together from infancy" (Kaffman 1977:216). Such relationships, he claims, "may

---

2. If correct, this analysis confutes Fox's attempt to salvage Westermarck's theory. The latter theory, according to Fox (1980:chapter 2), only applies to children who not only live together but also engage in intense physical interaction. Since, he argues, their physical contacts lead to sexual arousal, and since immature children have no means of physiological discharge, their painful frustration leads to a consequent sexual aversion for the children (later adults) who are responsible for their pain. If, however, children who live together have no physical interaction and, therefore, no history of painful sexual frustration, Westermarck's theory does not apply. The kibbutz case, according to Fox, supports this argument because it involves physical interaction in childhood followed by aversion at adolescence.

According to my analysis, however, it is not the physical interaction in childhood, but the sexual prohibition at adolescence in the face of powerful sexual stimulation that leads to sexual aversion in the kibbutz. By my argument, the sexual stimulation leads to sexual arousal, which is frustrated by sexual prohibitions, and the resulting painful tensions are defended against by repression and reaction formation which, if effective, lead to sexual aversion.

not be typical, but [they are] not all that rare either" (ibid.). Kaffman also reports that whereas in an earlier study of seventeen-year-old kibbutz children, 66 percent of the sample were opposed to sexual relations, in 1973 only 7 percent of the males and 11 percent of the females voiced opposition.

How, then, are the discrepancies between Kaffman's report and the earlier reports to be explained? And what light do these discrepancies shed on the conflicting interpretations of the earlier reports? Kaffman's findings are based on studies conducted some few years after two major changes had begun to take place in the kibbutz movement. In the first place, many kibbutzim changed the living arrangements in the high school dormitories from mixed to unisexual bedrooms. In many of them, too, the prohibition on teenage sexual behavior has been informally if not formally abolished. According, then, to my interpretation of the earlier findings, Kaffman's findings are exactly what one would expect from such changes: no longer suffering the severe sexual tensions aroused by a contradiction between their living arrangements and sexual norms, adolescents in those kibbutzim which had undergone these changes had no need to create psychological barriers (repression and/or reaction formation) to their sexual feelings. As more and more kibbutzim make these structural and cultural changes, we would then expect the sexual changes reported by Kaffman to become more widespread. It is difficult, however, to accommodate Kaffman's findings to Westermarck's theory. Since, according to that theory, sexual aversion results from joint living in childhood, and since no changes in the children's living arrangements were associated with the sexual changes reported by Kaffman, his data are clearly inexplicable by that theory.

If, then, my interpretation of the earlier reports is correct, why is it that the structural and cultural changes pointed to above have not had an even greater effect on the incidence of intragroup love affairs and marriage? There are at least two answers to that question. In the first place, the fact that individuals who live together in childhood (whether they are siblings or nonsiblings) acquire sexual wishes for each other does not mean, as I observed above, that these are their strongest sexual wishes. When we consider, then, that kibbutz peer groups, as Kaffman observes, are small and the range of sexual choice limited, and when we consider too the differential maturation rates of boys and girls, we would not expect a surge of sexual behavior within the peer group despite those changes. In the second place, since sexual attractiveness is hardly the only basis for marriage, we would not expect all couples who are sexually attracted to each other to wish to enter into a marriage.[3]

I would conclude, then, that the kibbutz case no more than the Chinese constitutes proof for the Westermarck theory. Indeed, if my analysis is correct, the kibbutz case provides strong support for the contention of the vast majority of incest theorists that individuals who live together (whether they are family or nonfamily members) do indeed develop and retain sexual feelings for each other unless they are inhibited by countervailing social and cultural pressures.

This analysis of the Israeli case is supported by yet another case, one which was reported only some few years following the claim that the kibbutz and Chinese cases support the Westermarck theory. This case, which has already been mentioned in a previous chapter, consists of brother-sister marriage in Roman Egypt. For two centuries, brother-sister marriage, according to Hopkins (1980:310), was a "frequent practice" in Roman Egypt. According to second century census returns, for example, 23 of 113 recorded marriages were between brother and sister. More important for the terms of this discussion is that these marriages, which were considered to be entirely "normal"— hence, not prohibited by an incest taboo—were based not on economic or other practical considerations, but on "love and sexual passion." Hence, when such marriages came to an end in the third century, it was not because love and passion between brothers and sisters came to an end, but because Egypt came under Roman law, which prohibited incest.

3. Those incest theorists—the so-called alliance theorists—who see the unchecked motivational disposition to incest as a barrier to the formation of interfamily alliances have primitive and prehistoric families as their model. Since the latter (hunting and gathering) families are frequently isolated from other families in their bands, mating with a family member is much more likely—unless it is checked by incest taboos—than in families in which a wide range of sexual partners, in addition to family members, are available. Physical isolation of the family, as we have previously observed, is an important condition for incest in modern families as well.

If, then, the Chinese case does not refute the generalization that siblings who are reared together develop incestuous feelings for each other, and if the kibbutz and Egyptian cases offer strong support for that generalization, we may now turn to the question of incestuous feelings in the dyad that is relevant to the Oedipal problem, the mother-son dyad.

There is nothing in the evidence summarized above regarding the existence of a motivational disposition to nuclear family incest which suggests that the boy's incestuous feelings for his mother are less strong than those for his sister. Indeed, given the nature of the mother-son bond in humans, it is reasonable to assume that, typically, his incestuous feelings for the mother are stronger by far than those for his sister, and that this generalization holds even when the mother is not seductive, as she is (according to my argument) in the Trobriands. Moreover, given the nature of the mother-child bond in humans, the incestuous feelings for the mother in our species, so I shall argue below, are much stronger than those found in any other species. In short, contrary to most incest theorists, I shall argue that if the (mother-son) incest taboo represents the transition from the state of nature to that of culture, it is because the intensity of the incestuous attachment to the mother is much stronger in human (culture) than in animal (nature) societies. A comparison of human with infrahuman primate societies—for convenience' sake this discussion will be restricted to primates, our closest animal relatives—can reveal why this is the case.

For obvious biological reasons it is the mother with whom any primate infant, human or infrahuman, sustains its most intimate emotional and physical relationship. It is she primarily who suckles, trains, and plays with him. It is her voice, her body, and her face that the infant knows best, and it is she whom above all others he seeks out for pleasure, protection, and comfort. As a consequence, it is the mother who is the primary object of the infant's emotional attachment. If, then, even the infant—as we observed in chapter 4—is a sexual creature and capable of sexual arousal, it is not unreasonable to assume that the early attachment to the mother has important libidinal overtones, and that the mother, therefore, is the object of the earliest libidinal attachment. Despite these similarities between humans and other primates, the incestuous attachment to the mother is much stronger and especially problematic in humans because of two important biological characteristics that are unique to humans: the suppression of estrus and prolonged infantile dependency.

Among infrahuman primates there is an incompatibility between sexuality and mothering because at the height of estrus, when the females are in a state of sexual "mania" or "frenzy," as the primatologists call it, they have little interest in mothering or, for that matter, in any other activity except sex. Hence, mothering can only occur during anestrus—the period in which the female is not sexually receptive—which, apart from the normal sexual cycle, begins immediately following pregnancy and continues until the end of lactation. When, at the end of lactation, estrus returns, the juvenile is already weaned, and since typically infantile helplessness does not extend beyond weaning, the mother's indifference to her offspring during estrus does not endanger their welfare since they are no longer dependent upon her for care and nurturance. Indeed, at the conclusion of weaning the juvenile's relationship with the mother is typically and abruptly severed. Thus, in those primate societies consisting of mother-child families, the juvenile is usually driven off by the mother when, at the conclusion of weaning, she enters estrus, while in those with biparental families, he is usually driven off by her consort. In either case, he usually joins a group of juveniles who, with some few exceptions, are permanently "peripheralized" (as the primatologists say).

Since, then, mother and son are separated following weaning, and since their separation is socially enforced at least until the son achieves maturity—when, in a few cases, he may force himself upon the dominant adult male(s)—there is no opportunity for his early attachment to the mother to become intensified by a continuing relationship with her. (For a more extensive treatment, see Bischof 1975; Chance and Jolly 1970; Fox 1980; Lancaster 1979; Rowell 1972.)

Among humans, the mother-child relationship is very different. Since infantile helplessness is prolonged, and cultural acquisition complex, it is necessary that the child remain dependent upon the mother (or mother surrogate) long after the completion of weaning. And since, with the suppression of estrus, the human female is not characterized by sexual mania, her interest in sex, though continuous, does not interfere with her motivation or ability to care for her young children. Since, then, there is no incompatibility between mating and mothering among humans, human offspring live with and remain dependent upon their mothers for many years, not excluding the "phallic" period (when the early libidinal attachment to the mother receives strong reinforcement) and puberty (when sexuality may erupt explosively).

In short, since the son's relationship with the mother may persist throughout childhood and even into puberty, thereby intensifying his early emotional attachment to her, and since that attachment is based on *both* libidinal and dependency feelings, it is reasonable to expect the incestuous attachment of the son to the mother to be much stronger in humans than in primates. For the same reason, one would expect the attachment to the mother to be much stronger than the incestuous attachment to the sister. Although brother and sister live together, they never have—indeed, they are prohibited from having—the intimate physical relationship that the son has with his mother.

Strangely enough, Malinowski (unlike most of his followers) fully recognized the strength of the boy's incestuous attachment to the mother, as well as the critical challenge that it posed for his contention that the Oedipus complex is confined to "patriarchal" families of the Western type. Indeed, in a long rhapsodic passage he expatiates in concrete detail on the erotic feelings of the young boy for his mother (*SR*:212–14). At the same time he also observes that since lovers employ the same organ zones and behavioral modes in their physical interaction with each other that mother and child employ in their interaction, the male's later induction into the "erotic life" may arouse in him "disturbing memories" of the relationship with his mother, because she "remains in the foreground of [his] emotional interests throughout his life." That being the case, Malinowski continues, before the boy reaches sexual maturity it is necessary that "all sensuality felt toward the mother become repressed." That is achieved by inculcating in the boy emotions of "reverence, dependence [and] respect" toward the mother so that if a "subconscious temptation of incest" is aroused when he is mature, it is muted by its "blending" with these nonsexual emotions.

The above analysis represents Malinowski's conception of what happens to the early incestuous attachment to the mother in the West (and some other societies), but it is not what happens (according to him) in matrilineal societies, in which the "passionate" attachment of the infant to the mother spontaneously disappears by the time the boy reaches the "phallic" stage of development, the very stage when genital love for her is normally expected to appear. Unfortunately, however, his argument on behalf of this claim, as was indicated in chapter 2, is less than convincing. In a nutshell, Malinowski nowhere indicates how or why the spontaneous disappearance of the boy's passionate attachment to the mother occurs. *That* it occurs, however, he is quite sure on the grounds (it will be recalled) that, when he asked the Trobriand men whether they wished to have intercourse with their mothers, they ridiculed the very suggestion. Such a response, he argued, proves that a "repressed Oedipus complex" cannot possibly exist in the Trobriands.

Although I have already dealt with this "proof" in chapter 2, it is nevertheless worth repeating because most other critics of the notion that incestuous motives might be repressed adduce exactly the same argument. Briefly, the argument is invalid on three counts. First, although it now seems unlikely that the boy's incestuous wishes in regard to the mother are ever—to use Freud's metaphor—"smashed" in childhood (as a result of castration anxiety), it does seem to be the case that in some individuals and in some societies those wishes do undergo a gradual process of extinction, coordinate with the cessation of childhood sexuality (sexual "latency"). Second, even in those individuals and societies in which incestuous wishes regarding the mother persist into adulthood, it is rare that the adult mother is the object of these wishes. Rather, it is the mother of childhood—or, rather, his mental representation of her—on whom the son's incestuous wishes remain fixated. In the latter event—to come to the third reason—the son's fixation cannot be discovered by the mere asking because, typically, it is not in conscious awareness, which is precisely what is meant—to use Malinowski's expression—by a *"repressed Oedipus complex."* To that extent Westermarck and his followers are correct when they argue that incest taboos do not have the function of prohibiting incest (with mother or anyone else), not because incestuous wishes (as they contend) do not exist, but because typically the implementation of the incest taboos in childhood has achieved its intended function. In short, from this perspective, the function of incest taboos is not to signal to *adults* that their incestuous wishes must be inhibited, but rather to banish such wishes from *children* before they become adults.

If, then, the implementation of the mother-son incest taboo (a subject to which we shall return) typically results in the disappearance of the incestuous attachment to the childhood mother—as a result either of extinction, on the one hand, or of repression and reaction formation, on the other—to challenge the universality of such an attachment on the grounds that in some society (or societies) adults do not consciously experience any sexual feelings for the mother is clearly misguided. By that criterion, such an attachment does not exist in any society, whether "patriarchal" or matrilineal, not at any rate in its "normal" members. In short the evidence for the universality of a motivational disposition to mother-son incest remains unaffected by this challenge.

Since, then, that evidence is very strong, and since (as we argued above) the existence of the incestuous dimension of the Oedipus complex renders its aggressive dimension all but axiomatic, the only appropriate response to the question, "Is the Oedipus complex universal?" is "How could it possibly not be?" Even in those primate societies in which females have no permanent consorts—the multimale societies of trooping monkeys—and in which, therefore, there can be no rivalry between son and father, powerful rivalry nevertheless exists between the peripheralized young males as a group and the dominant males who monopolize the females (Chance and Jolly 1970). In single-male primate societies, on the other hand, whether those of the monogamous gibbon (Carpenter 1940) or the polygynous hamadryas baboon (Kummer 1968), the rivalry is directly and explicitly between father and son.

In sum, there is only one obvious retort to the above riposte. If there were a human society in which mothers did not have male consorts—so that the son had no adult rival for the love of the mother—in such a society the Oedipus complex (by definition) would not exist. So far as we know, however, no human society of that type exists, or has ever existed. The "matrifocal" households—widely prevalent in the Caribbean (Smith 1956) and among lower class American blacks (Rainwater and Yancey

1967)—do not constitute an exception to that generalization because typically a husband-father is intermittently present or else the mother brings a series of temporary lovers into the household. That being the case, although there is no evidence one way or the other, I would also expect these New World matrifocal households to produce an Oedipus complex. This expectation is supported by the findings of Gough (1953) that an Oedipus complex is found among the Nayar, an Indian caste of the Malabar Coast, despite the fact that Nayar women typically take a series of lovers rather than living with a permanent consort.

That the Oedipus complex, according to this analysis, would be expected to be universal does not imply, I hasten to add, that it would also be expected to be cross-culturally uniform. On the contrary, since we know (from Western data) that the Oedipus complex is variable within societies, we would then expect that it would exhibit a wide range of variability across societies. That is the thesis I want to explore in the following section.

Cross-cultural Variability in the Oedipus Complex

Since the Oedipus complex may be said to have three important dimensions—structure, intensity, and outcome—in principle at least it could be expected to display cross-cultural variability in all three. Let us begin with its structure. By the "structure" of the Oedipus complex I mean the members—in addition to the boy himself—who make up the Oedipal triangle and who are the objects, therefore, of his sexual and aggressive wishes.

If in the classical Oedipus complex it is the boy's biological parents who are the objects of those wishes, that is not to be explained, surely, by the closeness of their genetic relationship, nor again by some instinctual vectorial dimension of the sexual and aggressive drives. Rather, that particular Oedipal triangle is best accounted for by the sociological fact that the boy and his biological parents, typically constituting a social group and inhabiting a common household, sustain certain modes of social relationships with each other. It is these relationships that account for the biological parents, specifically, becoming the objects of his sexual and aggressive wishes. Hence, variability in these relationships could be expected to result in corresponding and predictable variability in the structure of the Oedipal triangle. Thus, for example, if there were a society in which, rather than belonging to a common residential household, parents and children were distributed in different households, it might then be expected that the child's mother-surrogate (rather than his biological mother) would be the focus of his libidinal wishes, and that her consort (rather than his biological father) would be the focus of his aggressive wishes. At the moment, however, such a society is not known.

If, then, there is no theoretical reason why the adult members of the Oedipal triangle must consist of the boy's biological mother and father, it might well be the case that in some society this triangle consists of the boy, his sister, and his mother's brother. Malinowski's claim that this is the case in the Trobriands was rejected (in chapter 2) not on theoretical, but on empirical grounds: neither the composition of the Trobriand household nor the social relationships that obtain within the nuclear family display the characteristics that might expectably produce that particular structural variant of the classical Oedipus triangle. For exactly the same reason neither this nor any other structural variant of the classical Oedipus triangle has been reported at a total societal level for any other society, which does not mean that such a variant or variants may not occur in individual cases or in certain subgroups in some societies, or that some variant may not be reported in the future for some (as yet unknown) total society.

Although the structure of the Oedipus complex, while variable in principle, seems to be universal in fact, this is not the case in regard to its two other attributes—its intensity and outcome—in which cross-cultural variability is not only a theoretical expectation but an ethnographic fact. Since variability in the intensity of the Oedipus complex was discussed in the previous chapters, we shall focus here on variability in its outcome, especially since the latter attribute has important social and cultural consequences. Moreover, since the implementation of the incest taboo is a major determinant of its outcome, we shall limit our discussion to that determinant alone.

Since libidinal desires for the mother may be present, as we have seen, in the nursing infant, the implementation of the incest taboo may be said to begin with weaning, which is also the time when the child is usually banned from the mother's bed and when, in general, he is discouraged from continuing those more intimate forms of physical contact with the mother that she had previously permitted, if not actively encouraged. The diminution, if not cessation, of these intimate forms of bodily contact with the mother during this—the pre-Oedipal—period does not, of course, lead to the extinction of the boy's libidinal desires for her, especially since those desires are intensified when he enters the "phallic" stage of psychosexual development. At the latter stage, therefore, the mother-son incest taboo is implemented in all societies by still other means which (in varying degrees) result in its internalization, i.e., in the acquisition of a motivational disposition on the part of the boy to comply with the prohibition. These means and the process of internalization are conceived of differently by different theorists.

For cognitive theorists, the implementation of the mother-son incest taboo, like the implementation of any other cultural prohibition, is achieved by the usual processes of enculturation, i.e., by verbal instruction, including instruction in the punitive consequences attendant upon its violation. For social learning theorists that kind of instruction is not sufficient to achieve the internalization of the taboo unless it is accompanied by various socialization techniques—techniques of positive and negative reinforcement—which provide the boy with important incentives for complying with the taboo. Psychoanalytic theorists, who also stress the importance of socialization, emphasize the signal importance of castration anxiety as the motivational basis for compliance with the taboo. As they see it, the threats (negative reinforcement) which are used to sever his incestuous attachment to the mother lead to the son's fantasized expectation of castration as the punishment for incest with the mother.

Whether it is achieved by the one means or the other, if the implementation of the incest taboo leads to its internalization, compliance with the taboo is achieved either by the extinction of the boy's incestuous desire for his mother or by its repression, the latter often being accompanied by a reaction formation against the desire, i.e., by an emotional aversion to sexual contact with the mother. In sum, if the taboo is internalized, the boy's incestuous attachment to the mother either disappears entirely (extinction) or, although persisting unconsciously (repression), disappears from conscious awareness. Why the internalization of the taboo results in the one consequence rather than the other is a question concerning which there are many, but few satisfactory, answers.

Extinction and repression, however, are not the only possible outcomes of the incestuous attachment to the mother. If, for example, the implementation of the incest taboo by any of the processes mentioned above is only partially successful in promoting its internalization, the son's libidinal attachment to the mother is not extinguished, and although it may be repressed, it undergoes only weak or incomplete repression. In Bengal, for example, mother and son—so Roy (1975:125) observes—remain "highly cathected libidinal objects [for] . . . a lifetime." (For other parts of India, see also Carstairs 1956 and Kakar 1978.) Similarly, the typical male in the Mexican town of San Juan, according to Hunt (1971:129), "has never been able to transfer his libidinal energies from his mother to an outsider," thereby manifesting a "typical Mediterranean pattern." (For other parts of Mexico, see also Bushnell 1958.) That such an outcome is a "Mediterranean pattern" is readily discerned, for example, from Parsons's (1969) description of the mother-son relationship in Italy (Naples). The same pattern is also found, however, in East Asia. In Japan, for example, as Tanaka (1981:16) observes, the mother-son relationship is characterized by the "continuous presence of unresolved libidinality." In many societies in which the incestuous attachment to the mother is incompletely repressed, other means than those mentioned above are used for the implementation of the incest taboo, as we shall see below.

Let us first, however, turn from the incestuous attachment to the mother to briefly comment on the possible outcomes of the boy's hostility to the father, the other dimension of the Oedipus complex. Since, as we have seen, the boy's hostility to the father sustains a correlative relationship with his love for the mother, the outcome of his Oedipal hostility is systematically related to the outcome of his Oedipal love. In short, it is the entire Oedipus complex whose outcome may variously take the form of extinction, repression, or incomplete repression.

While all three outcomes may be found in a single society, as we know from clinical evidence in the West, it is usually the case (as I have been suggesting) that one of them is dominant. Since, however, the dominant outcome (as I have also been suggesting) is not the same in all societies, we may now say that this—the second dimension—of the Oedipus complex is cross-culturally variable not only in principle but in fact.

Although of some interest in itself, the cross-cultural variability in the outcome of the Oedipus complex is anthropologically important because its outcome has social and cultural consequences. Since, then, the differences in the psychological characteristics of these three outcomes are nontrivial, the differences in their variable social and cultural consequences are likewise nontrivial. The latter differences are especially marked when we compare societies in which extinction and repression are the dominant outcomes with those in which incomplete repression is dominant.

Operationally defined, a "weak" or "incomplete" repression of the Oedipus complex is one in which repression is insufficiently powerful to preclude the conscious arousal of the boy's incestuous wishes for the mother (and hence his hostile wishes toward the father) under conditions of incestuous temptation. Hence, those societies in which incomplete repression is the dominant outcome of the Oedipus complex are societies in which the implementation of the taboos on mother-son incest and father-son aggression by the enculturation and socialization techniques described above is not entirely successful in achieving their internalization. This being the case, rather than relying on the boy's own psychological resources—extinction, repression, and reaction formation—to ensure compliance with those taboos, many of those societies achieve compliance by means of social and cultural resources, as well.

In short, so far as their social and cultural consequences are concerned, the first notable difference between societies in which extinction and repression are the dominant outcome of the Oedipus complex and those in which incomplete repression is its dominant outcome is that the latter societies (much more often than the former) practice child extrusion and painful initiation rites. These customs (as was noted in a previous chapter) ensure compliance with the twin Oedipal prohibitions by reducing the opportunities for incestuous and aggressive temptation or by strengthening the incomplete repression of the boy's sexual and aggressive Oedipal wishes. Let us briefly examine each of these customs, beginning with child extrusion.

When boys—and in some societies, girls too—are extruded from the parental household, their subsequent residence, as the cross-cultural record indicates, is highly variable. It may be an age-graded dormitory, a men's house, a children's village, some other household, a boarding school, or the like. Whatever the conscious motives for these practices may be—depending on the society, they include the reduction of the son's rivalry with the father (Wilson 1949; Spiro 1958), the prevention of his witnessing the primal scene (Elwin 1968), economic apprenticeship (Aries 1962), educational advancement (Gathorne-Hardy 1977), the economic advantage of adoption (Powell 1957), and others— they have the consequence (among others) of separating the son from his parents, thereby reducing the opportunities for the arousal of his sexual and aggressive Oedipal wishes. When, at some later age, more frequent interaction with the parents is once again resumed, his libidinal and aggressive impulses have typically been rechanneled. Son extrusion in human societies has its analogue, it will be recalled, in the peripheralization of male juveniles in primate societies. By the latter process, the juveniles are deprived of the opportunity of acting upon their sexual and aggressive impulses toward their mothers and adult males, respectively.

The second consequence of the incomplete repression of the Oedipus complex—which, like the first, constitutes a cultural resource for enhancing the compliance with the taboos on mother-son incest and father-son aggression—is the practice of painful initiation rites. Although the conscious, culturally constituted explanations for these rites only infrequently relate them to the Oedipal issue we have been addressing here, the ethnographic descriptions of these practices and of the initiates' psychological reactions to them provide strong evidence for the thesis that these rites, like child extrusion, constitute an important cultural resource for ensuring compliance with the taboos on incest with the mother and aggression toward the father.[4]

If, however, child extrusion achieves this end by removing the son from the locus of Oedipal sexual and aggressive temptation, initiation rites achieve the same end (according to some

---

4. For four superb descriptions of these rites and of the emotional reactions of the initiates in New Guinea, I especially recommend Herdt (1980, 1982), Poole (1982), Read (1965), and Tuzin (1980).

theorists at least) by removing these Oedipal wishes from the son. That is, by hazing, isolation, physical torture, ordeals, and phallic mutilation (circumcision, subincision, and superincision), these rites arouse in the boys intense fear and anxiety—often, in my view, castration anxiety—regarding the father and/or the father-figure initiators (Fox 1980:159), thereby serving to break the boys' incestuous attachment to their mothers (Hiatt 1971:81) and inhibit their aggression to their fathers. In sum, these rites, I am suggesting, serve to strengthen the (incomplete) repression of the boys' Oedipal (sexual and aggressive) wishes, and in some cases they might perhaps lead to their extinction. That these painful and often brutal rites also provide a culturally sanctioned (and ritually limited) opportunity for men to express their complementary Oedipal hostility to boys—rationalized, of course, by the ideology of helping them achieve social and cultural maturity—seems equally obvious, as Reik ([1919] 1946) suggested some years ago.

I must hasten to say, however, that an Oedipal interpretation of these rites not only is *not* obvious to other commentators, but has typically been rejected by anthropologists (see Langness 1974) and psychoanalysts (see Lidz and Lidz 1977) alike. Since I believe that rituals, like most other cultural activities, have multiple meanings, I have little difficulty in accepting most of the sociological and psychological meanings that other commentators have attributed to these rites. But I have great difficulty in ignoring their Oedipal and complementary Oedipal meanings, which, in the light of recent descriptions (see footnote 4), are just too blatant to overlook. Indeed, from these descriptions I would argue that societies which practice initiation rites of the ferocity found in—and perhaps confined to—New Guinea and Australia are societies in which the incomplete repression of the childhood Oedipus complex is most pronounced.

As an illustration of their "blatant" Oedipal and complementary meanings, consider Herdt's (1982) description of the boy's initiation rite among the Sambia of Papua New Guinea. The first stage of the rite, which consists of forcible nose-bleeding, administered by the men on boys of seven to ten years, is a "violent assault whose effects are probably close to producing authentic trauma," the boys themselves referring to their fright by such expressions as " 'I feared they were going to kill me.' " If the boys resist the men and cry, as they often do, the men "have little pity" for them, and they are "severely dealt with by prolonging the action and thereby brutalizing it." Herdt is hardly exaggerating in calling it "an act of raw aggression." Similarly, in the third stage, performed for boys thirteen to sixteen, a line of warriors, appearing as ghosts and enemies, surround them and, plucking bows and arrows, hooting, and shouting, they again forcibly nose-bleed the boys, who are now in a state of "terror."

That this aggression both gratifies the complementary Oedipal complex of the men and is intended to contain the Oedipal wishes of the boys is indicated by Herdt's comments. Nose-bleeding is described by the Sambia as "punishment" for the boys for their insubordination to their fathers and elders. That this insubordination includes Oedipal insubordination is reflected both in the warning given the boys that they may never again so much as touch, hold, talk with, eat with, or look at their mothers and in the conscious and unconscious symbolic equation of nose and penis in Sambia thought and culture. Because of their early and exclusive attachment to them, Herdt comments, the boys "must be traumatically detached from their mothers and kept away from them at all costs." In later stages of the rite, those following puberty, references to the mother drop out, and, instead, the boys are admonished by the initiators to avoid other women, especially married women; should they disobey, they are warned, they will be killed. Indeed, beginning with the separation of the boys from their mothers at the first stage of the initiation rite until their marriage following the last stage, males are never again alone with a woman, and throughout that period ritual aggression is used by the older males to "instill [in them] fear and obedience" so that their avoidance of females will be maintained.

Although the Sambia begin their first stage of initiation in early childhood, it is important to note that there are important cross-cultural differences in the age at which these rites, as well as child extrusion, occur. In some societies they take place in childhood, in others not until puberty. Insofar, then, as these customs are (among other things) cultural resources for the implementation of the taboos on mother-son incest and father-son aggression, it may perhaps be assumed that those societies in which they do not take place until puberty are societies in which the boy's repression of his incestuous and aggressive wishes, though incomplete, is sufficiently strong to prevent them from passing through the repressive barrier throughout childhood, and that it is only at puberty, with the eruption of his sexual urges, that his own psychological resources are inadequate to that task. If that assumption is correct, it then follows that, conversely, those societies in which these cultural resources are already brought into play in childhood are societies in which the boy's psychological resources for coping with his Oedipal wishes are inadequate from the very beginning.

Whether the one or the other, however, if the Oedipus complex is incompletely repressed in childhood, there is a special urgency for containing the boy's Oedipal wishes either before or at the time he reaches puberty, for it is then that he is physiologically capable of acting upon his sexual wishes and physically capable of acting upon his aggressive wishes. That is the time, in short, by which it is especially urgent that cultural resources be brought into play either to strengthen the incomplete repression of his Oedipal wishes (painful initiation rites) or to reduce his opportunities for acting upon them (extrusion).

If, then, son extrusion and painful initiation are most likely to be practiced in societies in which the Oedipus complex is incompletely repressed, and least likely in those which exhibit the two other outcomes, we can now see that differences in the outcome of the Oedipus complex have other important consequences as well. Since, for example, societies in which the Oedipus complex is extinguished or fully repressed are unlikely to practice child extrusion, the family is more likely to remain an intact residential group than in those in which, as a consequence of the incomplete repression of the Oedipus complex, the son is extruded from the household. But not all intact family households are the same; among other things they vary importantly in their emotional texture. Thus, the emotional texture of the family in which the Oedipus complex is extinguished and in which, therefore, children can live together with parents in emotional comfort, without suffering intrapsychic conflicts regarding their sexual and aggressive Oedipal wishes, is very different from the emotional texture of the family in which the Oedipus complex is repressed and in which, therefore, the integrity of the family household is purchased at the cost of persistent unconscious struggles with Oedipal wishes. These differences, of course, are much more pronounced during puberty than during childhood.

Differences of another type distinguish societies which, because of incomplete repression of the Oedipus complex, practice painful initiation rites from those which, because of its extinction or full repression, have no need to practice them. Thus, in many tribal societies, initiation rites can be of unimaginable complexity, extending over a period of many years, and consuming a large proportion of their social and economic resources. Indeed, in many of these societies—most notably those of New Guinea—these rites may be said to dominate the lives of the members of the group, constituting the main focus of their interests and action (see Herdt 1980; Read 1965; Tuzin 1980). A funnel for so many social and economic resources, and for so much emotional energy, a cultural focus of this type has still other consequences. For example, it significantly limits the options of these societies for choosing alternative (and perhaps more productive) cultural means for the investment of emotional energy and the allocation of social and economic resources. Moreover, inasmuch as a cultural focus of this type is both a highly elaborated magical response to unconscious wishes and fears, as well as a stimulus for the arousal of still others, it may serve to reinforce the skewed ratio of magical to realistic thinking found in many of these tribal societies. If so, this would account not only for the high proportion of magical (alternatively, primary-process, prelogical, animistic) thinking that, in my view, is one of their singular psychological characteristics, but also for their seeming inability to evolve an alternative cultural focus (or foci) based on realistic (alternatively, secondary-process, logical, nonanimistic) thinking.

There are, of course, many other social and cultural consequences attendant upon the variability in the outcome of the Oedipus complex which, since their explication would require a separate book, can only be mentioned here. Thus, in societies in which unconscious Oedipal conflicts require persistent repression for their containment, the Oedipus complex may undergo structural transformations as a result of defensively motivated projections and displacements which importantly affect other social relationships and institutions. That, indeed, is Jones's (1924) contention regarding the boy's hostility toward the mother's brother in the Trobriands, which, so he argues, represents the displacement of his Oedipal hostility for his father. Gough (1953) interprets the nephew's hostility toward the mother's brother among the Nayar in the same manner.[5]

Kin relationships, however, are not the only social relationships in which repressed Oedipal conflicts are projected and displaced. Political (Lasswell 1960), religious (Erikson 1958), and economic (Brown 1959) institutions, to mention only a few, constitute some of the larger social arenas for the symbolic expression of a repressed Oedipus complex. Thus, to advert to its hostility dimension, rebellious attitudes toward authority figures often have their psychodynamic source in repressed Oedipal hostility, the former being a vehicle for the displacement or sublimation of the latter (see Erikson 1963; Feuer 1969; Rothman and Lichter 1982). The same process occurs in regard to the sexual dimension of the Oedipus complex. Thus, for example, the strong male involvement in the Marian cult in southern Italy (Parsons 1969) and Mexico (Bushnell 1958) is often interpreted as a sublimation of the repressed Oedipal attachment to the mother.

Since religion (because, perhaps, of its frequent use of family idioms) like politics (for the same reason) is an especially important cultural domain for the expression of repressed Oedipal conflicts, it might be added that other differences between societies in which the Oedipus complex is repressed in contrast to those in which it is extinguished may also be seen in such diverse religious phenomena as ritual circumcision and clitoridectomy, ascetic abstinences and self-torture, sexualized goddesses and witches, celibate priests and priestesses, mystical and trance states, and many others.

Although further examples would require a monograph, this brief discussion has perhaps been sufficient to suggest that the continuing debates over the Oedipus complex are debates not merely about a passing episode in the psychological develop-

5. Structural transformations in the initial formation of the Oedipus complex are also found in its symbolic expression in myth, as Paul (1980) has shown in his perceptive analysis of the hostility dimension of the Oedipus complex in Greek, Judaic, and Christian Oedipal myths.

ment of the child. Rather, they are debates about a psychological constellation which, as this discussion has attempted to show, has pervasive cultural, social, and psychological consequences.

The Making of a Scientific Myth

In the previous two sections I argued that although the universality of the Oedipus complex is rendered highly likely by the child's potentiality for sexual and aggressive arousal, inasmuch as the intensity and distribution of sexual and aggressive wishes are each a product of the social relationships that the child sustains with those adults who constitute his "significant others," in principle we would expect to find cross-cultural variability in the Oedipus complex as a function of the variability in those relationships. That this expectation is most probably actualized, however, in regard only to the intensity and outcome, but not the structure, of the Oedipus complex is not surprising. Since the classical Oedipal triangle—consisting of mother, father, and son—is determined by the twin facts that the child's early mothering figure is the first and most important object of his sexual wishes, and that his perceived rival for her love is the consequent object of his hostility, cross-cultural variability in this structure would be expected if, but only if, there were some range of variability in the social recruitment to the mothering role. Since at the *societal* level, however, it is the biological mother who is the child's central (if not exclusive) early mothering figure, and the biological father his most salient rival for her love in all known societies, it is understandable that the structure of the Oedipus complex, although cross-culturally variable in principle, is most probably invariant in fact.

This, of course, brings us back to our point of departure, the controversy over the Trobriand Oedipus complex. For the very nub of Malinowski's contention that the structure of the nuclear complex (as he preferred to put it)[6] is culturally variable not only in principle, but also in fact, consists of his claim that although the biological mother is the primary mothering figure in the

---

6. Since, for Malinowski, the Oedipus complex is a cultural product, he used "nuclear complex" as a cover term for all possible cultural variants, reserving "Oedipus complex" for that particular variant in which mother and father are the objects, respectively, of the child's sexual and aggressive impulses.

Trobriands, it is the sister who is the primary object of the boy's libidinal desires. Since that paradoxical claim was already shown in chapter 2 to be refuted by Malinowski's own evidence, there is no need to repeat that demonstration. Rather, in this final section, I wish to address the remarkable fact that this paradoxical claim has been accepted with almost no skepticism or critical inquiry for fifty years.

Given the powerful evidence (discussed earlier in the chapter) for the universality of the motivational disposition to mother-son incest, if it were reported that in some society the mother is not an incestuous object for the son, such a report would, of course, be rather surprising. But since the history of science is a history of persistent refutations of well-established generalizations, there would be no reason to greet such a report with special skepticism. In claiming, therefore, that it is a "remarkable fact" that Malinowski's report of such a finding in the Trobriands has not been greeted with sufficient skepticism, it is not because that report challenges an established generalization, but because in the context of Trobriand culture the absence of an incestuous attachment to the mother is twice anomalous.

The first anomaly consists in the fact that of the three types of incestuous desire that might, in principle, be found in any male, the desire of the son for the mother is, alone, reported to be absent in the Trobriands, while that of the father for the daughter is reported to be as strong as it is purported to be in the West, and that of the brother for the sister stronger by far. This gestalt is all the more anomalous since typically the boy's incestuous attachment to the mother is, if anything, much stronger than the other two; and it becomes still more anomalous when it is recalled that the incestuous attachment of the Trobriand daughter to the father, unlike that of the son to the mother, is reported to be of normally expected Oedipal intensity.

In claiming that because it is anomalous Malinowski's report should have been greeted with skepticism, I am by no means suggesting that its truth or accuracy should therefore have been impugned. If "anomaly" is glossed as "puzzle," and if we follow Kuhn (1962:chapter 4) in viewing science as a puzzle-solving enterprise, then, rather than impugning the accuracy of an anomalous finding, scientific skepticism merely signals the existence of yet another puzzle to be solved. In the case of this Trobriand puzzle, one simple solution immediately suggests itself. Since, as has already been observed, it is their physical and emotional intimacy that accounts for the son's incestuous attachment to the mother, part of the Trobriand puzzle would be solved if it were the case that the most intimate relationship of the young boy is with some woman (or women) other than the biological mother. If, moreover, it were also the case that this structural arrangement did not affect the relationship of the male to either his sister or his daughter, the other parts of the puzzle would be solved, as well, and the skepticism could be laid to rest.

Unfortunately, however, the ethnographic facts are the very opposite of this proposed solution. As we have seen in the previous chapter, all the conditions that highlight the mother-son relationship as the primary arena for the boy's most intense incestuous struggles in the "normally expectable" family are present in the Trobriands as well—and then some! In short, there is nothing in Malinowski's account that might solve the puzzle of why it is that in a family and socialization system of the Trobriand type the sister and daughter are the objects of the male's incestuous desires, whereas the mother is not. That, indeed, is why I characterized Malinowski's claim as anomalous.

Perhaps, however, the solution to this anomaly might be found by taking another tack. For just as the problem of inflation can be tackled from either the supply or the demand side of the market, the solution to an ethnographically anomalous finding can sometimes be found not in an antecedent, but in a consequent condition. Specifically, if the reported absence of a normally expectable incestuous attachment to the mother were accompanied by the absence of a normally expectable mother-son incest taboo, the former report would not then constitute an anomaly (although the absence of such an attachment would still have to be explained by some as yet unknown, and theoretically unexpected, antecedent condition). Unfortunately, the ethnographic reality is once again the reverse of the proposed solution: the mother-son incest taboo is, in fact, present in the Trobriands. Moreover, the presence of this taboo not only leaves the anomaly unresolved, but creates yet another: if the boy has no incestuous desire for the mother, why should there be a taboo prohibiting incest with her? This second anomaly, of course, could be resolved by simply rejecting the assumption on which it is based, viz., that taboos exist to prevent the practice of the tabooed actions. But that requires at least a brief discussion of the historical debates regarding incest taboos.

It was Frazer ([1887] 1910:vol. 4, p. 97 ff.) who first converted the above assumption about the function of taboos into the generally accepted theory of incest taboos. Since, following from that assumption, the function of incest taboos is the prevention of incest with their stipulated targets, the existence of these taboos, so Frazer argued, implies the existence of incestuous desire for those very targeted persons.[7] This theory, however, has had its opponents from its very inception. Most of them, following Westermarck's ([1906–8] 1924–26:vol. 2, p. 368) view that sexual aversion develops between family members who live in proximity to each other from an early age, argue that incest taboos are merely the institutionalized expression of sexual aversions.

Although the acceptance of this theory would resolve the anomaly of the reported co-occurrence in the Trobriands of a mother-son incest taboo and the absence of an incestuous desire for the mother, there are powerful grounds for rejecting it as invalid. One could point, for example, to the evidence in support of the motivational disposition to nuclear family incest which was summarized earlier in this chapter. Again, one could point to Lindzey's reformulation of Frazer's hypothesis in terms of the adaptive framework of evolutionary biology, a reformulation which, in my view, is unimpeachable. "It seems unlikely that there would have been universal selection in favor of such a taboo if there were not widespread impulses toward expression of the prohibited act" (Lindzey 1967:1055). Rather, however, than evoking these general empirical and theoretical grounds in

7. Why it is that all societies have wanted to prevent incest at least within the nuclear family is a question that has been variously answered, but all the proposed answers point to one or more of the following maladaptive consequences of the widespread practice of nuclear family incest which are precluded by compliance with incest taboos: (1) biological impairment attendant upon inbreeding (see Lindzey 1967), (2) collapse of the family authority structure, because of the sexual rivalry between father and son, with the attendant difficulty of cultural transmission (see Malinowski [1927] 1955:216), (3) structural breakdown of the family attendant upon role confusion (see Parsons 1954), (4) breakdown of social alliances attendant upon family endogamy (see Lévi-Strauss [1949] 1969:chapters 4 and 29).

refutation of Westermarck's theory, it is enough—and in this context much more relevant—to refute it on specific Trobriand grounds.

The latter grounds consist of evidence that proclaims loudly and clearly that rather than sexual aversion, at least some Tro-brianders who live in close propinquity develop strong sexual feelings for each other. That is how Malinowski, at any rate, describes the relationship between brothers and sisters in the Trobriands, and (to a lesser degree) between fathers and daughters. At the same time there are taboos in the Trobriands which both prohibit and (as Malinowski makes quite clear) are intended to prevent incest between the members of these dyads. For the Trobriands, then, there can be no doubt about the functional relationship between incestuous desires and incest taboos, so far at least as these two dyads are concerned. Hence, for the Trobriands the co-occurrence of the mother-son incest taboo and the absence of incestuous desires for her is clearly an anomaly, not because it violates a (disputed) theoretical assumption, but because in the Trobriand cultural configuration their co-occurrence is incongruous.

If, however, it were still contended that this finding is not anomalous—because the anomaly now derives from merely another theoretical assumption, that of pattern consistency—this contention would convert an unresolved anomaly into an unresolved dilemma. For if it were held, on the one hand, that the taboo on incest with the mother does not imply the existence of incestuous wishes for her, what possible explanation might then be offered for the taboos on incest with the sister and daughter which, in fact, do correspond to known incestuous wishes for them? And if it were held, on the other hand, that the taboos on sister and daughter incest are explained by known incestuous wishes for them, how could it then be contended that it is invalid to infer the existence of incestuous wishes for the mother from the taboo prohibiting incest with her?

Malinowski, himself a leading proponent of Frazer's theory of incest taboos, was keenly aware of this dilemma, and, it will be recalled, he attempted to resolve it by holding to both of its horns. That is, while he held that incest taboos are valid measures of incestuous wishes, he also held that in the Trobriands the taboo on mother-son incest is "weak." Hence, he argued, just as the strong incestuous desire for the sister in the Trobriands is reflected in a "strong" brother-sister taboo, the weak desire for the mother is reflected in a "weak" mother-son taboo. Unfortunately, however, the facts (see above) are otherwise: there is simply no evidence for the putative weakness—whether absolute or relative—of the mother-son taboo. In short, despite Malinowski's attempt to resolve it, the second anomaly in his reported absence of an incestuous attachment to the mother in the Trobriands remains—like the first—unresolved.

The fact, then, that neither of these anomalies can be resolved—or, to put it more cautiously, that neither has been resolved thus far—must surely constitute sufficient reason to be skeptical of the report that the Trobriand son has no incestuous attachment to the mother. That this report, then, has not received the skeptical reception that normally greets an anomalous scientific report is not only, as I said above, a remarkable fact, but one which itself constitutes an intriguing intellectual problem. Since its solution could shed important light on the influence of scientific paradigms on the acceptance and persistence of scientific ideas, it is to be hoped that an investigation of the problem might some day be undertaken by an intellectual historian or a historian of science.

Although the causes for the unskeptical reaction to this anomalous report are still to be discovered, its consequence—with some notable exceptions—has been an uncritical acceptance of the putative Trobriand matrilineal complex. I would suggest, then, that if this report had been subjected to the probing scrutiny to which anomalous scientific findings are usually subject, the matrilineal complex would have been rejected (on the grounds adduced in chapter 2) as empirically unsupported rather than achieving the status of an incontrovertible finding of anthropological science. Nevertheless, it is not its weak empirical foundation that led me to characterize the Trobriand matrilineal complex a "scientific myth." This characterization stems, rather, from the uncritical acceptance of the reported finding— the absence of an incestuous attachment to the mother—on which its plausibility hangs, despite the fact that this finding is not only once, but twice, anomalous.

A myth, Malinowski taught us, enjoys uncritical acceptance because it serves important functions for those who believe it to be true. It would be well, therefore, if our hoped-for historian were to address yet another question in the course of his investigations: what functions might have been served by the acceptance of *this* myth? Indeed, since the role of the "will to believe" in the acceptance of scientific ideas is as prominent as the role that William James attributed to it in the acceptance of religious doctrines, it is entirely possible that the answer to this second question might simultaneously provide the answer to the first.

References

Abernethy, Virginia
  1979   Dominance and Sexual Behavior. *American Journal of Psychiatry* 131:813–17.

Aries, Philippe
  1962   *Centuries of Childhood.* New York: Knopf.

Austin, L.
  1934   Procreation among the Trobriand Islanders. *Oceania* 5:102–18.

Bagley, Christopher
  1969   Incest Behavior and Incest Taboo. *Social Problems* 16:505–19.

Bak, Robert C.
  1968   The Phallic Woman: The Ubiquitous Fantasy in Perversions. *Psychoanalytic Study of the Child* 23:15–36.

Bakan, David
  1971   *Slaughter of the Innocents.* San Francisco: Jossey-Bass.
  1979   *And They Took Themselves Wives.* San Francisco: Harper and Row.

Barnouw, Victor
  1973   *Culture and Personality.* Homewood: Dorsey.

Beals, Alan R.
  1979   *Culture in Process.* New York: Hall, Rinehart and Winston.

Becker, Ernest
  1973   *The Denial of Death.* New York: Free Press.

Bettelheim, Bruno
  1969   *The Children of the Dream*. London: Macmillan.
Bibring, Grete L.
  1953   On the "Passing of the Oedipus Complex" in a Matriarchal Family Setting. In Rudolph M. Loewenstein (ed.), *Drives, Affects, and Behavior*. New York: International Universities Press.
Bischof, Norbert
  1975   Comparative Ethology of Incest Avoidance. In Robin Fox (ed.), *Biosocial Anthropology*. London: Malaby Press.
Brandes, Stanley
  1980   *Metaphors of Masculinity: Sex and Status in Andalusian Folklore*. Philadelphia: University of Pennsylvania Press.
Broude, Gwen J.
  1980   Extramarital Sex Norms in Cross-Cultural Perspective. *Behavior Science Research* 15:181–218.
Brown, Norman O.
  1959   *Life against Death*. Middletown: Wesleyan University Press.
Brunswick, Ruth Mack
  1940   The Preoedipal Phase of the Libido Development. *Psychoanalytic Quarterly* 9:293–319.
Burton, Roger V., and John W. M. Whiting
  1961   The Absent Father and Cross-Sex Identity. *Merrill-Palmer Quarterly* 7:85–95.
Bushnell, John
  1958   La Virgen de Guadalupe as Surrogate Mother in San Juan Atzingo. *American Anthropologist* 60:261–65.
Buxbaum, Edith
  1970   *Troubled Children in a Troubled World*. New York: International Universities Press.
Campbell, Donald T., and Raoul Naroll
  1972   The Mutual Methodological Relevance of Anthropology and Psychology. In Francis L. K. Hsu (ed.), *Psychological Anthropology*. Cambridge, Massachusetts: Schenkman Publishing Company.

Campbell, J. K.
  1974   *Honour, Family, and Patronage*. New York: Oxford University Press.
Campbell, Joseph
  1956   *The Hero with a Thousand Faces*. New York: Meridian Books.
Carpenter, C. R.
  1940   A Field Study in Siam of the Behavior and Social Relations of the Gibbon (*Hylobatis lar*). *Comparative Psychology Monographs* 16:1–212.
Carstairs, G. Morris
  1956   *The Twice Born*. Bloomington: Indiana University Press.
Cavallin, Hector
  1966   Incestuous Fathers: A Clinical Report. *American Journal of Psychiatry* 122:1132–38.
Chance, Michael R. H., and Clifford J. Jolly
  1970   *Social Groups of Monkeys, Apes, and Men*. New York: Dutton.
Christian, William A.
  1972   *Person and God in a Spanish Valley*. New York: Seminar Press.
Cohen, Yehudi
  1964   *The Transition from Childhood to Adolescence*. Chicago: Aldine.
Cormier, Bruno, Miriam Kennedy, and Jadwiga Sangowicz
  1962   Psychodynamics of Father-Daughter Incest. *Canadian Psychiatric Association Journal* 7:203–17.
Demarest, William J.
  1977   Incest Avoidance in Human and Nonhuman Primates. In Suzanne Chevalier-Skolnikoff and Frank E. Poirier (eds.), *Primate Bio-Social Development*. New York: Garland Publishing.
Devereux, George
  1953   Why Oedipus Killed Laius: A Note on the Complementary Oedipus Complex. *International Journal of Psychoanalysis* 34:132–41.
  1973   The Self-Blinding of Oidipous in Sophokles *Oidipous Tyrannous*. *Journal of Hellenic Studies* 93:36–49.

Edmunds, Lowell, and Richard Ingber
1977   Psychological Writings on the Oedipus Legend: A Bibliography. *American Imago* 34:374–87.

Elwin, Verrier
1968   *The Kingdom of the Young.* Oxford: Oxford University Press.

Ember, Carol R.
1978   Men's Fear of Sex with Women: A Cross-Cultural Study. *Sex Roles* 4:657–78.

Ember, Carol R., and Melvin Ember
1973   *Cultural Anthropology.* New York: Appleton-Century-Crofts.

Erikson, Erik H.
1958   *Young Man Luther.* New York: W. W. Norton.
1963   *Childhood and Society.* New York: W. W. Norton.

Fenichel, Otto
1945   *The Psychoanalytic Theory of Neurosis.* New York: W. W. Norton.

Feuer, Lewis S.
1969   *The Conflict of Generations.* New York: Basic Books.

Fortes, Meyer
1977   Custom and Conscience in Anthropological Perspective. *International Review of Psychoanalysis* 4:127–54.

Fortune, R. F.
1932   *Sorcerers of Dobu: The Social Anthropology of the Dobu Islanders of the Western Pacific.* London: Routledge.

Fox, Robin
1980   *The Red Lamp of Incest.* New York: Dutton.

Frances, Vera, and Allen Frances
1976   The Incest Taboo and Family Structure. *Family Process* 15:235–44.

Frazer, James George
[1887]   1910
            Totemism and Exogamy. London: Macmillan.

Freud, Sigmund
[1908]   1968
            Family Romances. *The Standard Edition of the Complete Psychological Works of Sigmund Freud*, Vol. 9. London: Hogarth Press.

[1909] 1968
        Analysis of a Phobia in a Five-Year-Old Boy. *Standard Edition*, Vol. 10.
[1910] 1968
        A Special Type of Choice of Object Made by Men. *Standard Edition*, Vol. 11.
[1916– 1968
  17]   Introductory Lectures on Psychoanalysis. *Standard Edition*, Vol.16.
[1923] 1968
        The Ego and the Id. *Standard Edition*, Vol. 19.
[1924] 1968
        The Dissolution of the Oedipus Complex. *Standard Edition*, Vol.19.
[1925] 1968
        Some Psychical Consequences of the Anatomical Distinction between the Sexes. *Standard Edition*, Vol. 19.
[1931] 1968
        Female Sexuality. *Standard Edition*, Vol. 21.

Fromm, Erich
  1949 The Oedipus Complex and the Oedipus Myth. In Ruth Nanda Anshen (ed.), *The Family: Its Function and History*. New York: Harper.

Galenson, Eleanor, and Herman Roiphe
  1980 The Preoedipal Development of the Boy. *Journal of the American Psychoanalytic Association*. 28:805–27.

Gathorne-Hardy, Jonathan
  1977 *The Public School Phenomenon, 597–1977*. London: Hodder and Stoughton.

Gebhard, Paul H., John H. Gagnon, Wardell B. Pomeroy, and Cornelia V. Christenson
  1965 *Sex Offenders: An Analysis of Types*. New York: Harper and Row.

Goldman, R. P.
  1978 Fathers, Sons, and Gurus: Oedipal Confliction in the Sanskrit Epics. *Journal of Indian Philosophy* 6:325–92.

Gough, E. Kathleen
  1953 Female Initiation Rites on the Malabar Coast. *Journal of the Royal Anthropological Society* 85:45–80.

Greenacre, Phyllis
    1968   Perversions: General Considerations regarding Their Genetic and Dynamic Background. *Psychoanalytic Study of the Child* 23:47–62.

Hall, Calvin S., and Vernon J. Nordby
    1972   *The Individual and His Dreams*. New York: New American Library.

Hartland, Edwin Sydney
    1910   *Primitive Paternity*. London: David Nutt.

Herdt, Gilbert H.
    1980   *Guardians of the Flutes: Idioms of Masculinity*. New York: McGraw-Hill.
    1982   Fetish and Fantasy in Sambia Initiation. In Gilbert H. Herdt (ed.), *Rituals of Manhood*. Berkeley: University of California Press.

Herskovits, Melville and Frances
    1958   Sibling Rivalry, the Oedipus Complex, and Myth. *Journal of American Folklore* 71:1–15.

Hiatt, L. R.
    1971   Secret Pseudo-Procreation Rites among the Australian Aborigines. In L. R. Hiatt and C. Jayawardena (eds.), *Anthropology in Oceania*. San Francisco: Chandler.

Hoebel, E. Adamson
    1972   *Anthropology: The Study of Man*. New York: Random House.

Honigmann, John J.
    1967   *Personality in Culture*. New York: Harper and Row.

Hopkins, Keith
    1980   Brother-Sister Marriage in Roman Egypt. *Comparative Studies in Society and History* 22:303–54.

Horney, Karen
    1932   The Dread of Women. *International Journal of Psychoanalysis* 13:348–60.

Hunt, Robert C.
    1971   Component of Relationships in the Family: A Mexican Village. In Francis L. K. Hsu (ed.), *Kinship and Culture*. Chicago: Aldine.

Jonas, A. David, and Doris F. Jonas
    1975   A Biological Basis for the Oedipal Complex. *American Journal of Psychiatry* 132:602–6.

Jones, Ernest
 1925   Mother-Right and the Sexual Ignorance of Savages. *International Journal of Psychoanalysis* 6:109–30.
Justice, Blair, and Rita Justice
 1979   *The Broken Taboo.* New York: Human Sciences Press.
Kaffman, Mordecai
 1977   Sexual Standards and Behavior of the Kibbutz Adolescent. *American Journal of Orthopsychiatry* 47:207–17.
Kakar, Sudhir
 1978   *The Inner World.* Delhi: Oxford University Press.
Kardiner, Abram
 1939   *The Individual and His Society.* New York: Columbia University Press.
 1945   *The Psychological Frontiers of Society.* New York: Columbia University Press.
Kaufman, I. Charles
 1970   Biological Considerations of Parenthood. In Anthony E. James and Theresa Benedek (eds.), *Parenthood.* Boston: Little, Brown.
Kitahara, Michio
 1976   A Cross-cultural Test of the Freudian Theory of Circumcision. *International Journal of Psychoanalytic Psychotherapy* 5:535–44.
Kluckhohn, Clyde
 1967   *Navaho Witchcraft.* Boston: Beacon Press.
Kottak, Conrad
 1978   *Anthropology: The Exploration of Human Diversity.* New York: Random House.
Kuhn, Thomas S.
 1962   *The Structure of Scientific Revolutions.* Chicago: University of Chicago Press.
Kummer, Hans
 1968   *Social Organization of Hamadryas Baboons.* Chicago: University of Chicago Press.
La Barre, Weston
 1970   *The Ghost Dance.* Garden City, New York: Doubleday.
Lancaster, Jane B.
 1979   Sex and Gender in Evolutionary Perspective. In Herant A. Katchadorurian (ed.), *Human Sexuality: A Com-*

parative and Developmental Perspective. Berkeley: University of California Press.

Langness, L.L.

1974   Ritual Power and Male Domination in the New Guinea Highlands. *Ethos* 2:189–212.

Lasswell, Harold D.

1960   *Psychopathology and Politics.* New York: Viking.

Leach, Edmund R.

1954   A Trobriand Medusa? *Man.* No. 158.

1967   Virgin Birth. *Proceedings of the Royal Anthropological Institute,* pp. 39–50.

Lessa, William A.

1956   Oedipus-Type Tales in Oceania. *Journal of American Folklore* 69:63–73.

1961   *Tales from Ulithi Atoll.* Berkeley: University of California Press.

Lévi-Strauss, Claude

[1949] 1969
        The Elementary Structures of Kinship. London: Eyre and Spottiswoode.

Lidz, Ruth W., and Theodore Lidz

1977   Male Menstruation: A Ritual Alternative to the Oedipal Transition. *International Journal of Psychoanalysis* 58:17–31.

Lindzey, Gardner

1967   Some Remarks concerning Incest, the Incest Taboo, and Psychoanalytic Theory. *American Psychologist* 22:1051–59.

Lustig, Noel, John W. Dresser, Seth W. Spellman, and Thomas B. Murray

1966   Incest—A Family Group Survival Pattern. *Archives of General Psychiatry* 14:31–40.

Malinowski, Bronislaw

[1922] 1961
        Argonauts of the Western Pacific. New York: E. P. Dutton.

1926   *Crime and Custom in Savage Society.* London: Kegan Paul, Trench, Trubner

[1927] 1955
        Sex and Repression in Savage Society. New York: Meridian Books. (*SR.*)

1929   *The Sexual Life of Savages in North-Western Melanesia.* New York: Eugenic Publishing Company. (*SLS*).

1935   *Coral Gardens and Their Magic.* New York: American Book Company.

1955   *Magic, Science, and Religion.* Garden City: Doubleday-Anchor Books.

Mandler, George
1963   Parent and Child in the Development of the Oedipus Complex. *Journal of Nervous and Mental Diseases* 136:227–35.

McDougall, Lorna
1975   The Quest of the Argonauts. In Thomas R. Williams (ed.), *Psychological Anthropology.* The Hague: Mouton.

Meiselman, Karin C.
1978   *Incest.* San Francisco: Jossey-Bass.

Money, John
1980   *Love and Love Sickness.* Baltimore: Johns Hopkins University Press.

Montagu, Ashley
1974   *Coming into Being among the Australian Aborigines.* London: Routledge and Kegan Paul (revised and expanded Second Edition).

Murdock, George Peter
1949   *Social Structure.* New York: Macmillan.

Neubauer, Peter B. (ed.)
1965   *Children in Collectives.* Springfield: Charles C. Thomas.

Neumann, Erich
1963   *The Great Mother.* Princeton: Princeton University Press.

Parsons, Anne
1969   *Belief, Magic, and Anomie.* New York: Free Press.

Parsons, Talcott
1954   The Incest Taboo in Relation to Social Structure and the Socialization of the Child. *British Journal of Sociology* 5:101–17.

Paul, Robert A.
1980   Symbolic Interpretations in Psychoanalysis and Anthropology. *Ethos* 8:286–94.

Poole, Fitz John Porter
  1982   The Ritual Forging of Identity: Aspects of Person and
          Self in Bimin-Kuskusmin Male Initation. In Gilbert H.
          Herdt (ed.), *Rituals of Manhood*. Berkeley: University
          of California Press
Powell, H. A.
  1957   *Analysis of Present-Day Social Structure in the Trobriands.*
          Ph.D. Dissertation, University of London.
  1969   Genealogy, Residence, and Kinship in Kiriwana. *Man*
          4:177–202.
Raglan, Lord
  1949   *The Hero*. London: Watts and Company.
Rainwater, Lee, and William L. Yancey
  1967   *The Moynihan Report and the Politics of Controversy.*
          Cambridge: MIT Press.
Ramanujan, A. K.
  1972   The Indian Oedipus. In A. Poddar (ed.), *Indian Lit-
          erature: A Symposium*. Simla: Indian Institute of Ad-
          vanced Study.
Rank, Otto
  1964   *The Myth of the Birth of the Hero*. New York: Vintage
          Books.
Read, Kenneth E.
  1965   *The High Valley*. New York: Scribners.
Reik, Theodore
  [1919] 1946
          Ritual: Four Psychoanalytic Studies. New York: Grove
          Press.
Richards, Cara E.
  1972   *Man in Perspective*. New York: Random House.
Róheim, Géza
  1932   Psychoanalysis of Primitive Cultural Types. *Interna-
          tional Journal of Psychoanalysis* 13:1–224.
  1950   *Psychoanalysis and Anthropology*. New York: Interna-
          tional Universities Press.
Rohner, Ronald P.
  1977   Why Cross-cultural Research? *Annals of the New York
          Academy of Sciences* 285:3–12.
Rothman, Stanley, and S. Lichter
  1982   *The Radical Impulse*. New York: Oxford.

Rowell, Thelma E.
1972   Female Reproduction Cycles and Social Behavior in Females. *Advances in the Study of Behavior* 4:69–105.
Roy, Manisha
1975   *Bengali Women*. Chicago: University of Chicago Press.
1975   The Oedipus Complex and the Bengali Family in India (A Study of Father-Daughter Relations in Bengal). In Thomas R.Williams (ed.), *Psychological Anthropology*. The Hague: Mouton.
Sade, D. S.
1968   Inhibition of Son-Mother Mating among Free-ranging Rhesus Monkeys. *Science and Psychoanalysis* 12:18–37.
Sarnoff, Charles
1976   *Latency*. New York: Jason Aronson.
Shepher, Joseph
1971   Mate Selection among Second Generation Kibbutz Adolescents and Adults: Incest Avoidance and Negative Imprinting. *Archives of Sexual Behavior* 1:293–307.
Sierksma, Fokki
1966   *Tibet's Terrifying Deities: Sex and Aggression in Religious Acculturation*. The Hague: Mouton.
Slater, Philip
1966   *The Glory of Hera*. Boston: Beacon Press.
Slavin, Malcolm Owen
1972   *The Theme of Feminine Evil*. Ph.D. Dissertation, Harvard University.
Smith, Raymond T.
1956   *The Negro Family in British Guiana: Family Structure and Social Status in the Villages*. London: Routledge and Kegan Paul.
Sofue, Takao
1981   Family and Interpersonal Relationships in Early Japan. Paper presented for the International Symposium on Religion and the Family in East Asia, National Museum of Ethnology, Osaka, August 30-September 7, 1981.
Spiro, Melford E.
1958   *Children of the Kibbutz*. Cambridge: Harvard University Press.

1968	Virgin Birth, Parthenogenesis, and Physiological Paternity: An Essay in Cultural Interpretation. *Man* 3:242–61.

1977	*Kinship and Marriage in Burma*. Berkeley: University of California Press.

1982	Collective Representations and Mental Representations in Religious Symbol Systems. In Jacques Maquet (ed.), *On Symbols in Anthropology: Essays in Honor of Harry Hoijer*. Malibu: Udena Publications.

Spitz, Renee

1945	Hospitalism. *The Psychoanalytic Study of the Child*, Vol. 1. New York: International Universities Press.

Stephens, William N.

1962	*The Oedipus Complex*. New York: Free Press of Glencoe.

Swartz, Marc J.

1958	Sexuality and Aggression on Romonum, Truk. *American Anthropologist* 60:467–86.

Talmon, Yonina

1964	Mate Selection on Collective Settlements. *American Sociological Review* 29:491–508.

Tanaka, Masako

1981	"Maternal" Authority in the Japanese Family. Paper presented for the International Symposium on Religion and the Family in East Asia, National Museum of Ethnology, Osaka, August 30–September 7, 1981.

Tuzin, Donald F.

1980	*The Voice of the Tambaran*. Berkeley: University of California Press.

Warner, W. Lloyd

1937	*A Black Civilization*. New York: Harper.

Weinberg, S. Kirson

1955	*Incest Behavior*. New York: Citadel.

Weiner, Annette B.

1976	*Women of Value, Men of Renown*. Austin: University of Texas.

Weisskopf, Susan (Contratto)

1980	Marital Sexuality and Asexual Motherhood. *Signs* 5:766–82.

Westermarck, Edward
[1906–8]1924–26
The Origin and Development of the Moral Ideas. London: Macmillan.

Whiting, John W. M., Richard Kluckhohn, and Albert Anthony
1958 The Function of Male Initiation Ceremonies at Puberty. In Eleanor E. Maccoby, Theodore Newcomb, and Eugene A. Hartley (eds.), Readings in Social Psychology. New York: Holt.

Wilson, Edward O.
1978 On Human Nature. Cambridge: Harvard University Press.

Wilson, Monica
1949 Nyakyusa Age Villages. Journal of the Royal Anthropological Institute 79:21–25.

Wolf, Arthur P.
1966 Childhood Association, Sexual Attraction, and the Incest Taboo: A Chinese Case. American Anthropologist 68:893–98.
1968 Adopt a Daughter-in-Law, Marry a Sister: A Chinese Solution to the Incest Taboo. American Anthropologist 70:864–94.
1970 Childhood Association and Sexual Attraction: A Further Test of the Westermarck Hypothesis. American Anthropologist 72:503–15.

Wolf, Arthur P., and Chich-Shan Huang
1980 Marriage and Adoption in China, 1845–1945. Stanford: Stanford University Press.

Zimmer, Heinrich
1962 Myths and Symbols in Indian Art and Civilization. New York: Harper Torchbooks.

Index